GETTING AND SPENDING:
The Consumer's Dilemma

GETTING AND SPENDING:
The Consumer's Dilemma

Advisory Editor
Leon Stein

*See last pages of this volume
for a complete list of titles*

PRICING POWER

&

THE PUBLIC INTEREST

A STUDY BASED ON STEEL

BY GARDINER C. MEANS

ARNO PRESS
A New York Times Company
1976

Editorial Supervision: EVE NELSON

Reprint Edition 1976 by Arno Press Inc.

GETTING AND SPENDING: The Consumer's Dilemma
ISBN for complete set: 0-405-08005-0
See last pages of this volume for titles.

Manufactured in the United States of America

Library of Congress Cataloging in Publication Data

Means, Gardiner Coit, 1896–
    Pricing power & the public interest.

    (Getting and spending)
    Reprint of the ed. published by Harper, New York.
    1. Price policy—United States. 2. Steel—
Prices—United States. I. Title. II. Series.
[HF5417.M38 1976]   338.5'2   75-39260
ISBN 0-405-08033-6

PRICING POWER AND THE PUBLIC INTEREST

PRICING POWER

&

THE PUBLIC INTEREST

A STUDY BASED ON STEEL

BY GARDINER C. MEANS

HARPER & BROTHERS
PUBLISHERS · NEW YORK

PRICING POWER AND THE PUBLIC INTEREST

THIS BOOK IS DEDICATED TO THE PROGRESSIVE
LEADERS OF BIG BUSINESS PRESENT AND FUTURE

CONTENTS

Contents

Contents

PART III

THE LOGIC OF ADMINISTRATIVE COMPETITION

Contents

CHARTS

TABLES

PREFACE

This book is written on the premise that big business is a good thing. It is here and here to stay.

At the same time, modern big business is basically different from the small-scale private enterprise on which most of the philosophy of a free enterprise system has been based.

The small private enterprise had little or no economic or political power and, in developing the philosophy of free enterprise, such little power as it had could be disregarded. Economic theory could deal with a forest of small enterprises whose activity was canalized in the public interest by the invisible hand of market forces.

Today the modern corporate enterprise is a huge collective. Typically, it combines the labor of tens or hundreds of thousands of workers and the capital of tens or hundreds of thousands of investors in a great engine of production serving millions of consumers. To think of it as a private enterprise is to deny its essential character. It is a different kind of enterprise and deserves a separate name. Here it will be called a "collective enterprise."

Because of its absolute size and because of its size relative to its markets, the huge collective enterprise has significant economic and political powers.

How these powers can be made to serve the public interest is one of the major problems of our day. It is signalized in the search for legitimacy and in the demand that corporate management should act with a social conscience.

Central to these powers is the power over price. Where competition is among a few big competitors, a significant degree of market power develops. Competition limits the range of pricing discretion, but does not assure its socially desirable use. Until a way has been found to canalize this power in the public interest, it is difficult to deal with other problems of corporate power, and once this problem has been resolved, a basis will have been provided for the discussion of other power problems.

This book is, therefore, focused on pricing power. It does not deal, except incidentally or by implication, with other problems of power involved in collective enterprise. Nor does it attempt to deal with the problem of full employment. In so far as the inflexibility of administered prices prevents the operation of Say's Law and accounts for wide swings in business activity, this presents another major problem which I aim to take up in a later volume.

This book brings together two concepts which I introduced into economic theory more than twenty-five years ago. The first is the concept of the separation of ownership and control. It was initially presented in *The Quarterly Journal of Economics* (1931) and certain of the economic and legal implications of this separation were developed by Adolf A. Berle, Jr., and myself in *The Modern Corporation and Private Property* (1932). The second concept is that of administered prices. It was first published in 1935 in Senate Document No. 13 (Seventy-fourth Congress) on *Industrial Prices and their Relative Inflexibility,* and some of its economic implications were developed by Caroline F. Ware and myself in *The Modern Economy in Action* (1936). The present book carries forward the logic of these concepts as they apply to the pricing power of collective enterprise.

Steel pricing has been chosen as the basis for analyzing pricing power, partly because of the economic importance of the industry, partly because of the availability of data and argument in the 1957–1959 Senate Committee Hearings on Administered Prices, and perhaps most importantly because the large rise in steel prices after 1953 sharpened the issues of public policy.

In the actual writing of this book, I have received encouragement, criticism, and suggestions from many people. Most important of all is that from my wife, Caroline F. Ware. In addition I owe special gratitude to the following who read the whole or major parts of the manuscript and helped materially in improving its quality: Adolf A. Berle, Jr., John Blair, James C. Bonbright, Robert F. Lanzillotti, Edwin G. Nourse, Romney Robinson.

GARDINER C. MEANS

Vienna, Virginia
June 1, 1961

PART I

THE DRAMA OF STEEL PRICES

CHAPTER I

PROLOGUE IN STEEL

On June 14, 1958, Senator Kefauver closed a speech to the Senate with the words "Let me emphasize that there are only 17 days left for the President to act." A poll among steel producers had shown an expectation that steel prices would be raised $4 to $6 a ton on July 1. The Senator called on the President to use the full powers of his office to hold off this expected increase and recommended a system of voluntary controls to hold the line on prices and wages.

Behind this call for public action lay three things: first, the specter of inflation—a 60 per cent increase in consumer prices had occurred since World War II; second, the specter of depression—industrial production had dropped 15 per cent in the preceding twelve months while unemployment had risen to more than 5 million; and third, the crucial role of the steel industry in a society built on steel.

Also behind this call lay an extensive Senate investigation of the administration of steel prices. In hearings on administered prices, during the summer and fall of 1957, the Kefauver Committee[1] questioned leaders of the steel industry and representatives of labor on the factors determining steel prices. Emphasis was focused on the $6 a ton price increase of July 1, 1957, which had followed a $5 increase in the winter of 1956–1957, an $8.50 increase in August, 1956, and increases totaling more than $27 in the preceding four years. These increases amounted to a rise of 45 per

---

[1] The Subcommittee on Antitrust and Monopoly of the Committee on the Judiciary, U.S. Senate, 85th Cong., 1st sess., pursuant to S. Res. 57.

3

cent in the index of finished steel prices during a five year period in which the wholesale price index rose only 6 per cent and the consumer price index rose less than 6 per cent.[2]

The hearings failed to resolve the question of the legitimacy of these price increases. Management placed major responsibility for the increases on increased costs due directly and indirectly to wage increases, particularly those required under the three-year labor contract signed in the summer of 1956. Labor defended the increased compensation under the three-year contract as legitimate and not requiring increased steel prices. The hearings did, however, reflect a serious public concern with the behavior of steel prices as another round of steel wage and price increases became iminent—the concern which was voiced by Senator Kefauver.

Faced with this considerable public concern, the United States Steel Corporation, largest producer and usually the leader in price changes, issued the following unprecedented statement:

The terms of our existing three-year labor contract, which is similar to the labor contracts of other steel producers, provide for another substantial employment cost increase to U. S. Steel on July 1, 1958. This new cost increase is about 5½ per cent—or more than 20 cents an hour. We have already incurred, without a price change, an additional 5 cent an hour so called cost-of-living increase on Jan. 1 of this year.

Since July 1 of last year when steel prices were increased, additional cost increases have been incurred—for example, State and local taxes, transportation costs and the cost of certain purchased goods and services.

It must be obvious to anyone that the matter of price adjustment would not even come up under present economic circumstances if it were not for the very substantial employment cost increase we now face.

United States Steel is constantly attempting to achieve economies in operation by emphasis on efficiency and technology. These new employment and other cost increases, however, cannot possibly be offset

[2] Ratio of increases in the Bureau of Labor Statistics Indexes of Finished Steel Products, Wholesale, and Consumer Prices from July, 1952, to July, 1957.

by these economies nor by any other foreseeable factors of increased productivity.

Some degree of relief through higher sales prices must therefore be given the serious consideration which it deserves. While costs are a major factor in any price determination, they are only one among many.

Any adjustment of sales prices can only be made in the light of all known commercial and economic factors, including competitive conditions in the steel industry, competition with other materials, underlying customer product demand, and economic climate and outlook, together with other factors.

United States Steel is continuing its study of all of these factors. The only point we have reached to date is not to attempt to change our prices until the situation clarifies itself.[3]

According to the *New York Times,* this statement "appeared to puzzle most observers of the industry."[4] The *Wall Street Journal* commented, "The fact any statement was volunteered was unusual in the light of the company's traditional reluctance to discuss prices in advance of any formal action,"[5] and suggested that U.S. Steel might be bidding for another ranking producer to take the lead in raising prices.[6]

On June 20, Senator Kefauver sent a telegram to the President saying, in part, "I again urge you to use the full powers of your office in order to prevent this disastrous occurrence. I am confident that if you would bring together the leaders of the steel industry and the United Steel Workers of America, a realistic hold-the-line price-wage program could be developed."[7]

On June 24, the President wrote to the Senator refusing to take public action.

[3] *Administered Prices:* Hearings before the Subcommittee on Antitrust and Monopoly of the Committee on the Judiciary, U.S. Senate, 85th Cong., Pts., 1, 2, 3, and 4; July 9, 11, 12, 13, 16, August 8, 9, 10, 12, 15, 16, 20, 21, 22, October 21, 22, 29, 30, and November 4 and 5, 1957 (Washington, D.C.: Government Printing Office, 1957 and 1958), p. 4476. Subsequent reference to this series of hearings will be made simply to *Hearings* with the pages indicated.

[4] *New York Times,* June 20, 1958.

[5] *Wall Street Journal,* June 20, 1958.

[6] *Ibid.,* June 23, 1958.

On June 25, the Alan Wood Steel Company, a small steel producer, announced that it was raising its price of steel an average of $6 a ton to be effective July 7, but only if other steel companies also raised their prices.

On June 26, President Avery C. Adams of Jones & Laughlin Steel Corporation, fourth largest producer, announced that his company would not raise steel prices unless The United States Steel Corporation did so.[7]

Also on June 26, Senator Kefauver released telegrams from the chairman of the board of the United States Steel Corporation and the president of the United Steel Workers of America in reply to questions on the imminent increase in steel prices. The steel company simply referred to the public statement already issued and reproduced above. The labor union official replied as follows:

IN ACCORDANCE WITH YOUR REQUEST OF THIS DATE CONCERNING THE WAGE INCREASES DUE UNDER OUR STEEL WAGE AGREEMENTS ON JULY 1ST, THE DETAILS OF THE INCREASE ARE AS FOLLOWS: AN AVERAGE 9 CENT WAGE INCREASE PLUS A FURTHER 3 CENT COST ARISING FROM CERTAIN IMPROVED FRINGE BENEFITS (SUNDAY AND HOLIDAY WORK PREMIUMS AND SHIFT DIFFERENTIALS). THE STEEL AGREEMENTS ALSO PROVIDE FOR THE RECOVERY OF THE LOSS IN PURCHASING POWER SUFFERED OVER THE PAST SIX MONTHS BECAUSE OF THE RISE IN CONSUMER'S PRICES. THESE PRICES HAVE RISEN BY ENOUGH TO REQUIRE A 4 CENT WAGE ADJUSTMENT.

EVEN AFTER THESE INCREASES BECOME EFFECTIVE, EMPLOYED STEELWORKERS, BECAUSE OF SHORT WORK WEEKS, WILL EARN LESS IN "REAL" WEEKLY PAY THAN THEY DID A YEAR AGO. THESE 1958 WAGE ADJUSTMENTS HAVE BEEN FULLY EARNED BY OUR MEMBERS THROUGH INCREASED PRODUCTIVITY. THE AVERAGE ANNUAL GROWTH IN OUTPUT PER MANHOUR IN THE PAST DECADE HAS BEEN LARGE ENOUGH TO OFFSET COMPLETELY THE RISE IN HOURLY WAGE RATES.

THE INVESTIGATIONS OF YOUR COMMITTEE ITSELF SHOWED THAT THE COST OF LAST YEAR'S STEEL WAGE INCREASE WAS MORE THAN OFFSET BY THE DECREASE IN SCRAP COSTS ALONE, YET, THE INDUSTRY IGNORED THIS COST SAVING AND THE PRODUCTIVITY INCREASE AND

[7] *Wall Street Journal,* June 27, 1958.

RAISED PRICES BY MORE THAN TWICE AS MUCH AS THE ALLEGED IN-
CREASE IN LABOR COSTS.

BOTH BECAUSE OF INCREASED PRODUCTIVITY AND LOWER MATERIAL
COSTS NO INCREASE IN STEEL PRICES SHOULD HAVE BEEN MADE LAST
YEAR, AND NONE ARE REQUIRED NOW. I SHARE WITH YOU YOUR CON-
CERN OVER RISING STEEL PRICES AND THEIR IMPACT ON THE ECONOMY.
AS YOU KNOW, SEVERAL MONTHS AGO I URGED THE CREATION BY THE
PRESIDENT OF A TOP-LEVEL COMMITTEE FROM INDUSTRY AND LABOR
TO CONSIDER THE PROBLEMS, INCLUDING INFLATIONARY PRICING, BE-
SETTING OUR ECONOMY. I AM STILL OF THE OPINION THAT THIS AP-
PROACH HAS GREAT MERIT.

DAVID J. MCDONALD,
PRESIDENT, UNITED STEELWORKERS
OF AMERICA[8]

July 1 came and went without an increase in steel prices, but
there was a widespread belief in the industry that prices would be
increased. Thus, the trade journal *Iron Age* predicted on July 3
that steel prices would be raised, that the increase would take
place in August, that the advance would average out to about
$5.50 per ton, and that the price boost would be on a "selective"
basis. The journal stated: "Not all steel products will be affected
at the outset. It is even possible that U.S. Steel will follow, rather
than lead, in establishing new prices on some products."[9]

On July 7 the Alan Wood Steel Company announced the with-
drawal of its price increase, the president of the company stating,
"We are disappointed that the big mills have not increased their
prices. We have no alternative but to stay competitive with their
prices."[10]

Then came the break. On July 29 the Armco Steel Corporation,
seventh largest in the industry, announced a price increase on hot
and cold rolled sheet and strip products averaging $4.50 a ton to
become effective July 31.[11] On July 30, Republic and Jones &

[8] *Hearings,* p. 4478.
[9] *Hearings,* p. 4481.
[10] *Wall Street Journal,* July 8, 1958.
[11] *Wall Street Journal,* July 31, 1958.

Laughlin announced that thèy too were increasing prices.[12] On July 31, United States Steel came into line and Bethlehem, National, Pittsburgh, Wheeling, and Youngstown immediately followed suit.[13] Thus, by August 1, prices for sheet and strip steel, roughly 30 per cent of total steel shipments, were up an average of $4.50 a ton or about 3 per cent.[14] In the following weeks the prices of many other finished steel products were raised so that the September index of finished steel prices showed an increase over June of 2.8 per cent, indicating an increase of nearly $4.40 a ton for the average of all finished steel products. Yet this increase occurred when the steel industry was operating at little more than half of its rated capacity.

The appeal to the President had failed. The appeal to management and labor in the industry had failed. Steel prices continued to rise in the face of a relatively low level of demand for steel and much unemployment in the industry.

This episode raises in sharp relief the major problem with which this book is concerned: the pricing power of big enterprise and means for achieving legitimate prices in an industry such as steel.

[12] *Wall Street Journal,* July 31, 1958.
[13] *Wall Street Journal,* Aug. 1, 1958.
[14] *Loc. cit.*

CHAPTER II

THE PROBLEM OF LEGITIMATE PRICES

Concentrated economic power . . . raises at once the question of "legitimacy."

A. A. BERLE, JR.
SCHOOL OF LAW, COLUMBIA UNIVERSITY*

The 1958 increase in the price of steel and the manner in which this increase was brought about sharply dramatize a central fact of our modern economy—the power of big business to determine prices. It raises basic and vital questions: Are the prices which result from the exercise of this power truly in the public interest? Are they, in this sense, *legitimate*? And if they are not, what can be done to bring about prices that do serve the public interest? It is the purpose of this book to seek an answer to these questions, at least in so far as manufacturing enterprise is concerned.

Today, one hundred and thirty big corporations account for nearly half of manufacturing output in the United States.[1] They are usually subject to active competition among the big three or the big four of an industry and to some competition from smaller enterprises. But such competition is not of a character to prevent price administration and a considerable degree of pricing power.

One cannot exaggerate the importance of finding a satisfactory answer to the problem posed by pricing power. Prices are at the

---

* *Power Without Property*, (New York: Harcourt, Brace and Company, 1959), p. 98.

[1] Edward S. Mason, ed., *The Corporation in Modern Society*, (Cambridge: Harvard University Press 1959), p. 5.

9

heart of every money economy. They are crucial to economic growth, to full employment and to the use which we make of our human and material resources. We cannot hope for a healthy, vigorous economy unless we can be sure that, in the presence of the economic power wielded by large-scale enterprise, prices will be "right."

IMPLICATIONS OF ADMINISTERED PRICES

The need to concern ourselves, consciously, with the rightness of price—with price legitimacy—arises directly from the presence of big business itself. Under the conditions on which classical economic theory was based, prices were *automatically* right. The "unseen hand" of market forces, not any conscious intervention of a price-setter, determined prices and assured their legitimacy.

According to the law of supply and demand, prices were assumed to be flexible and responsive to the situation in the market place. If demand exceeded supply, the price would rise, stimulating supply or dampening demand, until supply and demand were in line with each other. If supply exceeded demand, the price would fall until supply and demand were in balance.

For a market system dominated by this law, there was reason to think that the resulting prices would serve the public interest by directing resources into the most effective uses, except where the market was interfered with by efforts to obtain a corner on a particular commodity or by other rigging.

But we do not have such a market system in an economy dominated by large corporations. The decision to raise steel prices in the summer of 1958 did not reflect the automatic forces of the market place. It was an administrative decision and the resulting prices were administered prices.

In spite of vigorous competition in the steel industry, steel prices do not equate supply and demand. Competition alone does not bring the law of supply and demand into operation. Administered steel prices are set for periods of time and revised from time to time. At times, demand at the prices set may far exceed supply so that the filling of some orders has to be postponed and some go unfilled. At other times, supply may be greatly in excess of demand and efficient productive capacity may be idle. Only by chance is supply just equal to demand at the current price. And an excess of demand over supply or the reverse does not necessarily bring a change in price. Steel prices are not, and under modern conditions cannot be, set by the classical law.

Steel prices are only an outstanding example of administered prices. This type of pricing prevails widely throughout the economy, both in the market for goods and in the market for labor. And because such prices are not determined by the law of supply and demand, they present major problems of public policy with respect to inflation, with respect to depression, with respect to income distribution, and with respect to the effective use of resources.

There has been some confusion as to the meaning and implications of the term "administered price." By some it has been taken to imply criticism or opprobrium. But it was originally introduced as a neutral technical term to distinguish prices which are set by individual companies and kept constant for periods of time from those which are set by classical competition and the law of supply and demand.

The contrast between the two types of price is clearly evident in the steel industry where the prices of steel products are announced by management and may remain constant for months or years at a time, while the prices of steel scrap are in a constant state of adjustment. In the case of steel products, production is adjusted to the demand at the prices set even though supply—the amount the companies are willing to deliver at the administered prices— might be very much greater. In contrast, the price of steel scrap adjusts more or less continuously so that the amount of scrap offered at the current price just satisfies the demand and the market is just cleared.

Administered prices are not new, nor is the practice of price administration in itself objectionable. On the contrary, administered prices are an essential part of our modern economy. They can contribute to greater efficiency and lead to higher standards of living. Big industry could not operate without them. It is almost impossible to imagine an efficient modern steel industry without administered prices.

What is important is that administered prices lie outside of classical economic theory. The whole body of classical theory was in part a revolt against the price administration of the medieval guilds. It was built on the conception of prices as flexible and market-determined. At no point did it introduce the concept of price administration. Indeed, it is in part because classical theory excluded from its analysis prices which were set by administrative action that it provides no clear guide to the legitimacy of administered prices. It is this which makes the task undertaken by this study so important.

The implications of administered prices for public policy are far from clear. There is no body of economic theory which establishes the conditions under which administered prices will be so set as to serve the public interest. In the simple economic model provided by classical theory, where reliance on market forces gave legitimacy to the unlimited pursuit of individual gain, public policy toward private power over prices was clear: break up monopolies so as to make the law of supply and demand work or, if this could not be done, treat the monopolies as public utilities and regulate their prices. It is on this basis that our country chose to regulate the railroads and power companies and chose to apply antitrust laws to industry.

But most administered prices do not fall into either of these two categories. They are not set by competition, however much competition may influence them. Neither do most of them fall into the category of monopoly prices. They represent a third category which has only begun to be taken into account in economic analysis.

Since the classical mechanism does not operate to determine administered prices and give them legitimacy, we must ask: Where there is power to administer prices, what prices *are* legitimate and what are the conditions under which the prices set are *likely to be* legitimate? These are the questions with which this volume is concerned.

STEEL PRICES AS THE SUBJECT OF ANALYSIS

In order to have a solid basis for elaborating theory and formulating public policy, there is need for a body of data which reveals the actual manner in which administered prices are, in fact, set and how they relate to costs. But no such body of data is available. Outside of the regulated industries, the big corporations do not disclose their costs of operation as they relate to prices. Past efforts, such as the Temporary National Economic Committee investigations in 1939–1940, have not succeeded in developing a comprehensive picture of the pricing process and the relation of prices to costs.

The Senate hearings on administered prices, which began in 1957, provide the most substantial data, but without further analysis they do not offer a solid basis for theory or policy. In the case of steel prices and costs, the data were not presented by the industry in a manner or form which enabled the Senators or others, merely by reading the record, to determine the actual basis for steel prices or to appraise the legitimacy of the price increases. Only through a most careful scrutiny of the material presented there, and similar material, can the data be made to yield the relevant information.

The present study has, therefore, undertaken to make such an examination in order to provide a factual basis for considering the theoretical and policy implications of the pricing power of big manufacturing enterprise. Chief reliance for the facts on steel is placed on the data introduced at the hearings by the steel industry in defense of its price actions and particularly the material presented by the United States Steel Corporation.[2] These are the data on which the industry rests its case and invites the conclusion that its prices are legitimate.

Steel prices provide an unusually good basis for examining the problem of pricing power, not only because of the body of material presented at the hearings, but because steel prices are less complex than those of some other concentrated industries. Steel is produced according to fairly rigid specifications, so that an analysis of steel price behavior is not plagued by changes in quality. Moreover, steel is a basic industry. What happens in steel pricing has wide repercussions throughout the economy, both from the direct effect of steel prices and from the example of pricing action which may be followed by other industries.

THE STRUCTURE OF THIS STUDY

The first part of this study, "The Drama of Steel Prices," deals with the methods by which steel prices are set, the different reactions which could be expected under different types of inflation, and the actual behavior of these prices during the war influences and since 1953.

Because this is a pioneer attempt to lift the veil hiding the exercise of pricing power, the cumulative steps in the analysis have been presented in substantial detail in Chapters V and VI. The reader who is only interested in the conclusions of this analysis can omit these two chapters which are summarized in the beginning of Chapter VII. The evidence is marshaled in Chapters V and VI for those readers who need to be assured of the validity of the

[2] On occasions where a standard index such as that for wholesale prices or for productivity was introduced into the record, earlier or later values of the same index have been used to complete the picture. In some cases where data were supplied from nonpublic sources for certain years and not for others, rough interpolations have been made on the basis of standard indexes. In a few cases, data not derived from the hearings have been introduced.

conclusions or who are interested in the analytical and statistical procedures that can be used to extract the relevant information from published data for steel or other industries dominated by big enterprise.

The second part of the study, "Approaches to Legitimacy," is concerned with the traditional approaches to legitimacy reflecting the logic of classical competition and that of utility regulation where government intervenes.

Part III, "The Logic of Administrative Competition," will consider the logical implications of competition where prices are administered, comparing the results to be expected with those which would be regarded as legitimate under classical competition or under utility regulation.

The fourth part of the study, "The Logic of Collective Enterprise," will be concerned with the character of big business, its role in administering prices and its relation to the public interest. On this basis, a new approach will be proposed to the problem of legitimate pricing in concentrated industries like steel—an approach which involves neither the breakup of big business nor government regulation of prices.

CHAPTER III

THE ADMINISTRATION OF STEEL PRICES

We have published f.o.b. mill prices for standard steel mill products at each of our producing mills. This is the price we quote to all of our customers—large and small. In other words, we have a one-price policy. When a change is made in our f.o.b. mill price, the new price applies to all of our customers and to all unshipped orders on the books as of the date of change.

RICHARD F. SENTNER, EXECUTIVE VICE-PRESIDENT,
THE UNITED STATES STEEL CORPORATION*

Our first task is to see just how steel prices are actually set.

It is easy to imagine a single product, "steel," and speak glibly of the price of steel. But steel is a whole category of thousands of different products, each with its own price and even with different geographical prices for the same product.

The price structure in steel may not be as complex as the railroad rate structure, but it is amply complex. Simplification is brought by employing base prices for standard categories, such as cold rolled sheets or hot rolled bars, and then adding "extras" for differences in specification within the category, say an extra for especially thin or especially wide cold rolled sheets. A company can change the prices of all its products in a particular category at the same time by changing the base price for that category. Similarly, it can change the price of any individual item within the category by altering its extra. Thus, when the United States Steel Corporation announced its $6 price increase for July 1, 1957, over

* *Hearings*, p. 354.

a hundred different base prices were listed, and these applied to thousands of separate items. This is the more usual and more publicized form of price change. As a rule, the extras are seldom changed and books giving specific extras are published and often remain in use for years at a time while the base prices are more frequently changed. But sometimes, as in the winter of 1956–1957, a considerable change in prices is brought about by changes in extras.

We can follow the net effect of individual price changes through an index of finished steel prices or through such average-increase figures as the $6 a ton given by the U.S. Steel Corporation for July 1, 1957. But to understand how the individual prices are arrived at, we need to examine the industry as a whole.

The steel industry is fairly concentrated. Thus, in 1957 U.S. Steel had approximately 30 per cent of steel ingot capacity, and in 1956 the largest four companies, including U.S. Steel, had close to 60 per cent.[1]

These over-all industry figures are important; but much more important for the problem of pricing is the degree of concentration in specific types of product. The American Iron and Steel Institute prepared for the Senate Committee a compilation of the shipments of the major types of carbon steel products by the largest four shippers of each product and by the next largest four. Table 1 has been calculated from these figures. It shows the concentration in sales for the more important categories of steel products for the first half of 1957. The table covers four-fifths of all finished steel shipments and shows the proportion of total shipments of each product by the four and the eight largest shippers of that particular product. Of course, the companies that fall in the largest four and eight are likely to be different for different products as some steel companies make more of a speciality of one product than another. However, concentration in so far as it affects the price of a particular product is the concentration in the shipments of that particular product, not the concentration of steel shipments in total.

[1] *Hearings*, pp. 335, 1035.

Table 1—CONCENTRATION IN THE SHIPMENT OF
PARTICULAR FINISHED CARBON STEEL PRODUCTS:
FIRST SIX MONTHS OF 1957

Steel Product	Total Shipments in 1,000 Tons	Proportion of Particular Products Shipped by	
		Largest 4 Shippers of Product	Largest 8 Shippers of Product
Rails, Standard	740	100.0%	100.0%
Structural Shapes	3,407	91.6	97.8
Tinplate, Electrolitic	2,783	76.5	93.6
Wire Rods	522	75.9	93.9
Strip, Hot Rolled	768	72.5	87.1
Bars, Hot Rolled	3,498	71.6	88.3
Bars, Reinforcing	1,334	68.5	82.8
Bars, Cold Finish	591	67.2	89.0
Plates	4,745	65.5	81.6
Line Pipe	2,180	64.5	85.4
Wire, Drawn	1,408	64.5	82.3
Standard Pipe	1,517	63.5	92.7
Sheets, Galvanized	1,292	61.0	94.6
Oil Country Goods	1,362	59.7	90.8
Sheets, Hot Rolled	4,206	59.5	80.1
Sheets, Cold Rolled	6,019	53.9	81.7
Strips, Cold Rolled	520	50.6	80.0
All Other Steel Products	4,397		
Total Carbon Steel Shipments	41,289		

Source: Hearings, pp. 1022-1025.

As can be seen from Table 1, for each of the major steel products more than half was shipped by the four leading shippers of that particular product and four-fifths or more was shipped by the eight leading shippers of that particular product. For each of these seventeen products, the market was predominantly supplied by no more than eight large producers and in some cases by four large producers.

Even these figures do not indicate the full degree of concentration when we are concerned with problems of pricing. They represent concentration on a national basis and for broad categories of products, such as cold rolled sheets or plates. But pricing is only partly a problem of broad categories and national markets. A rolling mill on the West Coast is seldom a competitor in, say, the Detroit area. Thus, for reasons of transportation costs, the degree of concentration for any particular region is likely to be greater than that for the country as a whole. Similarly, some important companies may not produce the whole range of products in a particular broad category. If some companies concentrate on heavy plate and others on light plate, the concentration ratio is likely to be greater for the two separately than for the broader category. Just how much greater the concentration in relation to the market may be is difficult to determine and need not concern us here since the concentration indicated by the national figures for broad categories is sufficient to pose the problem of price administration.

This degree of concentration does not constitute monopoly. As long as there are four or five concerns actively competing with each other for business, each must be on its toes to maintain its share of the total business. In the absence of actual collusion or conspiracy to act as a unit in setting prices or controlling production, we do not have the single seller that is the mark of monopoly. With four or five producers serving each market, the situation is significantly different from that where, say, a single power company serves a particular area and is regulated as a monopoly.

On the other hand, when there are only a few companies selling in a particular market, we do not have the large number of sellers necessary for prices to be determined by the law of supply and demand. This "law" can work in the organized wheat and cotton markets through which thousands of buyers and sellers operate on the price. A small increase in demand and the price quickly rises;

a small increase in the supply and the price quickly falls. By such quick and usually frequent adjustments, the price moves to whatever level is necessary to equate supply and demand. It is this flexible price which is the basis of traditional economic theory. It is what traditional economists refer to as a competitive price. But it is not a price which is likely to be reached, except by chance, where sellers are few.

Experience has shown that when a few competing producers predominate in supplying a particular market with a particular product, the following developments can be expected. (1) Prices tend to be administered, and not sensitive to short-run changes in demand and supply. (2) Competing producers tend to set the same prices or maintain the same price differentials over considerable periods of time. (3) There is apt to be one producer who is looked to as the leader in making price changes. (4) Prices tend to be set in terms of longer run considerations and not in terms of the short-run variations in the demand and supply factors which dominate prices set by competition. Certainly this is the pattern of pricing that has developed in the steel industry.

THE ADMINISTRATIVE CHARACTER OF STEEL PRICES
The administrative character of steel pricing can be easily seen by comparing the prices and production for a number of major steel products. This is done in the following four charts which, in combination, represent approximately two-fifths of total steel shipments in the first half of 1957.

These charts indicate the changes in price and production for each category from 1947 to 1957 by showing the base price and the rate of production by months.

The first thing to notice in these charts is the step-like character of the price changes. The price will be constant for months at a time and then will be revised upward or downward by a sizable amount. The year and a half stretch of price stability from early

Chart I – TRENDS IN PRICE AND PRODUCTION, 1947-1957
(1947-1949 = 100)
(MONTH AT END OF QUARTER)

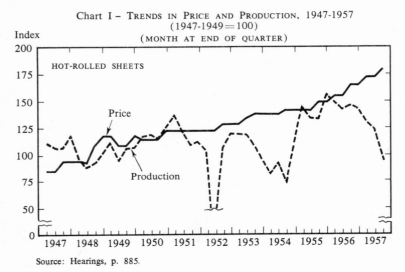

HOT-ROLLED SHEETS

Price

Production

Source: Hearings, p. 885.

Chart II – TRENDS IN PRICE AND PRODUCTION, 1947-1957
(1947-1949 = 100)
(MONTH AT END OF QUARTER)

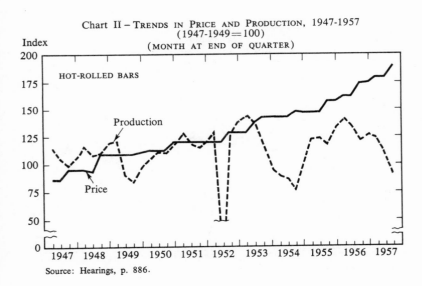

HOT-ROLLED BARS

Production

Price

Source: Hearings, p. 886.

Chart III — TRENDS IN PRICE AND PRODUCTION, 1947-1957
(1947-1949 = 100)
(MONTH AT END OF QUARTER)

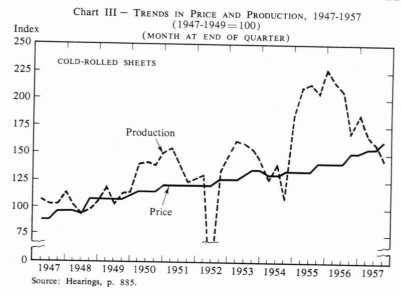

Source: Hearings, p. 885.

Chart IV — TRENDS IN PRICE AND PRODUCTION, 1947-1957
(1947-1949 = 100)
(MONTH AT END OF QUARTER)

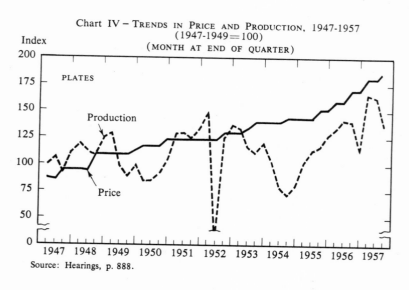

Source: Hearings, p. 888.

1951 to February, 1953 reflects the federal government's hold-the-line program, but for the rest of the period, the months of stability followed by price revisions represent normal steel price behavior. In the eleven years covered by the charts, the number of price changes varied from fifteen for plates to seventeen each for hot rolled sheets and cold rolled sheets. Thus, on the average, there were seven months of price stability between successive price changes. This is in great contrast to the behavior of the price of steel scrap which changed practically every month of the period as is shown in Chart V. The infrequency of price change is typical of a large body of administered prices.

The second thing to notice in the steel charts is the wide swings in production with little effect on prices. In the 1949 recession the hot rolled sheet price was reduced somewhat, but the other three items showed no decline in spite of a considerable reduction in demand. In the larger recession of late 1953 and 1954, the price of cold rolled sheets was reduced by 4 per cent while production declined 22 per cent and the other three prices remained the same or rose in the presence of even greater declines in production. In the still greater recession of 1957–1958, not one of these four steel prices was reduced in 1957 by as much as three-tenths of 1 per cent and all rose in 1958 in spite of a 40 per cent drop in production. Again this is in direct contrast with the behavior of steel scrap prices. As Chart V shows, steel scrap prices fell when the demand for steel scrap was low in the three recessions and rose when the steel scrap demand increased. In the case of scrap, the price adjusted to equate supply and demand. In the case of steel prices it did not.

In this particular respect, the prices and production in a concentrated but unregulated industry behave very much like the prices and production of regulated monopolies. In the case of railroads and public utilities, price (or rate) is arrived at by the joint activity of the monopoly and the regulating agency. But once the price is set it is likely to be kept constant for considerable periods

Chart V — COMPARISON OF TREND OF PRICE
AND PRODUCTION IN THE STEEL INDUSTRY
STEEL PRODUCTION, PRICE OF PIG IRON
& PRICE OF STEEL SCRAP, 1947-1957
(1947-1949=100)

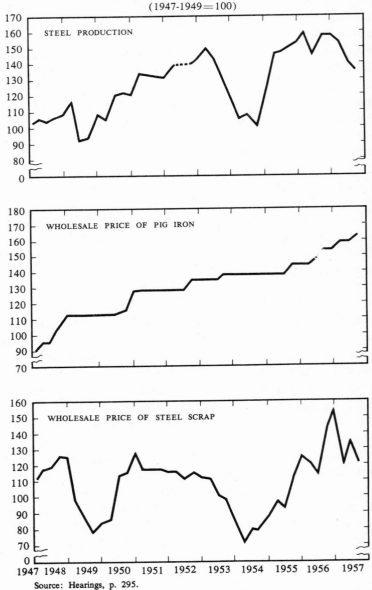

Source: Hearings, p. 295.

of time and production is adjusted to the demand at the particular price. If the demand for, say, electricity falls, generators will be shut down, but the price will not usually be reduced. And if demand exceeds capacity, as it sometimes does, the supply will be rationed by special measures restricting peak load use, but the price will not usually be increased. In these circumstances, as in the case of a privately administered price, the law of supply and demand does not operate.

The fact that we accept inflexible administered prices in the case of regulated utilities is important. It means that a price which is set administratively and kept constant for a period of time is not in itself regarded as contrary to public policy even though the price does not adjust to equate current demand and supply. This suggests that it is the level of prices arrived at by the private administration of price, not the inflexibility or the insensitivity to changes in supply and demand which is at issue.

IDENTICAL PRICING

A second characteristic of administered prices in the absence of monopoly is the tendency of different companies producing a standard product to set identical prices for the same product.

The general practice in the steel industry is for each company to publish price schedules at which it offers steel at each of its mills. For the most part these mill prices tend to be identical, though a standard differential may be maintained for mills which have an especially favorable location with respect to a particular market such as the closeness of Bethlehem's Sparrows Point Plant and U. S. Steel's Fairless Plant to the Eastern Seaboard market or that of National Steel's Ecorse Sheet Plant to the Detroit market. In addition, *within natural market areas,* freight will sometimes be absorbed to make delivered prices equal. Thus, if a customer is closer to one mill than another and is in the natural market area of both, the more distant mill may absorb the difference in freight so that the delivered price to the customer is the same as well as the mill price.[2]

The widespread identity of mill prices is well established. However, whether a particular mill will absorb enough freight to make delivered prices identical will depend on commercial policy and the particular conditions surrounding the particular order.

CONFUSION OVER THE MEANING OF A COMPETITIVE PRICE

In the steel hearings the question was raised whether identical prices can be regarded as competitive prices. It resulted in the following discussion:

MR. BLOUGH. If we offer to sell steel at the same price as a competitor at the customer's door, that is very definitely a competitive price with our customer. Now, it isn't a different price and, therefore, it isn't a non-competitive price, but it is a competitive price.

SENATOR KEFAUVER. You mean it will give him the right to decide whether he will buy his steel from you or Bethlehem Steel? That is the only difference; isn't it? That is the only competition? If you offer to sell a customer at the same price as Bethlehem, the only point of competition is whether they buy from you or whether they buy from Bethlehem, isn't it, or some other company?

MR. BLOUGH. That certainly isn't the only point of competition. There are many elements.

SENATOR KEFAUVER. What is the other point where you offer the same price?

MR. BLOUGH. Well you have quality, you have service, and you have many other aspects of competition, which are all very important elements.[3] . . . .

SENATOR KEFAUVER. Mr. Blough, do you regard it as true competition when another company matches your price to a thousandth of a cent per pound, or you match some other company's price to a thousandth of a cent per pound? Wouldn't it be more competitive if there were at least some slight difference in these prices?

I mean, what difference does it make who they buy from if the

---

[2] Of course, where the mill prices are the same and freight is absorbed to give the same delivered prices, only the latter are of interest to the buyer.
[3] *Hearings,* p. 310.

prices are going to be identical to one-thousandth of a cent per pound?

MR. BLOUGH. Mr. Chairman, I will try to go over this again so perhaps I can communicate. My concept is that a price that matches another price is a competitive price. If you don't choose to accept that concept, then, of course, you don't accept it. In the steel industry we know it is so.[4]. . .

MR. BLOUGH. There are lots of situations where the prices are different at the present time. Right now I could name a city where the price of a very important product is $5 a ton higher than our price, by a big producer.

SENATOR KEFAUVER. That being the case, if the prices are different, that is not competition?

MR. BLOUGH. I would say that the buyer in that situation who has a choice—remember now, I am talking about our published prices—the buyer in that situation has this choice. He chooses to buy from one company at $5 higher. He chooses to buy from our company at $5 lower. Now if you call that competition and a desirable form of competition, you may have it your way. I say the buyer has more choice when the other fellow's price matches our price.[5] . . . .

MR. BLOUGH. Now, again, your concept of competition, that one price has to be lower than another price at all times in order to be considered competitive is simply not a practical acceptable definition of competition of any business that I know of in the United States.

It is a concept of some people who aren't familiar with business, but it is just not a practical way of running any kind of a long-range, competitive manufacturing operation.[6]

Time magazine summarized this phase of the hearings in the following terms:

U.S. Steel Chairman Roger Blough offered another defense [of uniform prices], which would appeal to all lovers of Alice in Wonderland, and which seemed to defy the basic principle of a competitive economy. If all steel prices are the same, he contended, then the customer is free to buy from any producer he chooses. But if prices are different, then the buyer has no real freedom of choice because he must buy from the company that sells the cheapest.[7]

[4] *Hearings,* p. 312.
[5] *Hearings,* pp. 312-313.
[6] *Hearings,* p. 312.
[7] *Time,* November 18, 1957, p. 101.

A little consideration suggests that there is a good deal of Alice-in-Wonderland on both sides of this controversy. Partly the problem is semantic, but underlying the semantics is a crucial issue.

At the semantic level we have different meanings for competition. Up to a generation ago, theoretical economists used the terms "competition" and "competitive price" in a fairly standard fashion to refer to situations in which price is *determined* by the forces of supply and demand. In these situations, when demand was in excess of supply, individual sellers raised prices and when supply was in excess of demand individual sellers offered lower prices and brought the price down. It is this conception of a competitive price which is involved in "the basic principle of a competitive economy" to which *Time* refers. According to this principle the public would be well served if prices were competitive *in this sense*.

Also, in a competitive market, using competition in this sense, there can usually be only one price at a given time. On the other hand, there is no room for price administration. As in the case of wheat or cotton or scrap iron, the number of producers is so large that no one producer provides a significant proportion of the supply. It is not the identical prices in the steel industry that defy the basic principle of competitive economy, but the fact of price administration. Administered prices whether identical or different, are not competitive prices in the classical sense of the word.

In more recent years, some economists have broadened the concept of competition to include what chairman Blough called "the impossible paradox known as 'monopolistic competition.' "[8] This is competition among the few and is quite different from classical competition. Theoretical analysis suggests that if supply is dominated by a few producers and each acts to maximize its short-term profits, the result will not serve the public interest. Either there will be cut-throat competition damaging to consumers and workers as well as owners, or profits are likely to be excessive. Thus,

[8] *Hearings*, p. 202.

"monopolistic competition" defies the basic principle of a competitive economy. However, there is nothing inherent in the theory of "monopolistic competition" which would lead one to expect the inflexibility of administered prices.

Finally there is the business conception of a competitive price which Mr. Blough has clearly enunciated. According to this concept, if one competitor initially has a different price from that of another, the latter is "meeting competition" when he sets the same price and so his price is competitive, though obviously he is not engaged in price competition, i.e., he is not attempting to take business away from his competitor by offering a lower price. This business concept of a competitive price is a useful concept so long as its meaning is clear and *no attempt is made to imply that because a price is competitive in this business sense, it is competitive in the classical economic sense and, therefore, tends to serve the public interest.* Whether a price which is competitive in this business sense serves the public interest remains to be determined and is not determined by saying that two identical administered prices are competitive.

On the other hand, the fact that two prices are identical does not mean that they are not in the public interest. The railroads, while usually true monopolies over considerable parts of their lines, often do compete with each other between major centers. And when such competition occurs, the public regulatory agency *requires* that their prices be identical. This suggests that, in the absence of classical competition, identical prices as such, are not necessarily against the public interest. It is not their identity but their level that is significant.

PRICE LEADERSHIP IN STEEL

A third characteristic of administered prices where standard products are concerned is the tendency for price leadership to develop. When there are relatively few producers of a standard product and administered prices are once set—either identical prices or prices with geographical or other differentials—one particular producer is likely to be looked on as the leader in making major price changes, both upward and downward. This leader may be the largest producer or a producer that is strategically located or some historical development may determine who comes to be regarded as the price leader.

The successful price leader initiates the major price changes which are then followed by most other producers. In a seller's market when demand is strong, the smaller producers may lift some of their prices without action by the price leader and in a buyers market when demand is weak, small producers may shade their prices without action by the price leader, but as a rule the other large producers wait on action by the price leader. In exceptional circumstances, other producers may initiate changes in the prices for particular products or even initiate a general price change, but for the most part the price leader becomes the focus of pricing in the industry.

In the steel industry there is a long tradition of price leadership and this leadership has been provided by the United States Steel Corporation. Thus in hearings before the Senate Interstate Commerce Committee in 1936, the then President of U.S. Steel, Mr. Irwin testified:

MR. IRWIN. I would say we generally make the prices.
THE CHAIRMAN. You generally make the prices?
MR. IRWIN. Yes, sir. We generally make the prices, unless some of the other members of the industry think that that price may be too high, and they make the price.
THE CHAIRMAN. You lead off, then, with a price change either up or down at Gary; is that correct?
MR. IRWIN. Yes.[9]

Of course, this was under the old multiple basing point system of pricing which was discontinued in 1948. There may be more

[9] *Hearings,* p. 234.

exceptions to United States Steel's price leadership now with mill prices than under the more rigid basing point system, but the leadership role of United States Steel is still the dominant fact of steel pricing.

In more recent hearings Chairman Blough seemed reluctant to admit to such leadership.

SENATOR KEFAUVER. You say you didn't consult with them [the other major producers] and you don't know [why the other major producers changed their price on July 1, 1957], but it is a fact that substantially they followed your prices. You don't deny that, do you, Mr. Blough?

MR. BLOUGH. I would say that possibly one of the reasons that was going through their minds, although again I don't know, was the fact that we have a substantially uniform labor contract in the steel industry, and I suspect that their cost increases were going up at somewhat the same rate that ours were going up.

That may have been a motivating factor with them. And as to whether the prices in the steel industry are the same, I would like to say that in some instances they are the same and in many instances they are different.

SENATOR KEFAUVER. But anyway, Mr. Blough, it is well known, isn't it, and generally accepted, that while there are some differentials, the other prices went up substantially about the same as yours. Is that not characteristic and typical?

I am not saying there is any agreement, any understanding, any conversation. You fixed your price and generally the other companies went up about the same amount.

MR. BLOUGH. Well, now, Senator, if I am going to have an opportunity to answer that question, I would like to have the opportunity.

Now let me just answer it in my own way if I may. The statement has been made that United States Steel always raises the price and others follow. Now let me give you instances of where that did not happen.[10]

Mr. Blough then gave a few specific examples purporting to represent price changes initiated by companies other than U.S. Steel and followed by the latter. However, there was a question whether these examples were relevant to the problem of price

[10] *Hearings*, p. 231.

leadership because of strike conditions or a strong sellers market existing at the time. Senator Kefauver, therefore, asked for examples in a period in which there were neither strikes nor a seller's market. The committee staff and officials of U.S. Steel agreed that the year 1954 met these conditions and the Corporation supplied specific price data on nineteen cases in that year which purported to represent price changes *initiated* by competitors of U.S. Steel. Analysis by the committee staff disclosed that, in 18 of these cases, the price change merely narrowed or eliminated a premium which had previously been charged above U.S. Steel's price. After the change, the competitors price was at or above United States Steel's price. The staff's conclusion was that with one exception these eighteen cases did not ". . . show instances of price leadership, as it is commonly interpreted, by companies other than United States Steel."[11]

The one clear case of the failure of U.S. Steel's price leadership is instructive as it discloses a limit on U.S. Steel's power of price leadership. The case concerns the price of galvanized sheets. On July 3, 1954, U.S. Steel increased its price from $116.50 a ton to $120.00. Four days later Republic Steel increased its price from $116.50 to $117.00. In the face of this lower price by Republic, U.S. Steel retained its $120.00 price for nearly a month and then on August 5, 1954 it cut its price to the $117.00 price of Republic.

The leadership role of U.S. Steel in the price changes of 1956 and 1957 was brought out in the hearings. Evidence was presented showing the mill price changes by the ten leading steel companies in August, 1956, and in July, 1957, for fifteen major products which accounted for nearly 80 per cent of the output of carbon steel.[12] In all but two cases, the data for the three largest companies, U.S. Steel, Bethlehem, and Republic, showed the same base prices before the August 1956 revision, the same price in-

[11] *Hearings,* p. 956.
[12] *Hearings,* pp. 1338-1342.

creases both in August, 1956, and July, 1957, and the same base prices after the July, 1957, increases. In each of these cases U.S. Steel had posted the changes and the other two companies had followed suit. For the seven smaller big-ten companies, sixty-one of the seventy prices changed in August, 1956, were increased by the same amounts as United States Steel and sixty-six of the sixty-nine price changes in July, 1957, were identical. And even the departures from identical changes were minor and usually related to particular geographical factors. This is the substance of price leadership with a followership of more than 90 per cent.

Even the price changes in the summer of 1958 in which U.S. Steel *did not initiate* the changes, show the dominant role that company played in steel pricing. Thus, *Iron Age* for June 26 stated "from a practical standpoint no other major steel company can replace U.S. Steel as a price leader. No other steel firm will announce a price increase July 1 if U.S. Steel does not." When Alan Wood Steel Company, with its less than one-tenth of 1 per cent of the nation's steel capacity, announced its price increase on June 26, its president, Mr. Wood, stated: "We realize that our company is too small to maintain a price level different from that of our larger competitors. In the event the other steel producers do not change their prices by July 7 or in the event they increase them by amounts other than those we have announced, we will have have no alternative other than to be competitive with their prices."[13] When Mr. Hood, president of U.S. Steel, issued his statement saying that his company would not increase prices on July 1, but would wait to see what happened, *Steel* magazine stated: "Some observers interpreted it as a plea that some other company should take the pricing initiative."[14] A. L. Adams, president of Jones and Laughlin Steel said his company wouldn't raise steel prices unless U.S. Steel did and asserted, "We have no intention of committing commercial suicide and assuming the role of price

[13] *Wall Street Journal,* June 26, 1958.
[14] *Hearings,* p. 4382.

leader."[15] When Armco Steel, followed by Republic Steel and Jones and Laughlin, announced price increases to take effect July 31, the *Wall Street Journal* reported that the "sentiment" was that U.S. Steel would join up, but if not, those that had increased their prices would be forced to rescind their increases. And one big company, Inland Steel, stated that it would not attempt to raise prices unless the number one steel producer—U.S. Steel—first took such action. The *Wall Street Journal* quoted Inland as saying "to do otherwise would cause us a severe loss of business."[16]

In effect, U.S. Steel put it up to the other members of the industry to guess what price it would find acceptable, and the industry guessed right. Thus U.S. Steel's price policy was still the guide to the industry. This makes the price policy of U.S. Steel the key to an understanding of prices for the industry as a whole. In the following sections we will examine the principles of pricing adopted by this company, and then the departures from identical prices by other companies.

THE UNITED STATES STEEL CORPORATION'S POLICY IN PRICING
U.S. Steel's officials have indicated two basic principles which underlie its current pricing policies; first, a one-price policy, and second, a rejection of the aim of maximizing profit either in the short- or the long-run in favor of a responsible policy of fair prices.

The one-price policy was emphasized by Chairman Blough at the hearing as follows: "We tell everybody what our price is, and we have a one-price policy, as I think you know. We sell to everybody at the same price."[17] Mr. Sentner, executive vice-president in charge of sales, elaborated this in the following words. "We have published f.o.b. mill prices for standard steel mill products at each of our producing. mills. This is the price we quote

[15] *Hearings*, p. 4490.
[16] *Hearings*, p. 4383.
[17] *Hearings*, p. 311.

to all our customers—large or small. In other words, we have
a one-price policy. When a change is made in our f.o.b. mill price,
the new price applies to all our customers and to all unshipped
orders on the books as of the date of change."[18]

In addition, the corporation may absorb freight so as to meet
"a lower delivered price of a competitor when necessary and
commercially desirable in order to participate in the business of
an individual customer."[19] Thus, if a customer is closer to the
mill of a competitor which has the same mill price as U.S. Steel,
the *delivered cost* to the customer of steel from U.S. Steel would
be higher than the *delivered cost* from U.S. Steel's competitor because of the extra freight. In some situations U.S. Steel will absorb
this *extra* freight so as to make its delivered price "competitive."
Whether U.S. Steel will in fact absorb the extra freight is a matter
of "commercial policy" and will depend on the particular circumstances. However, only a relatively small part of total sales appear to involve such freight absorption and the company does
not absorb freight to reduce its delivered price *below* that of its
competitor's delivered price.

The system of mill pricing by the price leader for most of its
output gives stability and determinateness to steel prices and is
generally adopted by the other giants of the industry.

The second major element in U.S. Steel's price policy is that of
responsibility. In the hearings, the attitude of responsibility was
repeatedly expressed, but its meaning was never made very clear.
Fortunately, Dr. A. D. H. Kaplan of Brookings Institution and his
two associates in their book, *Pricing in Big Business,* report the
results of extensive interviews with the high officials of U.S. Steel
in which they sought to discover just how prices were set.[20] They
report one official as saying, "U.S. Steel has never tried to price to

---

[18] *Hearings*, p. 357.
[19] U.S. Steel Corp., *Annual Report,* 1953, p. 12.
[20] A.D.H. Kaplan, Joel B. Dirlam, and Robert F. Lanzillotti, *Pricing in Big Business, A Case Approach* (Washington, D.C.: The Brooking's Institution, 1958), pp. 13-24, 166-175.

maximum profit, not only in the short-run, but even in the long-run."[21] And that another official "summarized the company's pricing policy as bottomed on the expectation of earning over the years a net return, after taxes, of around 8 per cent on investment."[22]

Dr. Kaplan summarizes his findings as follows: "According to public statements by Mr. Fairless and other officials of U.S. Steel, the corporation aims at a "fair return" at assumed norms of operation; its policy is to sell 'at the lowest price consistent with cost and reasonable profit.' "[23] Mr. Fairless gave a more elaborate statement of this policy in testimony before the TNEC.[24] "A price is reasonable if it nets a reasonable return to our company; if it permits us to pay good wages to our employees, to keep our facilities in excellent condition, to keep our equipment abreast of the developments within the industry, also if possible, to pay a fair return to the owners of this business." One high ranking official referred to this as the Corporation's "public utility" approach.[25]

In the 1957 hearings, Mr. Sentner, executive vice-president in charge of sales, presented U.S. Steel's policy with respect to the marketing of steel and steel pricing. In part he said:

> As a practical matter, we cannot consider the steel market in terms of an isolated moment in time. We must examine markets both in the near term future and over longer periods of time. . . . We are, of course, sensitive to the fact that the total steel market moves upward or downward with changing conditions; but we cannot base our commercial planning on sporadic week-to-week or month-to-month fluctuations. . . .
>
> Our pricing is the product of management judgment applied to long-range commercial planning, as well as to the day-to-day administration of our commercial affairs. It, of course, recognizes the need for sustaining long-term sales relationships with customers.
>
> United States Steel endeavors—to the extent competition permits—

[21] *Ibid,* p. 23.
[22] *Ibid,* p. 169.
[23] *Ibid,* p. 169.
[24] *Investigation of Concentration of Economic Power,* Hearings before the Temporary National Economic Comm. 76th Cong., 2d sess. (1939), Pt. 19, p. 10526.
[25] Reported by Kaplan, *et al., op. cit.,* p. 168.

to sell its products at prices which will recover its costs and yield a profit which will prove attractive to investors in United States Steel. . . .

It has been suggested that when demand is temporarily in excess of supply, steel mill products should be sold to the highest bidder. During such periods this type of expedient pricing might indeed yield a handsome quick profit. However, this would be a shortsighted policy and would surely lead to serious discrimination among our customers. . . .

Thus, there is no place in our commercial planning or policy for auction-type pricing of our steel products. In periods of strong demand we exercise restraint in our pricing.[26]

No mention is made of behavior in weak markets, but it could properly have been added that in weak markets the policy is to exercise restraint also in cutting prices.

Mr. Sentner was clear in indicating that United States Steel does not seek to maximize profits in the short-run and there is ample evidence that this is so. His testimony was vague as to what long-run policy sought to achieve other than a profit which will "prove attractive to investors in United States Steel." Mr. Hood, president, made the long-run policy somewhat more clear in the following words:

In all of these endeavors we seek to make it crystal clear that:
1. It is in the interest of the stockholders that there be equitable compensation for the employees.
2. It is in the interest of the employees that there be equitable return for the stockholders.
3. It is in the interest of the customers, the employees, the stockholders, and the public that, after payment of employee compensation and other costs, and stockholder dividends, there be a remaining profit to maintain United States Steel in healthy financial condition to meet the new and ever-expanding needs of this Nation.[27]

But beyond this point it is not possible to determine from the hearings what basis is employed in arriving at an "equitable return for the stockholders," or at the "remaining profit" after dividends

[26] *Hearings*, pp. 353-355.
[27] *Hearings*, pp. 361-362.

needed "to maintain United States Steel in healthy financial condition."

The rate of return on book value was clearly rejected as a fair basis, both because the postwar inflation had changed the value of the dollar and because the depreciation charges allowed by standard accounting procedures were insufficient to cover the replacement of depreciated plant and equipment.[28]

Mr. Tyson, Chairman of U.S. Steel's finance committee, suggested that: "A more realistic measurement of profit propriety is to compare the stock market valuation of the facilities on which the profit is earned with what it nowadays would cost to reproduce those facilities."[29] He actually compared the stock market "valuation of not over $80 a ton" for U.S. Steel's existing capacity with the "minimum of $300 per ton to create brand new, completely integrated ingot capacity." This would seem to imply that the amount of profits on partly worn-out and in some degree obsolescent plant should be the same as if it were brand-new undepreciated plant with the latest technical improvements. Certainly the figure for the cost of new plant which is not adjusted for the depreciated conditions of the existing plant and the superior design possible with a new plant can throw no light on the reasonableness of profits on old plant. However, these considerations are somewhat academic since there is no indication that the comparison of stock market value and the cost to reproduce was actually used as a basis for measuring equitable return.

Some stress was also placed by company officials on the rate of profit per dollar of sales, but again there is no indication that this is the basis of determining an equitable return to investors.[30]

The question was still further confused in the Steel hearings by Mr. Blough's testimony on pricing. Asked why, on July 1, 1957, United States Steel had only raised the price of steel $6

[28] *Hearings,* p. 246.
[29] *Hearings,* p. 248.
[30] *Hearings,* pp. 277. See also pp. 381-382.

a ton instead of $7 or $8 or $9 or $10, Mr. Blough replied, "In the light of all the factors it was our judgment that the price that we raised steel on July 1 was approximately the price at which it could have properly been raised at that time. . . ."[31] And later when asked, "Just what do you mean by your 'best judgment,' " he stated, "This is what we mean by that: The factors which bear upon the judgment of anyone who is attempting to determine what level of price he will attempt to charge are many. I will try to mention the major factors which we consider."[32] He then gave the following six factors, elaborating on each . . .

(1) First of all, we must consider what is happening to our costs.

(2) The second point . . . is the competitive situation that we face.

(3) We also know that if our prices are not changed, [when costs go up] that our profits are very quickly going to be wiped out. . . .

(4) Now one other thing . . . that we have got to take into account is what is happening to us with respect to depreciation.

(5) We took into account what we anticipated would be our future cost situation.

(6) We took one other thing into account. We took into account the publicly stated desire of not only the President of the United States but of many other people in this country, to act as conservatively as all of us possibly could in this type of situation.[33]

He then added: "Now, those are some of the factors, and I am sure that my associates would have additional factors of their own which they probably took into account."

On its face, this looks straightforward, though it sheds little direct light on what is regarded as a fair profit. However, an examination of what is meant by "our costs" does throw a strange and confusing light on "fair profit." In his discussion of labor costs, Mr. Blough considered only the increase in costs *per hour of employment,* not costs *per ton of steel.* Nowhere in his elaboration did he introduce changes in productivity as a factor affecting costs,

[31] *Hearings,* p. 229.
[32] *Hearings,* p. 296.
[33] *Hearings,* pp. 296-298.

or discuss the costs of steel *per ton,* or other unit of output. Similarly, in his discussion of the changes in "overall costs," Mr. Blough took the total cost of material, power, etc., and divided it *by the total hours of employment* and not by the *total tons of steel produced.*

This use of labor and material costs *per hour of employment* and not *costs per ton of steel* is nowhere discussed or justified in Mr. Blough's testimony. Yet it radically alters the meaning of "costs" in his exposition of the six major factors which enter into U.S. Steel's pricing decisions. This matter is so important that the whole of Mr. Blough's elaboration of the role of costs in pricing is given below, with emphasis added:

> First of all, we must consider what is happening to our costs. I want to make it clear to you that what is happening to our costs is of prime importance because, as is indicated on the building over here on Pennsylvania Avenue, the Archives Building, "What is past is prologue."
> That certainly is true with respect to costs in steelmaking.
> Now, what we have understood about our costs are not the detailed little items that you are trying to get. We based our judgment; I cannot speak for anyone else in the organization, but I am talking about my own thinking.
> My own thinking, so far as costs, was along this line: We have incurred on the average, for the last 17 years, cost increases *per hour of employment* of approximately 8.1 per cent every year as the year rolled around; and last year the cost was increased about 10 per cent, not 8.1 per cent. That is an average for 17 years.
> We know that as those costs go up, we incur an increase overall, *per hour of employment* of 8.8 per cent. Now the relationship, therefore, when our employment costs go up approximately 8 per cent, our total costs go up more than 8 per cent.
> In this case, I knew from the data that you already have received, that our employment costs were going up approximately 6 per cent. We knew that. Now, what would our total costs go up, approximately, based upon our best judgment of what would affect us? And the answer is, it would go up approximately 6½ per cent total cost. You will recall that as against that 6½ per cent, which is an estimate on

my part at this point, we increased our price 4 per cent. Now we certainly take into account what our problems are with respect to cost.[34]

As can be seen, this explanation of the way in which "what is happening to costs" enters into pricing makes *no* reference to costs per ton of steel. Yet it is costs *per ton* of steel which are important for pricing and there is no close relation between labor costs or overall costs per hour of employment and labor or overall costs per ton of steel. If the employment cost *per hour* goes up 10 per cent and output per man-hour goes up 10 per cent, the labor cost per ton of steel would remain the same. The increase in labor cost per hour would not reduce profits per ton of steel nor would it justify an increase in price. Indeed, if steel prices were adjusted for changes. in employment costs *per hour* without regard to changes in output per hour of labor, the gains from increased productivity would go solely to increase profits.

The same would be true for overall costs except that a following of the Blough approach would add to the price of steel, not only increases in employment costs per hour which did not increase the employment cost per ton of steel, but an entirely fictitious increase in raw material costs. This peculiar result arises because, in his overall index of cost, Mr. Blough has in effect included nonlabor costs (raw materials, power, etc.) divided by man-hours of employment. If the prices of raw materials were constant and nonlabor costs *per ton* remained constant, the nonlabor cost *per man-hour* of employment would rise with every increase in output per man-hour. Yet this apparent increase in nonlabor costs would be entirely fictitious, reflecting neither an increase in cost per ton nor an increase in the prices of raw materials or other nonlabor items of input.

Since it is part of the ABC of business training that it is changes in cost per unit of output, not changes in cost per hour of employment, that are relevant to the pricing of a product, it is hard to understand or explain Mr. Blough's peculiar use of increases

[34] *Hearings,* pp. 296-297.

in costs *per hour of employment* and not *costs per ton* as a major factor in determining steel prices and his complete neglect of costs per ton or of changes in productivity as important factors. This, in turn, seriously confuses the question of what is meant by "an equitable return to stockholders."

Nor is this confusing concept of costs confined to Mr. Blough's testimony. Mr. Tyson, Chairman of the finance committee of U.S. Steel, presented a formal statement which Mr. Blough referred to as "a statement on the cost facts of United States Steel."[35] In this he introduced a chart showing indexes of employment costs *per employee hour* and total costs *per employee hour* from 1940 to 1956 and explained:

"It is in our most major cost that the most disturbing inflation is most readily observed. Ever since just before World War II our employment costs per hour . . . have been experiencing a continuous high-speed inflation."[36] Then he presented a second chart showing the seventeen-year rise of employment costs per hour of employment, in wholesale prices, and in steel prices, and income per dollar of sales. Of this he said, "In this diagram you will note the ever-rising employment costs per hour which are compared, on the basis of 1940 = 100, with the lesser rises in wholesale prices and steel prices."[37] In his formal statement, he presented no index of steel production per hour or of steel costs per unit of product or any other figures of costs that would seem to be relevant to pricing. Indeed, his presentation of "the cost facts of United States Steel" simply does not discuss the changes in the actual costs of producing steel and serves to reinforce the confusion as to the role of costs in pricing introduced by Mr. Blough.

It is difficult to regard seriously this comparison of the rise in steel prices with the rise in overall costs *per hour of employment* on which the steel officials place such stress, particularly in the absence of *any* data on the rise in the cost of making steel. Whether

[35] *Hearings,* p. 237.
[36] *Hearings,* p. 244. See also p. 255.
[37] *Hearings,* p. 245.

this material on steel "costs" was presented in order to mislead the public as to the relation between the rise in the costs of producing a ton of steel and the rise in steel prices or whether it is simply a part of the sound-effects of collective bargaining is not clear. What is clear is that it helps to confuse rather than clarify the method by which U.S. Steel arrives at its published prices.

In this situation we can either surrender to confusion or accept Dr. Kaplan's conclusion that the corporation seeks neither to maximize profits in the short-run nor in the long-run, but aims at reasonable prices, as "reasonable" is interpreted by the responsible corporate executives in the light of costs, competition and other conditions surrounding the production and marketing of steel. Just what this means and how close it comes to producing results that are "reasonable" from the point of view of the public interest can best be considered by examining what has actually happened. This will be done in the remaining chapters of Part I.

THE AREA OF DISCRETION

But one important conclusion can be drawn at this point. This is that the price leader in steel operates within an area of pricing discretion such that within a significant range it can set one price rather than another.

The power to choose between pricing to maximize short-run profit or long-run profit is in itself a reflection of a considerable area of discretion whenever the two aims would produce different results. Thus, in a sellers' market when demand is in excess of capacity, maximizing of short-run profit could be expected to result in a high price in relation to costs; in a buyers' market when supply is in excess of demand, it could be expected to result in a lower price in relation to costs. Where pricing is in terms of long-run considerations, these extremes of price fluctuation would be avoided.

The area of discretion is further widened when a company aims at a "reasonable" price rather than aiming at profit maximizing in either the short or the long-run. It is this area of discretion over price plus the importance of steel to the economy that makes the pricing of steel a matter of such important public concern.

That the price leader in steel has an area of discretion in setting its steel prices does not mean that it can set any price it chooses. Obviously, the price must cover its costs and yield a profit if the enterprise is to remain healthy and continue to serve its productive function in our society. Likewise the leader cannot set and maintain a price which its major followers find too high. In a sellers' market, the smaller companies may charge a premium over the leader's prices; and in a buyers' market they may set prices below those of the leader. Geographical or other differentials are likely to develop. But in the main, there is an area of discretion between the two limits of necessary profits and followership by competitors within which the price leader exercises judgment.

In the hearings, Mr. Blough was reluctant to admit of such an area of discretion. The first time he was asked by Senator Kefauver, ". . . when you talked about best judgments does that not indicate . . . you have a so-called area of discretion in which you can use your judgment?" he replied that he did not understand what was meant.[38] On a later occasion, after testimony had been introduced showing how impossible it was for a farmer to "administer" the price of his eggs or get a price other than that determined by the market, he agreed that when he and his officers arrived at a price increase of $6 they operated within an area of discretion which an eggseller does not have.[39]

Mr. George M. Humphrey, chairman of the board of National Steel Corporation, and former Secretary of the Treasury of the United States, showed no hesitation in agreeing to the existence of an area of discretion in pricing as the following colloquy indicates:

[38] *Hearings*, p. 296.
[39] *Hearings*, p. 308.

SENATOR WILEY. From a discussion of administered prices by the witnesses, the subcommittee gets the impression that top management has a very wide discretion in deciding how high steel prices should be. Do you say that is correct?

MR. HUMPHREY. I say it is. They have a very heavy responsibility with respect to it, and they have many limitations within which they have got to operate.[40]

That the price leader does in fact have an area of discretion in pricing was made clear by Mr. Blough when he closed his formal statement to the Kefauver Committee with the following words: "So, in the light of these facts and all of these responsibilities, I commend to the thoughtful consideration of this committee the question of whether or not our price action was responsible and in the public interest."[41]

This is the question which will be explored in the following chapters.

[40] *Hearings,* p. 852.
[41] *Hearings,* p. 214.

CHAPTER IV

STEEL PRICES AND TYPES OF INFLATION

And so, Mr. Chairman, if we are going to investigate steel prices at this hearing, by all means let us investigate steel prices; but in so doing let us not delude ourselves or anyone else into the notion that we are thereby striking at the roots of inflation!

ROGER M. BLOUGH,
CHAIRMAN OF THE BOARD,
THE UNITED STATES STEEL CORPORATION*

Is the public well served by the steel prices which emerge from this far-from-clear pricing process? Have the steel price increases of recent years in fact been in the public interest? Has the pricing power of the price leader, U.S. Steel, been used responsibly? It is not easy to answer these questions because of the extensive rise of prices which has occurred since the depths of the depression in 1932. The difference in the behavior of administered prices from that of market prices, the lags and leads in adjustment, and the problem of capital values confuse the issue of what is a responsible exercise of pricing power.

If only one kind of inflation were involved, the problem would not be so difficult. But actually three different types of inflation have contributed to the big rise in steel prices and each type has its own peculiar characteristics growing out of the special conditions under which it occurred. This chapter will examine these different types of inflation and their relevance for the movement of steel prices. This will provide essential background for in-

* *Hearings.* p. 207.

terpreting the actual movement of steel prices in relation to other prices and to costs, which will be considered in subsequent chapters.

THE THREE TYPES OF INFLATION

During the last thirty years, there have been five periods of sharply rising prices, as can be seen from the movements of the Wholesale Price Index shown in Chart VI. The first two were essentially similar and involved recoveries from depression in the 1930's. They represent a type of inflation quite different from the inflation of classical theory. The second two involved war, and were more nearly like the inflations of classical theory. The most recent rise is a third type, differing from both the recovery and the war inflations. It involved simultaneous inflation and recession. How different these three types of inflation are can best be seen by considering first the classical conception of inflation.

THE CLASSICAL CONCEPTION OF INFLATION

Up to a generation ago the conception of inflation was clear and simple. Economists distinguished between two types of price movement: (1) those changes in price which were primarily adjustments within the price structure, with no significant effect on the level of prices, and (2) those which were primarily changes in the price level. Thus, in a period in which the price *level* remained relatively stable, all sorts of price changes could be expected as the demand and supply of particular products shifted. If demand shifted from bread to meat, the price of bread would come down and that of meat would go up. If the demand for clothing shifted from cotton to wool, the same relative shift in prices would occur. If the cost of producing an item fell, its price would go down. If the cost of producing another item increased, its price would go up. Even though the price level as a whole remained fairly stable, there

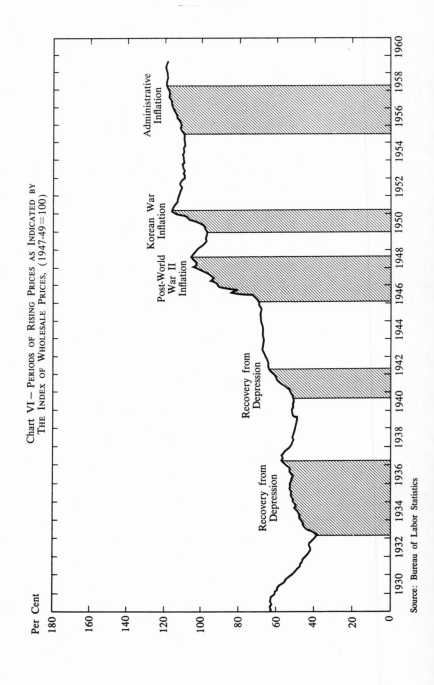

Chart VI – Periods of Rising Prices as Indicated by The Index of Wholesale Prices, (1947-49=100)

Per Cent

Administrative Inflation

Korean War Inflation

Post-World War II Inflation

Recovery from Depression

Recovery from Depression

Source: Bureau of Labor Statistics

would be a continuous shifting and change in individual prices. It would only be the level that was stable.

In addition, the level of prices might also change. Such a change was attributed, not to shifts in the demand and supply for particular goods, but to general changes in the demand for goods relative to the supply of goods. A general rise in prices would result from an offering of more money for goods at the current price level than the amount of goods offered for money at that price level. Indeed, the traditional type of inflation was often referred to as the result of too much money chasing too few goods. When the level of the demand for goods rose relative to the supply, it was expected that the level of prices would rise and when the level of demand fell relative to the supply of goods, it was expected that the price level would fall. Thus, the concept of a general rise or fall in prices became a part of economic analysis and was regarded as something distinct from changes in relative prices.

Of course, a general change in price level was almost certain to be accompanied by changes in the relation of different prices to each other just as, at a stable price level, some prices would be going up and others down. What is important here is that changes in price level were thought of as distinctly different from changes in relative prices, and as something which happened to all prices to exactly the same extent. Thus, if the price level rose 10 per cent, with some prices rising more than others, it was thought of as a perfectly general rise, that is, a rise of, say, 10 per cent in each price, combined with changes in relative prices. In fact, the changes in relative prices were usually thought of as pretty much the changes in relative prices which would have occurred if the price level as a whole had remained stable. The relation between individual price changes and a general change was like that between a tide and individual waves in the ocean. Any point on the surface of the water would be in constant motion up or down due to the waves, while, at the same time, the tide was raising or lowering the whole level.

In traditional thinking, changes in the price level arose solely from changes in the relation between the demand for and supply of money. At a given level of prices and incomes, individuals and businesses in the community would find it convenient to hold a certain amount of money, and this was the demand for money.[1] If the demand for money were constant and the money supply— the total amount of money outstanding—were just equal to it, the price level would be stable. It would also be stable if the money demand and supply both increased or declined by exactly the same amount. But, if they behaved differently, one changing relative to the other, the price level would change.

For example, if the money supply was just equal to the demand for money at an initial level of prices and incomes, and there was no initial change in the demand for money but the money supply was increased, the price level would rise. In one rigid formulation of the theory, if the money supply were doubled, the price level would double. More reasonable formulations of the theory recognized that the level of prices would be effected by the *method* of increasing the money supply as well as by the amount of increase. This is because the process of changing the money supply can also affect the *demand* for money. A rapid expansion in the money supply might make people so uncertain of the future value of money that there would be "a flight from money," that is, the demand for money would fall. This would combine with the in-

[1] It should be noted that the terms *"demand"* and *"supply"* without qualification are, by custom, used in significantly different ways when applied to money and when applied to goods. With goods, such as wheat, we could speak of the gross supply of wheat and the net supply of wheat referring, respectively, to the total stock of wheat at any time and to the amount that would currently be offered for sale, at different prices. When the supply of wheat is referred to without saying gross or net, it is customarily the net supply that is referred to. When the supply of money is referred to without saying net or gross, it it is customarily the gross supply that is meant, i.e., the total stock of money outstanding. Similarly with demand, the demand for wheat customarily refers to the net demand while the demand for money customarily refers to the gross demand, i.e., the demand for cash balances or what is the same thing, the demand for money as a store of value.

crease in supply to lift the price level more than if the same increase in the money supply occurred more slowly and without producing a change in the demand for money. But in both cases the price level would be determined by the relation between the demand for and the supply of money.

It was the essence of this traditional theory that the price level would continuously adjust so as to keep the demand and supply of money just equal. It was also a logical conclusion from this theory that the changes in the price level would automatically maintain employment at close to the optimum level so that excessive unemployment would be automatically self-correcting. Fortunately we do not need to go into the mechanism by which this was brought about, though we will presently have to go into the reasons why this automatic corrective does not operate in our actual economy. Finally, this theory of price behavior allowed for only one type of inflation, monetary inflation.

It is important to notice that this theory rested on the assumption that all prices were market prices like those of wheat, cotton, and steel scrap, with their flexible adjustment equating the supply and the demand for each particular good. The theory excluded administered prices, which tend to be inflexible and do not equate the supply and demand for goods except by chance. Indeed, as has already been suggested, the classical theory was initially developed in important measure as an attack on the inequities and restrictions involved in the price administration of the medieval guilds.

Today, administered prices (including administered wage rates) are a dominant characteristic of our economy. And the introduction of administered prices into the theory of prices and employment give that theory new dimensions: (1) administered prices alter the character of a monetary inflation, and (2) they create the possibility of the two additional types of inflation that will be discussed after the change in the character of monetary inflation has been examined. All three types contribute to the complexity of price movements and the difficulty of appraising the behavior of steel prices.

A MONETARY INFLATION WITH ADMINISTERED PRICES

The change in the character of a monetary inflation in the presence of administered prices is primarily in the process of inflation rather than in the end result. Even in the presence of administered prices it could be expected that an increase in the money supply relative to the demand for money at an initial price level would *ultimately* result in a general increase in prices comparable to the end result of a classical inflation. But the *process* of inflation could be expected to be different.

In the classical inflation, an increase in the supply of money increased the demand for goods more or less all along the line. With the general increase in demand, it was expected that prices would move up more or less together. Thus, while some specific prices might go up little and others a great deal because of specific factors, the average for any sizable group of prices representing a variety of products would go up by about the same amount as another similar group. And as the inflation progressed, different random groups would keep pretty much abreast of each other. In this sense, the inflation would be general and the price *level* would rise.

But the inflexibility of administered prices alters the process. When the money supply is increased and demand rises all along the line, the flexible prices of traditional theory can be expected to rise so as to equate supply and demand. In contrast, administered prices can be expected to remain relatively stable so that demand exceeds supply, forward orders build up, deliveries are delayed, and some customers go without. But then, under the pressure of rising costs, administered prices are successively raised.

This means that the price adjustment to the increased money supply can be expected to take place in two stages: one of monetary adjustment and the other of relative price adjustment. In the first stage, market prices can be expected to go up rapidly while administered prices go up much more slowly. This can be expected to continue until the *average* of market and administered prices is high enough to raise the demand for money to the level of the increased supply. This would bring the first stage of adjustment to a close with no further tendency for the average of prices to rise.

The second stage would be a readjustment in the relation between market and administered prices. If market and administered prices, as groups, were in reasonably good balance with each other before the increase in the money supply, the rise in the *average* of prices which equates the supply and demand for money would at the same time produce an unbalanced relation between market prices and administered prices. Market prices, as a group, would be altogether too high and administered prices, as a group, would be too low. However, once the supply and demand for money was equal, the *average* of prices could be expected to remain fairly constant, but administered prices could be expected to continue their rise and market prices could be expected to drop until something like a reasonable balance between the two was again achieved. Thus, in the second stage, market and administered prices could be expected to move in opposite directions.

The *end result* to be expected of a monetary inflation, therefore, would be a general rise in the price level regardless of whether all prices were market prices or whether some were market and others administered; in the latter case, however, the *process* would be different from the traditional "general" rise. In the analysis of steel price behavior, this difference in process is of crucial importance, as we shall see.

THE WAR INFLATIONS

This two-stage monetary inflation is the kind of inflation which occurred after World War II and during the Korean War.

During World War II the money supply of this country more

than doubled, but the inflationary pressure from this increase was largely contained after the spring of 1942 by government price control. However, when price control broke down in 1946, prices were free to adjust to the excess supply of money and a rapid rise in prices occurred. The two-stage process of adjustment is clearly shown in the first panel of Chart VII. This panel shows the be-

Chart VII – WAR-INDUCED MONETARY INFLATIONS IN WHOLESALE PRICES, 1945-1950 AND MID-1950-1952

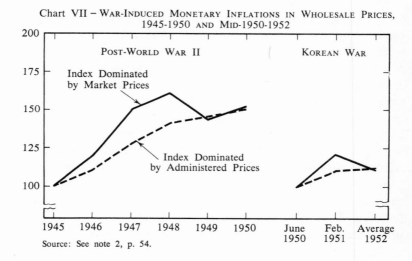

Source: See note 2, p. 54.

havior of two wholesale price indexes, one dominated by market prices (e.g., wheat, hogs, cotton, clothing, leather, lumber), and the other dominated by administered prices (e.g., cigarettes, auto tires, cement, steel, and the prices of new automobiles to dealers).[2]

[2] The market-dominated index is the weighted average of the five major groups in the Bureau of Labor Statistics Wholesale Price Index which are dominated by market prices: farm products, processed foods, textile products and apparel, hides, skins and leather products, and lumber and wood products. The administration-dominated index is the weighted average of the five major groups which are dominated by administered prices: tobacco and bottled beverages, rubber and rubber products, nonmetallic minerals, metal and metal products, and machinery and motive products. Of the

In the postwar inflation, as the chart shows, there was a rapid rise in the market-dominated index culminating in 1948 at a level 60 per cent above the 1945 average and then a decline so that the average for 1950 was only 52 per cent above the 1945 level. In contrast, the administration-dominated index rose much more slowly, in 1948 reaching an average of only 43 per cent above the 1945 level, but continuing to rise another 11 percentage points so that the average for 1950 was 54 per cent above the 1945 level. For the period as a whole, the two indexes rose by about the same amount. One could say that the monetary inflation—the general pressure of too much money chasing too few goods—was over by 1948, but with a very distorted price structure in which market prices averaged too high relative to the new price level and administered prices averaged too low. This distortion of prices at the wholesale level was largely corrected in the subsequent period, with the inventory recession and recovery from mid-1948 to mid-1950 carrying market prices index below and then back to approximately the level reached by the administration-dominated index.[3]

This same type of two-step inflation occurred also during the Korean War but on a much smaller scale, as can be seen in the

remaining five groups in the BLS Wholesale Price Index three, (fuel, power, and lighting materials; chemicals and allied products; and furniture and other household durables) involve such mixtures of market and administered prices that neither group clearly dominates while the other two (pulp, paper, and allied products; and miscellaneous products) are not available prior to 1947. The groups included in the market dominated index and the administration dominated index constitute three quarters of the weight of the 1960 BLS wholesale price index and carry nearly equal weight, 35.3 per cent and 39.4 per cent respectively.

[3] It should be noted that if monthly data had been used to compile the indexes, the differential behavior would have been increased since the market-price index reached a peak early in 1948, when it was several points above the average for the year while the administration-dominated index was several points below the year's average. On the other hand, monthly data would also show that in June, 1950 just before the outbreak of the Korean War, the readjustment in the relation between market and administered prices was not complete, just as the recovery from the recession was not complete.

second panel of Chart VII. From the beginning of the Korean War in June, 1950 to February, 1951 when the wholesale price index reached its peak, the market-dominated index rose 20 per cent while the administration-dominated index rose only half as much. Then market prices tended to fall while administered prices tended to continue their rise so that by 1952, the average war increase was about the same for both indexes.[4] Certainly by 1953 the main impetus of the two war inflations had spent itself and the price structure was in approximately the same balance as it held in 1942 and 1929.

This two-stage character of monetary inflation is important for the analysis of steel price behavior for two reasons. First, it gives us reason to expect that in a period of monetary inflation, steel prices will first lag behind the average rise since they are clearly administered prices and then continue to rise when market prices are falling. And second, it means that, in comparing the behavior of steel prices with that of other prices or with the behavior of costs, the relevant comparison can be seriously distorted by the time periods over which the comparison is made. For example, the fact that steel prices rose much more than the wholesale price index from 1948 to 1950 would cast no light on the legitimacy of the greater price rise, because the price structure was badly distorted in 1948. The choice of periods over which comparisons are made thus becomes a crucial matter.

PRICE RECOVERY FROM A DEPRESSION

The rise of prices occurring in a recovery from depression is quite different from that of a monetary inflation. This is partly because

[4] It should be noted that if one combines the two war periods and measures the changes in the two indexes from 1942 when the general order for freezing prices was issued to the first half of 1953, the net rise in the market-dominated index and the administration-dominated index is about the same, 70 and 76 per cent, respectively. Also by the first half of 1953, both indexes had risen by almost exactly the same amount above their 1929 level, 77.7 and 77.6 respectively.

a deflation in the presence of administered prices differs so markedly from that envisaged in traditional theory and provides a starting point for a rise in prices quite different from that traditionally assumed. Therefore, we shall have to consider the deflationary fall in prices as well as the subsequent rise.

In traditional monetary theory, a deflation should be just the opposite of a monetary inflation. A general drop in demand, due to a money supply too small in relation to the demand for money, could be expected to bring not only a drop in the general index of prices but also a drop more or less all along the line. And if all prices were market prices, this could be expected.

But where a major body of prices are administered, the inflexibility of administered prices and their relative insensitivity to changes in demand can be expected not only to modify the process of adjustment, but also to bring about a different end result—the unemployment of men and machines. When the demand for money exceeds the supply of money (which also means that the demand for goods is less than the supply), flexible market prices can be expected to drop, thus tending to reduce the demand for money as traditional theory prescribed. But administered prices can be expected to remain the same or to drop only a little, while the drop in the demand for goods whose prices are administered would result in a reduction in sales, production, and employment. And because peoples' real incomes would be reduced by unemployment, their demand for money would also be reduced. Thus, the initial deflationary excess in the demand for money relative to the supply would be corrected partly by a fall in prices, particularly those made in the market, and partly by a fall in employment and real incomes. At the same time—because market prices would drop much more than administered prices—the price structure would become distorted. This first stage of adjustment in a recession would be just the reverse of the first stage in a monetary inflation.

A comparable second stage in adjustment would occur if the smaller initial change in administered prices were simply a matter of lag, as it appears to be in the case of monetary inflation. Then administered prices could be expected to descend successively to lower levels until the whole of the deflation adjustment took the form of price reductions and optimum employment was re-established. In that case, the completed process of adjustment would mirror the two-stage adjustment of a monetary inflation: first, a drop in market prices with a smaller drop in administered prices until *monetary* balance was established, and then a continued fall in administered prices and some rise in market prices until *price* balance was re-established.

But actual experience and theory both clearly suggest that the adjustment to a monetary deflation involves more than a lag in administered prices. There is no evidence of a tendency for an administered price to continue down once the initial stage of adjustment has been completed.

This situation arises naturally from the action of price administrators. First, they tend to administer prices in terms of total costs, and while operating costs per unit tend to go down in a recession, with any reduction in raw material prices and wage rates, their overhead costs per unit go up with a lower rate of operation.[5] Second, in so far as their raw materials include items whose prices are administered, the prices of the latter on the average will not have declined as much as market prices. And third, wage rates are a form of administered price and in a major deflation show a behavior intermediate between market prices and the more inflexible administered prices. As a result the initial adjustment to deflation, which creates a distorted price structure and unemployment, does not appear to set up conditions under

[5] Some economists regard the inclusion of overhead costs in the setting of administered prices as irrational and not likely to serve the best interests of individual business enterprises. Perhaps this conclusion arises from an inadequate analysis of the economics of price administration. In any event, inclusion of overhead costs in the regulation of public utility rates is a standard part of the process of pricing in the public interest, and this procedure also appears to be extensive on the part of private price administrators. The rationale for this behavior is developed in Chapter XIV.

which automatic forces would correct the price distortion and the excess unemployment.

It also follows that, with the recovery of demand, a reverse process can be expected to take place, with market prices tending to rise faster than administered prices. With full recovery, the rise in the wholesale price index thus would tend to bring market prices and administered prices back into balance. In this way, a price rise in a period of recovery is an integral part of the recovery itself and can operate to improve the balance in the price structure. If such a rise in the average of wholesale prices is called an inflation, it is a *good* kind of inflation and lies outside the scope of traditional inflation theory. Because it is an integral part of the recovery process, such a beneficial price rise is often called "reflation" to distinguish it from the harmful monetary inflation.

REFLATIONS FROM THE BIG DEPRESSION

The two periods of price rise following the big depression belong to this reflation type of price rise. This can be seen in Chart VIII which shows the behavior of the market-dominated and administration-dominated indexes from 1929 to 1942. Between 1929 and 1932, as demand declined, the market-dominated index dropped more than 40 per cent while the administration-dominated index dropped less than half as much. Then in the recovery period to 1937, the market-dominated index rose twice as fast as the administration-dominated index. If recovery had continued and the two indexes had continued to rise at the same rates, another year and a half or two years of recovery would have brought the two indexes to the same relation they held in 1928 and 1929 before the big depression.

However, the recession of 1938–1939 intervened, and full employment was not achieved until early 1942 under the stress of war demand. In this recession, as in the big depression, market-dominated prices fell sharply while the administration-dominated index fell much less. Then, in the recovery, market prices recovered their position while the administration-dominated index rose only gently. By early 1942 when full employment was achieved, the two indexes had come close together and were almost exactly at the same level as in 1928 and 1929, although for the average of 1942 market prices were somewhat above their 1928–1929 level.

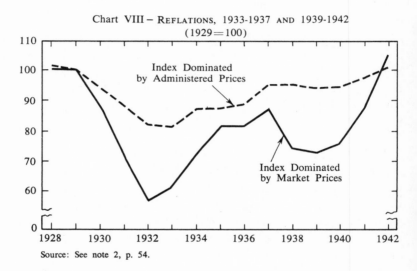

Chart VIII – REFLATIONS, 1933-1937 AND 1939-1942
(1929 = 100)

Source: See note 2, p. 54.

In these two periods of rise in the wholesale price index (1932 to 1937 and 1939 to 1942), we have a type of inflation with a significance quite different from that of monetary inflation. In both monetary inflation and reflation the price rise comes from an increase in demand and in both cases the big rise tends to come in market prices. But in monetary inflation the big rise of market prices distorts the price structure and requires readjustment; in reflation it corrects a distortion in the price structure that has already developed as a result of the previous recession.

This distortion and correction of the price structure in depression and recovery has an importance for the analysis of steel prices. It means that, in some years, market prices and administered prices tend to get seriously out of balance with each other and the use of any such year as a base for comparing the behavior of steel prices with other prices or costs is likely to distort the results. To be valid, comparisons must be made between periods in which the price structure is distorted to the same degree or, better, between periods in which the price structure is in close balance. In the present study, the latter procedure will be adopted as far as possible.

ADMINISTRATIVE INFLATION

Administered pricing also introduces the possibility of a third type of price rise, one which increases the average of prices and raises the price indexes, but is neither monetary inflation nor reflation from a depression and.which can bring about both inflation and depression at the same time. As this type of inflation is initiated by a movement of administered prices, it can conveniently be referred to as an administrative inflation.

And administrative inflation is made possible by the area of discretion within which price administrators do their pricing. As we have seen, the price administrator, usually the management of a corporation, operates within an area of discretion in which economic forces alone do not determine price. As a result, it is likely to be able to increase its price by a small percentage even though there is no change in demand or costs. In the case of wage rates, too, a union is likely to operate within an area of discretion so that it can use more pressure or less to get a higher wage rate. And this in turn could increase business costs to an extent that could produce price increases. Thus, with administered prices (including wage rates) it is possible to have rising prices without any monetary cause or excess demand for goods.

Some people have referred to this nonmonetary inflation as a cost-push inflation in the belief that it arises from excessive wage increases. But theoretically it could originate either with labor or management, and a more neutral term is needed. It is because this type of inflation could not occur in the absence of price administration that the term "administrative inflation" is here adopted to distinguish it from the classical monetary inflation.[6] This expression is neutral with respect to labor and management and implies that this type of inflation is associated with administered prices.[7] It does not imply, of course, that any individual or small group intentionally creates the inflation.

An administrative inflation differs from a monetary inflation in a second important respect. It is likely to lead to a recession in business activity and unemployment unless it is followed by monetary expansion. A rise in administered prices, with market prices unchanged, would usually have the effect of increasing the demand for money since more money would be necessary to command a given amount of buying power. If the money supply was not increased, the extra demand for the limited supply of money would produce a contraction in the demand for goods and in unemployment, in much the same way that, in the absence of administrative inflation, a contraction in the money supply would usually produce a recession and unemployment. The recession would also tend to force down market prices somewhat so that the average of prices and the price indexes would not go up as much as the rise in administered prices alone would require.

---

[6] See *Hearings,* p. 84.

[7] Some economists have used the terms "demand inflation" and "supply inflation" in place of "monetary inflation" and "administrative inflation." "Demand inflation" might conceivably be acceptable since this type of inflation involves an initial excess in the demand for goods relative to supply. However, it also involves an excess in the supply of money relative to the demand and so could equally well be called a supply inflation. The term "monetary inflation" clearly designates an imbalance between the demand and the supply of money which results in the reduction in the value of money. On the other hand, an administrative inflation does not involve any initial change in either the supply of goods or the supply of money. In essence it is the product of administrative decisions. For this reason, the term "supply inflation" seems quite inappropriate.

THE POST-1953 INFLATION

There is considerable evidence that the inflation of wholesale prices in the years following 1953 was of this administrative type. As can be seen from Chart IX, the index dominated by market

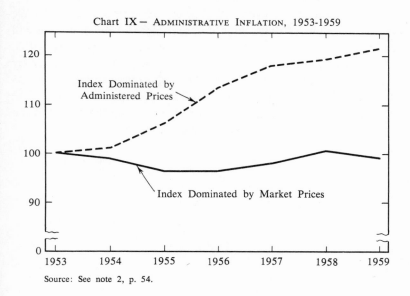

Chart IX — ADMINISTRATIVE INFLATION, 1953-1959

Source: See note 2, p. 54.

prices remained relatively stable and was at practically the same level in 1959 as in 1953. In contrast, the index dominated by administered prices rose more or less continuously and was 20 per cent above its 1953 level by 1959.

It is quite clear that the rise in the *average* of prices after 1953 was not due to a monetary inflation. There was not a *general* excess of demand, because this would have been reflected in a rise in market prices. Also there was considerable unemployment and two minor recessions during the period, clear evidence that production was not generally pressing on capacity.

Similarly the price rise after 1953 was not a case of reflation, for in 1953 employment was high. Indeed, if it were a case of reflation, we would expect market prices, not administered prices to rise the most. It is the rise of administered prices without a rise of market prices which distinguishes the inflation since 1953 from the reflations following depression and from the monetary inflations associated with the two wars.

In analyzing the recent behavior of steel prices, we shall have to take account of these three different types of inflation. We will be concerned primarily with the rise of steel prices since 1953. But much of the controversy over this rise turns on whether by 1953 steel prices had completed their adjustment to the war inflations. This will be the crucial question examined in the next chapter. The succeeding chapter will then take up the nature of the increase in the administrative inflation after 1953.

CHAPTER V

STEEL PRICES AND THE WAR INFLATIONS

Economic arithmetic tells us that the new cost-push inflation can never be terminated until inflation in the biggest and most basic cost, employment cost, is terminated.

ROBERT C. TYSON, CHAIRMAN, FINANCE COMMITTEE,
THE UNITED STATES STEEL CORPORATION*

Apparently the industry believes that any time—whether demand is high or low, whether it is rising or falling—is a good time to raise prices. . . . It raises prices when supply exceeds demand, when the reverse is true, and when the two factors are in balance. It raises its prices when profits are high, when they are low, and when they are moderate. It raises prices when costs go up, when costs go down, and when costs remain stable.

OTIS BRUBAKER, RESEARCH DIRECTOR,
UNITED STEELWORKERS OF AMERICA**

Between 1942 and 1953, finished steel prices doubled. Was this a legitimate response to the war inflations? Or was it an excessive increase? Some rise in steel prices and in steel wage rates was implicit in these monetary inflations and was therefore legitimate, or at least should be laid to the monetary authorities and not be blamed on either management or labor in the steel industry. Our concern here is to ask whether the whole of the increase in steel prices was legitimate. Was the rise sufficient to adjust steel prices and wage rates to the new level? Were steel prices raised by more than a legitimate amount, or by less?

* *Hearings,* p. 244.
** *Hearings,* pp. 420-421.

The present chapter will explore this problem. It will consider first the movement of steel prices relative to the general rise in price level. It will then examine the rise in operating expenses, covering the cost of labor, materials and services purchased, and finally it will examine the rise in the "producer margin"—the revenue remaining after operating expenses have been met. It is this margin that must cover taxes and provide the recovery of capital represented by the charges to depreciation and the return on the capital investment.

WHEN DID THE MONETARY INFLATION START?

Before the behavior of steel prices in the war inflations can be analyzed, it is necessary to indicate why 1942 has been adopted as the dividing line between the reflation from the great depression and the war-induced monetary inflation.

In the Senate hearings, the representative of U.S. Steel presented charts with 1940 as a base and discussed the rise of steel prices, steel wage rates, and other prices from that base to more recent times.[1] Yet in 1940 the reflation from the great depression was little more than half complete. Wage rates in 1940 were still depressed, over eight million workers were unemployed and the wholesale price index had recovered only a little more than half of its depression drop.[2] On the other hand, finished steel prices were already above their pre-depression level by 1940. Thus, the use of 1940 as a base would combine the reflation after 1940 with the war inflation and start the measurement of the adjustment of steel prices to monetary inflation with a highly distorted price structure in which steel prices were high in relation to the average of prices and to wage rates. We could expect a

[1] *Hearings,* p. 257.

[2] Source: Bureau of Labor Statistics. The depression drop in the wholesale price index was from 62.9 average in 1928 and 62.7 in July, 1929 (the 1929 peak) to 38.8 in February, 1933. The recovery to 1940 was to an average of 51.1 and a peak in December, 1940, of 52.0.

greater rise in other prices than in steel prices before they would be in balance and such a relative rise should be attributed to reflation, not to the monetary inflation. For this reason 1940 represents a most unsatisfactory base.

Equally unsatisfactory is the base used at the Senate hearings by the representatives of labor. For their "longer range comparisons" of the movement of prices and costs, they used 1947 as a base.[3] This was a year in the middle of the postwar inflation which also had a highly distorted price structure but one distorted in the opposite direction. Steel prices and steel wage rates had both lagged way behind the procession of rising prices and both needed to rise more than average in order to complete their adjustment to the monetary inflation. Thus the use of 1947 as a base involves a condition of unbalance in prices which is just as unsatisfactory as that of 1940.

If the monetary inflation had taken place in peace time, the most appropriate base for measuring monetary inflation would be a period after reflation was complete and before the monetary inflation had made headway. But World War II interfered with the reflation. In 1941, the last year before this country entered the war, the reflation was still incomplete. In that year unemployment was still large, averaging over 5.5 million.[4] Even at the end of the year unemployment was still 3.6 million. Also the reflation of prices was not complete. In 1941 the wholesale price index for the year was still nearly 10 per cent below the pre-depression level and at the end of the year was still 3 per cent below. Thus, because the reflation was still some way from completion, 1941 is not a good year for measuring the effects of the war inflations though it is very much superior to either 1940 or 1947.

The reflation was complete by the spring of 1942. By May of that year unemployment dropped below 2.6 million for the first time since 1929, and when the general price freeze was instituted

---

[3] *Hearings*, pp. 518, 520.
[4] Source: U. S. Dept. of Commerce, Bureau of the Census.

in early 1942, the wholesale price index had just recovered its pre-depression level.

Also, the indexes of market-dominated and administration-dominated prices had returned to approximately their pre-depression relations, as we have already seen.

If 1942 had been a peacetime year, there would be no hesitancy in adopting it as a base. But this country had just entered the war and the war disruptions were already affecting the economy. More than 3 million persons had been added to the armed forces and new recruits had taken the place of workers drawn off from the civilian labor force. And of particular importance, for this analysis, the product-mix for the steel industry shifted in the direction of special military steels and away from the standard carbon steels which constitute the great bulk of steel production in peacetime and dominate the price indexes for finished steel. This makes 1942 not altogether satisfactory as a base and the same applies with even greater force to the other war years in which the inflationary pressures were largely suppressed by price control.

Since 1941 is unsatisfactory as a base because of the incompleteness of reflation and 1942 is unsatisfactory because of war disruptions, can we use a shorter intermediate period? If we could use quarterly data in our analysis, we might use the last quarter of 1941, or the first quarter of 1942 as a base since, in these quarters, the reflation was more nearly complete and the actual war disruptions had not progressed very far. However, much of the data we have to use in the analysis, such as labor productivity, comes only in annual series and for some series such as steel production, seasonal factors make quarterly data more difficult to handle. Therefore, an annual base is required, at least until more refined data are available.

A look at the longer history of the relative movement of market and administered prices makes it clear that 1942 is the appropriate dividing line between reflation and the war inflation. This movement is reflected in Chart X, which presents as a continuous series the market-dominated and the administration-dominated price indexes already discussed. As can be seen from the chart, market prices and administered prices as groups tended to bear approximately the same relation to each other in the three full-employment periods 1929, 1942, and 1953. At other times between

Chart X — Relative Movements of Market and Administered Prices at the Wholesale Level, 1928–1959

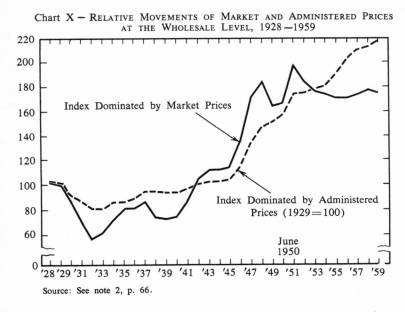

Source: See note 2, p. 66.

1929 and 1953 their relation was distorted either by depression or by the process of monetary inflation. Even under the war control of prices from 1942 on, some distortion developed as price control was more effective in stabilizing administered prices than in stabilizing market prices. As a result, by the end of the war, market prices had already incurred some measure of monetary inflation while administered prices had on the whole risen little beyond their 1942 levels. The chart makes it clear that between the depression and the war inflations, 1942 is the most appropriate base year for measuring the beginning of the war inflations.

By 1942 steel prices had fully recovered from the effects of the great depression and were in much the same relation to long-run costs as before the depression.[5] The index of finished steel prices in 1942 was nearly 7 per cent above its 1926–1929 level while the wholesale price index was only 2 per cent above. Labor costs per ton, low in 1940 and 1941, had just a little more than recovered their pre-depression level. So had the prices of raw materials required for steel-making. And the rate of return on capital *before taxes* was somewhat higher than the before-tax rate of return realized in 1929, a difference sufficient to take care of the moderate increase in peacetime corporate tax rates. Thus in 1942 the rates of return on capital *after peacetime taxes* were at about the same level as in 1929. If one treats the special war taxes as a temporary war charge to be paid by capital, then steel prices in 1942 bore about the same relation to total costs as they had before the great depression.

The year 1942 also had the advantage that, like 1953, it was a year of high employment in which the steel industry was operating at close to capacity. This means that the war inflations are bracketed by two years of comparable rates of operation.

STEEL PRICES VERSUS WHOLESALE PRICES

The rise in steel prices from 1942 to 1953 was part of the general war inflation but steel prices rose much more than wholesale prices and after the end of the war rose more steadily. For the whole period the wholesale price index rose only 72 per cent compared with the doubling of the finished steel price index. The difference in the behavior of the two indexes can be seen in Chart XI.

In the first part of the period, from 1942 to 1948, steel

[5] The justification for this assumption is given in more detail in Appendix A.

prices lagged well behind the big rise in the wholesale price index. During this period it can be said that the slower rise of steel prices helped to slow up the inflation. With the high postwar demand for steel, the industry could certainly have obtained higher prices and still operated at capacity as the extensive black

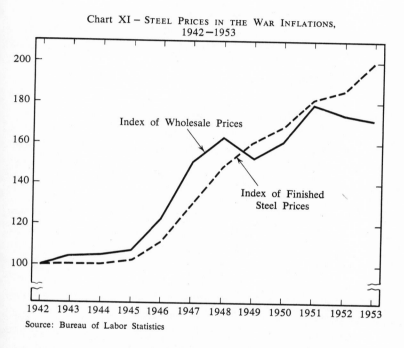

Chart XI – STEEL PRICES IN THE WAR INFLATIONS, 1942–1953

Source: Bureau of Labor Statistics

market in steel attested. However, in the fall of 1948 and throughout 1949 the wholesale index came down while steel prices rose somewhat so that by the middle of 1950 steel prices had risen more from 1942 than the wholesale price index.

Then the Korean War broke out with its inflationary impact. Both the wholesale price index and steel prices rose, with wholesale prices again advancing more rapidly than those of steel until early 1951. But then again the wholesale price index began to come down while steel prices continued to rise. By 1953 the rise in steel prices had far surpassed that of the wholesale price index. As indicated, the wholesale price index was only 72 per cent above its 1942 level, while that of finished steel prices was 100 per cent above.

The fact that steel prices rose much more from 1942 to 1953 than wholesale prices is clear. This fact needs explaining. Was the greater rise forced by increased costs, as steel management contends?

THE RISE IN OPERATING EXPENSES

In a general monetary inflation, it is to be expected that labor costs, material costs, and the costs of services will rise. The rise in these expenses of production can force a rise in product prices and our first problem in appraising the legitimacy of the steel price rise to 1953 is to examine these increased expenses.

Unfortunately the type of data presented at the steel hearing does not allow a very precise estimate of the rise in operating expenses in the actual making of steel. The most reliable data are the costs per ton of steel for production workers. But for the expenses for nonproduction workers and for raw materials and services purchased, only industrywide data was presented and this includes the labor costs for non-steel-making activity, such as railroad operation, cement making, and coal mining, carried on by the steel corporations. It is the custom in the industry to treat these industrywide figures as a fair index of the expenses of steel making and since the latter is a high proportion of the total this is not unreasonable. However, some margin of error is introduced by the gross character of the figures. A more accurate picture of the rise in the expenses of steel production would have been given if the expenses of steel production had been segregated from those of other activity.

THE RISE IN PRODUCTION LABOR COSTS

Most of the discussion of labor costs in steel has centered around the labor costs for production workers and the figures for this part of the total labor cost are more reliable than those for salaried workers and will be considered first. Even for production workers, there is no generally accepted index of labor costs per ton of steel production. However, data presented at the hearings do allow us to derive two indexes of the labor cost for production workers, one based on data supplied by management and one on data supplied by labor. Fortunately these indexes do not differ greatly for the aggregate rise in the period from 1942 to 1953, though the timing of the rise differs a little.[6] The difference between the two indexes is due solely to the inclusion or exclusion of controversial figures for certain fringe benefits. If we were concerned with absolute costs per ton, this difference would be important, but for the 1942 to 1953 period as a whole the two indexes rise in almost the same degree. This can be seen in Chart XII which also shows the rise in the index of finished steel prices.

Even the most cursory look at Chart XII makes it clear that the rise in steel prices in the war inflations ran far ahead of the increase in labor costs due to the wage increases of production workers. The estimates for the war years and 1946 suggest that labor costs acted to squeeze earnings. But after 1946 both the management and the labor estimates show the rise in labor cost running much below the rise in steel prices when both rises are measured from the 1942 base. If steel prices were in reasonable relation to labor costs in 1942, the *extra rise* in steel

[6] Both management and labor presented the same index of man-hours per unit of steel output, the index developed by the Bureau of Labor Statistics. Management also supplied figures for the average cost to management of employing an hour of labor, including the cost of all fringe benefits. Labor introduced the BLS figures for average hourly wages which includes some fringe benefits but not all. By multiplying the index of output per hour by the cost of an hour of labor, one obtains an index of the labor cost per ton.

prices up to 1953 in excess of the general rise in the price level cannot be justified by increased labor costs so far as production workers are concerned. Indeed the rise in this element of labor

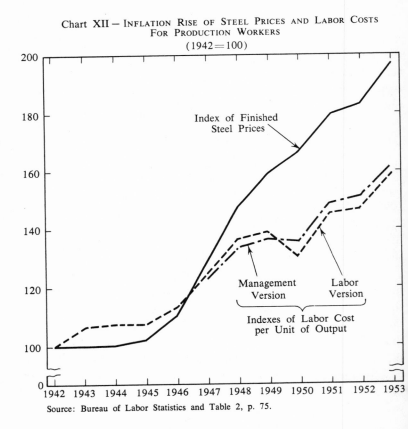

Chart XII — INFLATION RISE OF STEEL PRICES AND LABOR COSTS FOR PRODUCTION WORKERS

(1942 = 100)

Index of Finished Steel Prices

Management Version

Labor Version

Indexes of Labor Cost per Unit of Output

Source: Bureau of Labor Statistics and Table 2, p. 75.

cost appears to have been less than the rise in the wholesale price index in the same period—60 or 65 per cent as compared with 72 per cent for wholesale prices.

It is also significant that while wage rates, including fringe benefits, increased faster than the cost of living, the extra increase for the period as a whole amounted to a cumulative annual rate which was only about that of the increase in national productivity. This is shown in Chart XIII which gives not only the rise in the consumer price index and in the average hourly wage rates plus

Table 2—PRODUCTION LABOR COST PER UNIT
OF STEEL OUTPUT: 1941–1953

| | Index of Output Per Man-hour[a] 1947–49 = 100 | Average Hourly Earnings[b] (dollars) | Employment Costs Per Hour[c] (dollars) | Index of Labor Cost Per Unit of Output | |
				Labor[d] Estimate 1942 = 100	Management[e] Estimate 1942 = 100
1941	86.3	.941	.99	94.7	94.8
1942	(88.4)[f]	1.018	1.07	(100.0)	
1943	(90.6)	1.116	1.17	(107)	
1944	(92.6)	1.157	1.21	(108)	
1945	(94.8)	1.179	1.23	(108)	
1946	(97.0)	1.281	1.33	(114)	
1947	99.2	1.439	1.49	126.2	124.0
1948	99.4	1.580	1.63	138.0	135.4
1949	101.6	1.646	1.70	141.1	138.3
1950	110.8	1.691	1.85	132.5	137.8
1951	111.5	1.89	2.06	147.3	152.1
1952	116.0	1.99	2.16	149.2	153.8
1953	117.0	2.16	2.33	160.4	164.6

[a] *Hearings,* inserted by management, p. 1451; inserted by labor, p. 534. Source: BLS.

[b] *Hearings,* inserted by management, p. 1451; inserted by labor from 1947 to 1953, p 534. Source: BLS.

[c] *Hearings,* inserted by management, p. 1451. Source: U. S. Steel.

[d] *Hearings,* inserted by labor from 1947 to 1953, p. 534. Source: BLS. New base computed.

[e] *Hearings,* inserted by management, p. 1453. New base computed.

[f] Bracketed figures are rough estimates made by arbitrarily allocating productivity gain from 1941 to 1947 equally between years on a cumulative basis.

Subsequent figures published by the American Iron and Steel Institute show a higher level of employment cost per hour in each year but substantially the same per cent increase from 1942 to 1953 (1.113 to 2.440), an increase of 119.2 per cent as compared with 119.8 per cent.

fringe benefits for production workers, but also gives the latter
index deflated for the cost of living. The chart indicates that
there were only minor gains in real steel wage rates during the
later stages of World War II. Indeed, the increases in wage rates
could hardly keep up with prices so that up to 1948 steel wages
show almost no *real* increase. Then in 1949 and 1950 consumer

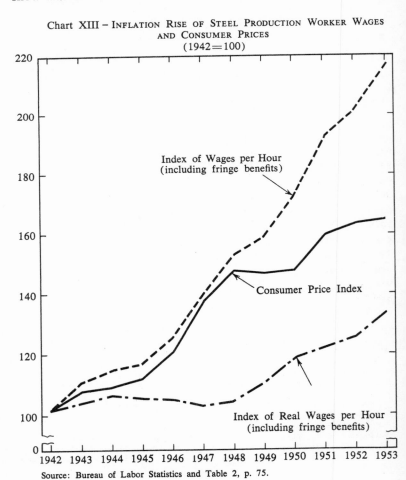

Chart XIII – INFLATION RISE OF STEEL PRODUCTION WORKER WAGES
AND CONSUMER PRICES
(1942=100)

Index of Wages per Hour
(including fringe benefits)

Consumer Price Index

Index of Real Wages per Hour
(including fringe benefits)

Source: Bureau of Labor Statistics and Table 2, p. 75.

prices remained fairly stable while wage rates increased to give a boost to real wages. In the Korean War both consumer prices and steel wage rates rose, with the latter rising enough faster to give a moderate increase in real wage rates. For the period as a whole, real wage rates increased at a cumulative rate of 2.6 per cent a year compared with a cumulative increase of 2.6 per cent a year in steel productivity. In the same period productivity in the private economy as a whole showed a cumulative increase of 2.5 percent a year.[7]

It is reasonable and legitimate that in a period of monetary inflation wage rates (including fringe benefits) should go up in

Table 3—STEEL PRODUCTION WORKER WAGES AND
CONSUMER PRICES: 1942–1953

	Average Hourly Earnings	Additional Fringe Benefits as Estimated by Management	Index of Hourly Earnings Plus Fringe Benefits 1942=100	Consumer Price Index 1942=100	Real Index of Hourly Earnings Plus Fringe Benefits 1942=100	Cumulative Expansion Curve at Annual Rate of 2.6% a Year 1942=100
1942	1.02	.05	100.0	100.0	100.0	100.0
1943	1.12	.05	109.3	106.1	103.0	102.6
1944	1.16	.05	113.0	107.9	104.7	105.2
1945	1.18	.05	114.8	110.3	104.0	107.9
1946	1.28	.05	124.1	119.8	103.8	110.6
1947	1.44	.05	139.0	137.0	101.4	113.4
1948	1.58	.05	152.1	147.6	103.2	116.3
1949	1.65	.05	158.8	146.0	108.7	119.3
1950	1.69	.06	172.7	147.0	117.4	122.4
1951	1.89	.17	192.5	159.2	120.8	125.6
1952	1.99	.17	201.5	163.0	124.5	128.9
1953	2.16	.17	217.4	164.1	132.3	132.3

Source: Table 2 and BLS.

[7] Source: Joint Economic Committee, 85th Congress, 1st session, 1957, *Productivity, Prices and Incomes*, p. 89

proportion to the general inflation plus the increase in national productivity, and this is what they appear to have done between 1942 and 1953. Thus, in so far as production workers are concerned, the rise in wage rates up to 1953 appears to have been legitimate and cannot explain the fact that steel prices rose more than the index of wholesale prices.

Also in 1953 steel wages bore about the same relation to wages for the whole of manufacturing as they had borne in 1942 and in 1929. In the interval between these three dates there had been considerable variations in the relation, some due to the big depression and some due to the differential effects of inflation. But 1929, 1942 and 1953 were all years of high steel and high manufacturing activity, so that the figures for average hourly earnings are comparable and therefore suitable for measuring the real changes in wage rates. The figures are shown in Table 4.

Table 4—RATIO OF STEEL WAGE RATES TO WAGE RATES FOR ALL MANUFACTURING

1929	1.19
1942	1.19
1953	1.22

Source: Steel and the Postwar Inflation, Otto Eckstein and Gary Promm for the Joint Economic Committee, 86th Cong., 1959, p. 16.

These figures suggest that, by the end of the war inflations, steel wage rates had not run significantly ahead of the rise in wage rates for manufacturing as a whole.

We can thus conclude that between 1942 and 1953, wage rates for production workers rose only in proportion to the monetary inflation and the rise in national productivity while the increase in the productivity of production workers was such that the production labor cost per unit of output rose less than 65 per cent while the wholesale price index rose 72 per cent and finished steel prices rose 100 per cent. Clearly the rise of steel prices by more than the general inflation in this period cannot be attributed to the rise in the wages of production workers.

THE RISE IN TOTAL LABOR COSTS

So far we have only covered the wage increases of production workers and the total labor cost of producing steel involves an increasing proportion of workers not directly engaged in production. If the wages and salaries of such workers increased in the same proportion as those of production workers and their productivity increased to the same extent, the total labor cost per unit of output would closely follow the labor cost per unit for production workers alone.

It is fair to assume that salaries went up in about the same proportion as wage rates but it is not appropriate to assume that labor productivity for nonproduction workers went up in the same degree as that of production workers. There has been a long-run tendency, already mentioned, for a larger proportion of the labor force in steelmaking to be made up of salaried workers not directly attached to production. Between 1942 and 1953 the Bureau of Labor Statistics compilation shows an increase of only 2 per cent in production workers and 38 per cent in nonproduction workers so that, while salaried workers constituted only 11 per cent of employees in 1942, they constituted 14 per cent in 1953.[8] It is therefore reasonable to assume that total labor costs per unit of output went up somewhat more than labor costs for production workers alone though no figures were provided at the hearings to give a direct estimate of the greater increase.

However, some light can be thrown on ·this question by analyzing figures compiled by the American Iron and Steel Institute for the great bulk of the industry. The Institute provides

[8] *Background Statistics Bearing on the Steel Dispute* (Washington, D. C.: Bureau of Labor Statistics, 1959), p. 22.

figures for total employment costs, covering both production and nonproduction workers. These figures include both the direct payments to labor and the cost of fringe benefits. If we had an index of steel production which took account of changes in product mix, we could divide it into the total of employment costs and derive an index of the employment cost per unit of output.

Unfortunately we do not have such an index of steel production for this period because of the war character of the product mix in 1942.[9] We can, however, obtain an approximate index of real steel output by an indirect method. The institute supplies figures of total sales for the same group of companies whose employment costs are compiled. We can deflate these figures for the change in the level of steel prices and thus obtain an index of real steel production which takes account of the change in product mix. Such an index is given in Table 5 for 1942 and 1953 and is divided into the dollar value of sales to give an index of the employment cost per ton of a standard mix.

According to these figures, the increase in employment cost per unit of output from 1942 to 1953 was 83 per cent, a figure which is higher than the 60 to 64 per cent figures obtained for production workers alone. The figures are reasonably consistent in the light of the greater increase in nonproduction workers. The 83 per cent increase in total labor cost per unit of output is above

[9] We have figures for the tons of steel ingots and castings produced each year and the tons of products shipped. But neither of these is a good index for the real production of steel since, in 1942, a much larger proportion of production was in special and more highly fabricated steels which require more labor to produce. In a very real sense an average ton of steel in 1942 represented more "production of steel" than an average ton in 1953 when the product mix was more normal. If we were to divide total employment costs by the reported tons produced or shipped, we would get figures which were altogether too low for the increase in labor costs. Actual calculations show an increase in labor cost per ton from 1942 to 1953 of only 53 per cent when tons of steel production are used and 49 per cent when tons of steel shipments are used. These values are not consistent with those already obtained directly for production workers.

Table 5—TOTAL EMPLOYMENT COSTS PER UNIT OF STEEL
OUTPUT FOR THE STEEL INDUSTRY: 1942 AND 1953

	1942	*1953*
Sales (in millions)	$5,874	$13,091
Index of Finished Steel Prices (1942=100)	100.0	199.9
Index of Steel Production (sales deflated by price index)	58.74	65.49
Total Employment Costs (in millions)	2,196	4,477
Index of Total Employment Costs per Unit of Output	100.0	182.9

Source: Derived from AISI and BLS data.

the 72 per cent increase in the level of wholesale prices but below
the approximately 100 per cent increase in the index of finished
steel prices. Thus, the rise in total labor costs can account for
some of the extra rise in steel prices above the wholesale index,
but only a part.

THE RISE IN MATERIAL COSTS

The rise in material costs per ton from 1942 to 1953 is even
more difficult to pin down with a reasonable degree of accuracy.
We lack not only an appropriate index of steel production but
also a corresponding index of prices for the materials going into
steel-making. The available wholesale price series give us some
clue as to what happened to the prices of particular steel ingredients but do not indicate how to weight them in an index to
show their combined movement.

The price rise for the most important ingredients in steelmaking is indicated in Table 6.

In this table the first three items—ore, scrap, and coking coal—
apply directly to the steel industry. The index for fuel and power

Table 6—CHANGES FOR MAJOR MATERIALS
USED IN STEELMAKING: 1942–1953

Iron Ore	+112%
Iron and Steel Scrap	+ 67%
Coking Coal	+101%
Fuel, Power and Lighting Materials	+ 65%
Combined Major Raw Material Index	+ 91%

Source: BLS. The combined index uses the following weights: iron ore 40; scrap 20; coal 20; fuel, power and light. 20.

applies to a broad industrial category and may only approximately reflect the price of the specific fuel and power items used in steelmaking.

Examination of these figures suggests that a properly designed index of prices for the materials required for producing a standard mix of steel products would show a greater rise than that of the wholesale price index. The largest single material cost in making steel is iron ore and this increased more than the price of steel. Coking coal also increased as much as the price of steel. On the other hand two items, scrap iron and steel and fuel and power, increased much less, tending to offset in some degree the greater rise in ore prices. A crude price index for these four steelmaking items, giving double weight to iron ore would show a rise of 91 per cent. These figures suggest that the combined cost of materials rose nearly as much as the price of steel.

A somewhat higher figure is suggested by the data on combined material and service costs published by the institute. In Table 7, the latter figures are divided by the index of production already developed to give an index of the cost of materials and services purchased per unit of output. These figures suggest an increase of 114 per cent between 1942 and 1953 in the material and service cost per unit as compared with the 83 per cent increase in the total labor cost per unit.

When the data for labor and for material and service expenses are combined they suggest an increase of 99.5 per cent in total operating expenses between 1942 and 1953, almost exactly the percentage increase in finished steel prices.

Table 7—MATERIAL AND SERVICE COSTS PER UNIT OF OUTPUT FOR STEEL INDUSTRY: 1942 AND 1953

	1942	*1953*	*Change*
Total Material and Service Expenses (in millions)	$2,552	$6,088	+132.4%
Index of Production (deflated sales)	58.74	65.49	+ 8.6%
Index of Material and Service Cost per Unit of Output	43.44	92.96	+114.0%

Source: AISI. For production index see Table 5. Figures cover 92 per cent of total production in 1942 and 94.5 per cent in 1953.

These estimates are crude, primarily because the data used include nonsteelmaking activity but also because the index of output is only approximate. But they do suggest that the main increase in operating expenses per ton *in excess* of the general rise in wholesale prices did not come from the rise in production worker wages but from nonproduction labor costs and from the increased cost of raw materials and purchased services, particularly the latter. Also they suggest that, as far as operating expenses are concerned, the increase in costs would justify a steel price rise greater than the general rise in wholesale prices. Whether the whole of the greater rise was justified would depend on the increased requirements for taxes, depreciation and profits which have to be financed out of the producer margin remaining after operating expenses have been met.

THE RISE IN THE PRODUCER MARGIN

If steel prices went up just about as much as operating expenses per unit of production, then the producer margin per unit remaining after meeting operating expenses must also have gone up in approximately the same proportion. It is this producer margin out of which the producer must meet taxes, recover his capital as plant and equipment wear out or become obsolete or his mineral reserves are depleted, and obtain a return on the capital still in use. An index showing the change in this producer margin from 1942 to 1953 is given in Table 8 and indicates an increase of 101 per cent in the funds remaining per unit of production after the payment of operating expenses.

Table 8—PRODUCER MARGIN FOR THE STEEL INDUSTRY: 1942 AND 1953

	1942	*1953*	*Change*
Producer Margin (sales less operating expenses) (in millions)	$1,126	$2,526	
Index of Production (deflated sales)	58.9	65.5	
Producer Margin per Unit of Output	19.2	38.6	+101.0%

Source: AISI. For production index see Table 5. Figures cover 92 per cent of total production in 1942 and 94.5 per cent in 1953.

These figures indicate that after paying for operating expenses, approximately twice as much was left per unit of output to cover taxes and to provide a recovery of capital and a return on investment. Whether this was sufficient to provide an adequate return to capital is a question which turns partly on the effect of higher peacetime tax rates and partly on the whole complex problem of adjusting capital values for the general rise in the price level.

THE EFFECT OF INCREASED TAX RATES

In both 1942 and 1953 heavy war taxes were levied on corporate income. These were special war measures and in discussing the reasonableness of the rise in steel prices it is appropriate to treat these as special levies against the stockholders and disregard them. However, the peacetime tax rates on corporate income were quite different before 1942 and after 1953. In 1939, approximately 20 per cent of the steel industry's net income was taken in federal income taxes while in 1955, after the excess profits tax was eliminated, close to 50 per cent was taken.[10] This increase in tax rates absorbed a considerable part of the increase in the producer margin.

A rough idea of this effect can be obtained by adjusting the actual figures of net income before taxes in 1942 and 1953 for these peacetime rates and calculating the increase in taxes per unit of output. Also by subtracting taxes at these peacetime rates from the producer margin, we can obtain figures on the return to capital, including both the return *of* capital through depreciation and depletion charges and the return *on* capital. These estimates are made in Table 9 and show an increase of 286 per cent in tax payments per unit of output and of only 53 per cent in the return to capital per unit of output.

We can accept the idea that the industry is willing and able to pass on to customers the increase in taxes. But this leaves only an increase in the general magnitude of 50 per cent in the funds available for recovery of capital and for a return on capital. Was this sufficient to reflect the increase from 1942 to 1953 in the capital being used by the steel industry? This is our final and perhaps most difficult question to answer.

[10] The AISI compilation for most of the steel industry shows 19.6 per cent of net income before taxes going to federal taxes in 1939 and 50.2 per cent in 1955.

Table 9—TAXES AND CAPITAL RETURN PER UNIT OF
PRODUCTION FOR THE STEEL INDUSTRY:
1942 AND 1953
(Estimated for peacetime tax rates)

	1942	*1953*
Producer Margin	1,146	2,591
State, Local, and Misc. Taxes	95	191
Federal Taxes (assuming 20% & 50% tax rates)	151	866
Total Taxes	246	1,057
Capital Return	900	1,534
Index of Production (deflated sales)	58.9	65.5
Index of Taxes per Unit of Output	100	386
Index of Capital Return per Unit of Output	100	153

Source: AISI. Figures cover 92 per cent of total production in 1942 and 94.5 per cent in 1953.

THE RISE IN CAPITAL COSTS, 1942 TO 1953

There is much evidence that the capital per unit of output rose significantly from 1942 to 1953. A considerable part of the steel plant in existence in 1953 was constructed at the higher postwar prices and adds directly to the average capital required per unit of output. Also consideration must be given to the effect of price increases on the 1953 value of plant and equipment acquired when prices were lower.

The increase in the average capital arising *directly* from the higher prices paid for new plant is reflected in the published figures of the steel industry. These show a rise of 37 per cent in the book value of the net fixed capital per ton of steel capacity and a rise of 31 per cent in the book value of the total capital (fixed plus working capital) per ton as can be seen in Table 10.

If one adopted book values which closely reflect the historical cost of plant and equipment, it would appear that the 50 per cent increase in capital return per unit of output was more than sufficient to cover the increase required by the increase in capital per unit of output.

Table 10—BOOK VALUE OF CAPITAL PER TON OF CAPACITY FOR REPORTING FIRMS IN THE STEEL INDUSTRY: 1942 and 1953

	1942	*1953*	*Increase*
Net Working Capital (in millions)	$1,368	$2,249	
Net Fixed Capital (in millions)	3,006	5,698	
Total Capital (in millions)	4,374	7,947	
Total Capacity (in million tons)	81.6	112.5	
Working Capital per ton of Capacity	16.76	19.97	+13.2%
Fixed Capital per ton of Capacity	36.84	50.60	+37.4%
Total Capital per ton of Capacity	53.60	70.57	+31.7%

Source: AISI adjusted as indicated. Both capital and capacity figures are the average of the beginning of the year and the beginning of the following year and represent 91 per cent of total industry capacity in 1942 and 93 per cent in 1953. Two adjustments have been made in the AISI figures. In 1935, U.S. Steel Corp. wrote up its depreciation account by $270 million, thereby reducing the book value of its net fixed capital by that amount. Then in 1948 it reversed this adjustment, reducing its depreciation account and increasing its net fixed capital. Since the 1942 figures for net fixed capital come before the revaluation and the 1953 figures come after, the revaluation is applied to the 1942 figures in order to make them more comparable with those of 1953. What other adjustments are needed to make the figures in the two years exactly comparable on an historical cost basis is not clear.

Also the 1959 figures of net fixed capital include an adjustment for excessive amortization. See Appendix D, Table 39.

However, steel management clearly rejects book values as a measure of the capital actually used. In the Senate hearings the issue came to a head over the question of depreciation. Chairman Blough referred to "inadequate depreciation allowances"[11]

[11] *Hearings*, p. 213.

and introduced into the hearings record an address on "Steel's Depreciation Problem," by Benjamin F. Fairless, before the American Iron and Steel Institute, of which he was president.[12] In this address Mr. Fairless said:

The purpose of depreciation is to recover over the lives of facilities the dollars originally invested in them. The dollars when recovered are presumed to be sufficient to buy enough equipment to keep even with the wearing out of existing equipment. And they would be, if there were stability in the buying power of the dollar.

But the simple fact is that the buying power of the dollar has not been stable. We have had 15 years of continuous cost inflation; and facilities for the steel industry now cost immensely more than they used to.[13]

The same theme was developed in the hearings by Mr. Tyson, chairman of the finance committee, the United States Steel Corporation. He said:

I start with the indisputable fact that, because of inflation, to construct or purchase new plant or equipment today costs a vastly greater number of dollars than the plant or equipment being replaced cost 20 or more years ago. Yet the depreciation on these old plants is required for tax purposes to be based on the relatively small number of dollars paid for them long ago. As a result the depreciation currently allowed is quite insufficient to equal what has to be paid out when the old facilities are modernized or replaced. . . .

Few people realize the extent of the deficiency in depreciation. United States Steel has calculated the number of dollars of wear and exhaustion that would have been needed in each year since 1939 to equal in each year's dollars the portion of the buying power originally expended which was used up in the year's production.

In every year since 1939 . . . the wear and exhaustion recorded . . . failed to equal that needed for recovery of buying power. The 17-year aggregate deficiency was $904 million.[14]

The position taken in these statements and elaborated in the Senate hearings on steel seems to combine three separate ideas.

[12] *Hearings*, p. 1148 ff.
[13] *Hearings*, p. 1150.
[14] *Hearings*, p. 246.

One is that depreciation charges should recover as many dollars over the useful life of a plant as it will cost to replace it when it is worn out. A second is that depreciation charges should recover as many dollars as would represent the same buying power as was initially invested in it. The third is that depreciation charges should recover as many dollars as would represent the wear and use of a plant if it were reappraised each year in the light of current construction costs.

At first reading it may seem that these are only three different ways of stating the same idea. This would be true if there were no changes in prices or technology. But where such changes occur the three requirements can lead to quite different results.

Take first the difference between recovering enough dollars to buy a new plant and recovering equal buying power. Suppose that a plant costs $1 million, has a useful life of twenty years and capital is to be recovered one-twentieth each year. At the end of ten years half a million of the capital will have been recovered. Then suppose that at the end of the tenth year the price level doubles so that a new plant would now cost $2 million. To recover $2 million over the life of the plant, the rate of depreciation would have to be *tripled* in the second ten years. But to recover the same buying power as was invested, the depreciation rate would only have to be *doubled*. During the first ten years, half a million would have been recovered *in dollars of the same buying power as those which were invested* and after the price level had risen only the remaining half-million of capital would have to be recovered through depreciation charges and double the rate of depreciation would be sufficient to do this. But this would not recover the $2 million necessary to buy the new plant.

Not only are the two requirements different but only the second makes economic sense. There is no reason why the dollars charged as depreciation should be equal in amount to the cost of a new plant. If an enterprise charges dollars of equal purchasing power to those invested it is "kept whole." Whether the enterprise maintains the buying power of capital recovered in the early years of a plant is a matter of good management not of depreciation policy.[15] For this reason we must reject the idea that depreciation charges should recover as many dollars as are required for the purchase of a new plant.

This leaves two principles by which depreciation and also capital values could be maintained. Values could be adjusted so that the buying power of the capital recovered was equal in general buying power to that invested. Or values could be adjusted by reappraising plant in the light of its reproduction cost. These can be called, respectively, the buying power principle and the reproduction cost principle. The difference between them will be apparent as the two principles are applied, as will be their relation to the principle of historical cost according to which most corporate accounts are kept.

THE BUYING-POWER PRINCIPLE

In conception, the buying-power principle is relatively simple and easy to apply. It is only necessary to adjust the depreciation and the value of capital measured on the basis of historical costs for the changes in the buying power of the dollar.

Thus, if one has the dates when capital was invested in

[15] In this example: if the half-million of capital recovered in the first ten years had been invested in securities and, like the price level, had doubled in value, then the half-million recovered at the initial price level, and now grown to $1 million plus the $1 million of depreciation collected in the second ten years, would provide the $2 million needed for the new plant. Or take the more likely case that the half-million of capital recovered in the first ten years was reinvested in plant at the initial price level. Then half the initial investment would have been recovered and reinvested at the same level of buying power. For that part of its capital the enterprise would be kept whole and would still be whole, if the price level doubled and depreciation rates were doubled on both the original and the subsequently acquired plant. On the other hand, if depreciation rates were tripled so as to recover $2 million from the original plant, and the same principle was applied to the plants bought out of the capital recovered in the first ten years, the enterprise would be more than whole.

plant or equipment, the accumulated depreciation based on historical cost for the plant and equipment acquired in each year and
a general index of prices, one can calculate the current depreciation charge which would be necessary to recover capital with
a dollar buying-power adjusted for the change in the real value
of the dollar.[16]

Similarly one can calculate the value of the capital still remaining to be recovered. As long as the accounting records
are kept on the principle of historical cost, the difference between
the historical cost and the accumulated depreciation charges represents the unrecovered capital valued at historical costs. If the
price level has risen in the meantime, it is only necessary to
multiply the unrecovered capital calculated on the historical cost
basis by the rise in price level. Thus, if in one year a million
dollars is invested in equipment having an expected useful life
of ten years, and is being depreciated at the rate of $100,000 a
year, at the end of six years $600,000 of the historical cost will
have been recovered, leaving $400,000 of the historically in-
vested capital still to be recovered. Should the price level double
in the meantime, the buying power value of the unrecovered cost
would be double its value in historical cost dollars, or $800,000.
The revaluation of depreciation charges and of the unrecovered
remainder of the capital investment, therefore, is both simple in
theory and relatively easy to apply when the necessary book
values are available year by year.

It is not possible to apply this procedure to the book values
reported by the steel industry with precision because we do not
have the purchase dates on all the steel properties. However, we
do have the industry's fixed capital expenditures from 1942 on,
and can roughly estimate the book value of the fixed assets still

[16] For example, if $1 million worth of capital were invested in equipment
in one year, and the appropriate annual depreciation charge calculated on
the historical cost basis were $100,000, a subsequent doubling of the price
level would make it necessary to recover $200,000 a year in order to
recover capital of the same real value as that of the capital invested.

Table 11—ADJUSTMENT OF THE CAPITAL EMPLOYED
BY THE STEEL INDUSTRY IN 1953 TO 1953 DOLLARS
(in million dollars)

Date of Acquisition	Fixed Capital at Cost[a]	Estimated Depreciation and Depletion[b]	Estimated Net Fixed Capital at Cost	Index of the Buying Power of the Dollar[d]	Estimated Net Fixed Capital in 1953 Dollars
Before 1942	$4,689	$3,445	$1,244[c]	164.1	$2,041
1942	265	194	71	164.1	117
1943	239	159	80	154.6	124
1944	136	82	54	152.1	82
1945	148	79	69	148.8	103
1946	365	170	195	137.2	268
1947	554	222	332	119.8	398
1948	642	214	428	111.3	476
1949	483	129	354	112.4	398
1950	505	101	404	111.3	450
1951	1,051	140	911	103.1	939
1952	1,298	87	1,211	100.8	1,221
Totals	$10,375	$5,022	$5,353		$6,617

	Book Value	Book Value Adjusted to 1953 Dollars	Per cent Increase
Net Fixed Capital (in millions)	$5,353	$6,617	+23.6%
Working Capital (in millions)	2,253	2,253	
Total Capital (in millions)	$7,606	$8,661	+16.6%

[a] Annual data and total from AISI. The assumption is made that all plant and equipment acquired after 1941 was still in use in 1953. If detailed figures were available this minor source of error could be corrected.

[b] Annual data estimated on the basis of a 15-year average life and straight line depreciation. Total from AISI.

[c] This estimate for the net book value in 1953 of the fixed capital acquired before 1942 is consistent with other information. For example, the net book value of fixed assets at the end of 1945 was down to $2,079 million, of which close to $700 million represented acquisitions after 1941. The $707 million net book value given above would mean that approximately half of the cost not written off by the beginning of 1942 was written off between 1942 and the beginning of 1953.

[d] As measured by the consumer price index. If the wholesale price index had been used the net results would have been essentially the same. The wholesale index rose a little more but also earlier.

on the books in 1953 and acquired before 1942. This has been done, and the resulting book values adjusted to 1953 dollars are shown in Table 11.

According to these rather crude calculations, an adjustment of the net fixed capital for the 1953 buying power of the dollar would increase the capital approximately 24 per cent. This is a notably small increase considering the great decline in the value of the dollar.

The smallness of the increase can be accounted for by the fact that two-thirds of the net book value of fixed capital at the beginning of 1953 represented plant and equipment acquired during the preceding five years after most of the price rise had already occurred. The estimate does suggest, however, that if the buying power principle is the appropriate principle of valuation, something like 24 per cent more fixed capital was employed in 1953 than the book values indicate.

When the book values per ton of capacity for 1953 are revised upward by this amount, as in Table 12, they indicate an increase in net fixed capital per ton of 59 per cent between 1942 and 1953, instead of the 37 per cent indicated by the books.

However, the total capital per ton of capacity would not be

Table 12—INCREASE IN REAL CAPITAL PER TON FOR THE STEEL INDUSTRY: 1942–1953

	1942	*1953*		*Increase*
		Book Value	*Adjusted to 1953 Dollars*	*1942 to 1953 on Buying Power Basis*
Working Capital per Ton of Capacity	$16.76	$19.97	$19.97	+19.2%
Fixed Capital per Ton of Capacity	36.84	50.60	58.52	+58.9%
Total Capital per Ton of Capacity	$53.60	$70.57	$78.49	+46.4%

increased by as large a percentage since working capital is presumably valued on the books at approximately current prices
and does not require revaluation. When working capital and
net fixed capital (valued in 1953 dollars) are combined, the
increase in total capital per ton from 1942 to 1953 amounts
to approximately 46 per cent.

This crude figure of 46 per cent increase in total capital per
ton of steel capacity suggests that the 53 per cent increase in
capital return per unit of output would just about provide the same
rate of recovery of capital and the same rate of return on capital
in 1953 as in 1942, provided the capital was valued in 1953
dollars. If these figures are accepted, and valuation is on the
basis of the real buying power of the dollar, one must conclude
that the doubling of steel prices between 1942 and 1953 is justified by the combination of the increase in operating expenses, the
increase in peacetime taxes, and the increase in capital invested.
The conclusion also follows that the whole of the adjustment
required by these three factors had already taken place by
1953, so that no further increase would have been required
except as additional costs, taxes, or capital investment per ton
occurred.

How reliable the foregoing estimates may be is another matter.
The over-all figures for the industry may not be wholly comparable from year to year. Methods of accounting change, rapid
amortization after 1950 distorts the capital picture, and in other
ways the aggregate figures for the industry as a whole can be
misleading. Nor has it been possible to go back of the figures
published for the industry to make the extensive adjustments
which would be required to be sure of comparability.

However, it has been possible to take the capital figures for
the United States Steel Corporation and to make the major
adjustments required to make the data for 1953 reasonably comparable with those for 1942. The actual adjustments to provide
comparability and the adjustments for the general buying power

of the dollar are given in Appendix B and yield the end results given in Table 13.

As can be seen from this table, the estimated increase in capital per ton of capacity was less for U.S. Steel than the somewhat cruder figures suggest for the industry as a whole, whether one compares book values or adjusts the 1953 book values for the general change in the value of the dollar.

Table 13—NET CAPITAL EMPLOYED BY THE UNITED STATES STEEL CORPORATION PER TON OF CAPACITY: 1942 AND 1953

	1942	(in millions) 1953		Increase from 1942 to 1593	
	Book Values	In Current Dollars	In 1953 Dollars	Historical Cost Basis	Buying Power Basis
Net Working Capital	$16.47	$ 8.99	$ 8.99	−45.4%	−45.4%
Net Fixed Capital	43.85	53.17	61.79	+21.3%	+40.9%
Total Capital	$60.32	$62.16	$70.78	+ 3.1%	+17.3%
Assuming same working Capital per Ton in 1953 as in 1942: Total Capital per Ton		$69.64	$79.26	+15.5%	+31.4%

Source: Appendix B.

When the principle of historical cost is applied, the figures for U. S. Steel show an increase of 21 per cent from 1942 to 1953 in the net fixed capital per ton of capacity compared with the cruder figure of 37 per cent for the industry as a whole. Similarly, the increase in total capital per ton of capacity is less: 3 per cent as compared with the crude industry figure of 32 per cent.

When the historical cost figures are revalued to take account of the decline in the value of the dollar, the value of U. S. Steel's fixed capital per ton of capacity in 1953 is raised by 17.4 per cent if the wholesale price index is used to measure the value of money, and by 18.8 per cent if the consumer price index is used. When the higher of these figures is used, the 1942–1953 increase in net fixed capital per ton for U.S. Steel comes to 41 per cent as compared with 59 per cent for the industry, and in total capital per ton to 17 per cent as compared with the industry's 47 per cent.

The smaller increases in the values of capital per ton of capacity for U. S. Steel arise in considerable part from the very low level of its working capital, which dropped from $16.47 per ton of capacity in 1942 to $8.99 per ton in 1953. If working capital per ton in 1953 had been the same as in 1942, the increases in capital per ton would have been 15 per cent on the historical basis and 31 per cent on the buying power basis.

This evidence tends to confirm the conclusion that if book values are used, the rise in price which allowed something like a 50 per cent increase in capital return per unit of output was more than enough to cover the increase in operating costs and in peacetime taxes, and to maintain the rates of recovery and return on capital. If the value of capital in 1953 is adjusted for the general price rise, the increase in price was of just about, or only slightly greater than, the magnitude necessary to cover the increase in costs including taxes and to maintain the rates of recovery and return on capital.

Thus, if one values capital on the principle of historical cost, the rise in steel prices from 1942 to 1953 was more than enough to cover the increase in operating expenses, the increased peacetime taxes and the increase in capital. If one values capital on the buying-power principle, which requires recovery of capital and return on capital in dollars of the same general buying power as those invested, then the increase in steel prices was sufficient to yield just about the same rate of return on the revalued capital as prevailed in 1942.

CAPITAL VALUES BASED ON REPRODUCTION COST

In the Senate hearings, the steel industry representatives based their argument that book values understated the capital actually involved in steelmaking on the grounds (1) that the general buying power of the dollar had fallen, and (2) that it would cost a great deal more to reproduce the existing facilities. As we have seen, adjusting historical costs for the change in the buying power of the dollar in 1953 increases the value of fixed capital per ton by from 17 to 24 per cent. Yet some of the figures presented at the hearings imply more than a doubling of the value of capital per ton. These much higher estimates involve the cost of constructing new plant.

For example, U. S. Steel's executive vice-president, M. W. Reed, presented figures showing "the large percentage increases in prices paid by U.S. Steel for a representative number of practically identical facilities which have been purchased in different years from 1923 to 1956."[17] In describing these figures, Mr. Reed gave particular emphasis to the rise in the cost of blast furnaces and gave the increase in the cost of four blast furnaces built in recent years which were "practically identical" with blast furnaces built in 1930, as follows:

A furnace built in 1943 cost 2 times a 1930 furnace
                    1948   " 3 1/3 " " 1930   "
                    1952   " 4 3/4 " " 1930   "
                    1957   " 5 1/4 " " 1930   "

Our concern is particularly with the figures for 1943 and 1952 which suggest that the cost of constructing *a blast furnace* more than doubled between these two years.

Data to a similar effect but focused on depreciation were presented by Mr. Robert C. Tyson, chairman of U. S. Steel's finance committee. He introduced an exhibit, reproduced here as Chart

[17] *Hearings,* p. 1126.

XIV, which showed for each year from 1940 to 1946 "regular depreciation" (presumably wear and exhaustion recorded on an historical cost basis), the "total wear and exhaustion needed" as estimated by U. S. Steel, and special amortization and depreciation charges recorded. According to this exhibit, the depreciation

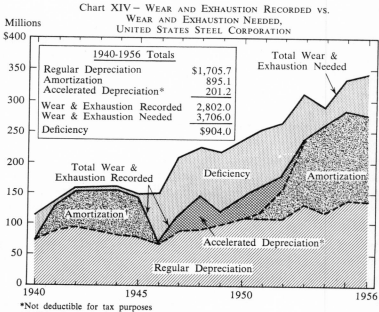

Chart XIV – Wear and Exhaustion Recorded vs.
Wear and Exhaustion Needed,
United States Steel Corporation

1940-1956 Totals	
Regular Depreciation	$1,705.7
Amortization	895.1
Accelerated Depreciation*	201.2
Wear & Exhaustion Recorded	2,802.0
Wear & Exhaustion Needed	3,706.0
Deficiency	$904.0

*Not deductible for tax purposes
†Additional amortization due to ending of emergency period allocated to years 1941-1945

Source: Hearings, p. 259.

needed to cover wear and exhaustion over the whole seventeen-year period exceeded the amounts actually charged through regular and special charges by approximately $900 million. Indeed, the depreciation needed, according to these estimates, amounted to approximately $3.7 billion in the seventeen-year periods, while regular depreciation based on historical costs amounted to only approximately $1.7 billion, a deficit of $2 billion. These figures suggest a much larger increase in the value of fixed capital due to inflation than that suggested by the general buying power estimate.

The great difference is emphasized if we focus on the value in 1953. U. S. Steel estimates that the depreciation needed in 1953 amounted to approximately $310 million while regular de-

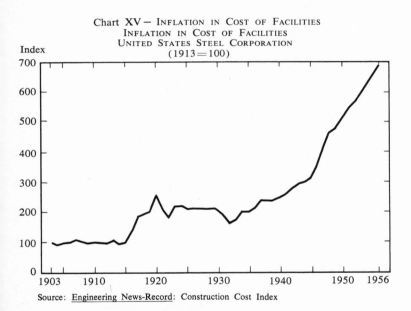

Chart XV — INFLATION IN COST OF FACILITIES
INFLATION IN COST OF FACILITIES
UNITED STATES STEEL CORPORATION
(1913 = 100)

Source: Engineering News-Record: Construction Cost Index

preciation amounted to only approximately $130 million.[18] Thus the needed depreciation as estimated by U. S. Steel was 2.4 times the "regular depreciation." If we apply this ratio to the historical value of U. S. Steel's fixed properties—their historical cost less regular depreciation—it gives a value for U.S. Steel's net fixed capital of close to $4.8 billion in 1953. This is to be compared with the approximately $2 billion value on the historical cost

[18] These figures are read from the Chart XIV and cannot be given with precision.

basis and the value of close to $2.4 billion on the general buying power basis. If the proper value to be placed on the fixed assets employed in steel making is of the magnitude suggested by these figures, then the 50 per cent increase in the amount available for recovery and return on capital from 1942 to 1953 would not be sufficient to provide for adequate depreciation and depletion charges and allow the same rate of return as in 1942. We must examine the argument behind the presentation of these figures as well as the figures themselves.

The basic argument underlying these figures involves the well-known principle of reproduction cost. According to this principle the value of an existing capital asset is what it would cost to reproduce it at the current price level less a depreciation adjustment to take account of the fact that part of its useful life has been used up. But this statement contains two uncertainties. One is uncertainty as to just what is being reproduced. The other is just what adjustments need to be made for depreciation.

Just what is it that is to be reproduced? Is it the *physical plant and equipment* so that one estimates the cost of building as nearly as possible identical plants regardless of improvements in design and materials that have occurred since the existing plants were acquired? Or is it the *service performed* which is to be "reproduced"? Should the reproduction cost of a blast furnace be the cost of building an exact replica of the furnace built fifteen years ago or should it be the cost of building the most modern and up-to-date furnace possible?

On this question the economist must say that what it would cost to construct an identical or practically identical plant is irrelevant to the problem wherever technical advance makes a different and better plant the one that would be built if the existing plant were destroyed.

There can be cases where no technical advance has occurred. For example, take a fifteen-year-old warehouse. If it were to be destroyed, it might be replaced by a practically identical building

with the same ground area, the same number of floors, the same
steel and cement construction, and the same characteristics in
other ways significant for its usefulness. Then one could take the
cost of building a replica of the existing building as its reproduction cost new, and deduct from this the appropriate depreciation
for the fifteen years of use. This would give a figure of value
based on the *reproduction cost* of the old building and could provide the capital basis for charging depreciation and determining
the return on capital for the current and future years.

But a blast furnace or a steel rolling mill is quite a different
matter. Technical progress is constantly making the plant constructed in earlier years obsolete or obsolescent. If a fifteen-year-
old blast furnace were destroyed, it is almost certain that it would
not be replaced by a replica of the old furnace. Rather, the
furnace built to replace it would be technically superior, would
probably have a greater output and would probably cost less per
ton of capacity to build than a new furnace built at the same prices
for labor and materials but as a replica of the old. It is the cost of
the function, in this case the cost per ton of capacity, which is
significant for reproduction cost as it relates to pricing.

Furthermore, technical progress affects the adjustment for depreciation. As long as value is based on historical costs, whether
or not adjusted for price level, the procedure for recovering the
capital over the life of the plant or equipment is set up at the outset
in terms of its expected life and according to some acceptable
depreciation formula.

But where one turns to reproduction cost, one is necessarily rejecting historical cost as a basis of value. One is taking the actual
present as the basis and, therefore, must take into account not only
the cost of the most modern plant and equipment which might be
built but also any superiority which it may have over the existing
plant and equipment. To the extent that the new plant would be
superior to the old, either because it could produce a better product
or use less materials or require less labor per unit of output, the

existing plant is to that extent obsolete and this fact must be taken into account in the adjustment for depreciation.

This point can be made clear by an extreme example. Suppose that the new plant would save so much in materials and labor per unit of output that its combined operating expenses and costs of capital, including both depreciation and a return on capital, were less than the operating expenses alone for the existing plant. Then the latter would be obsolete and its reproduction cost adjusted for this fact would be zero. The whole of the reproduction cost would be offset by the technical superiority of the new plant. Even though the old plant might still represent unrecovered capital on the books of the enterprise, it would not represent capital when valued on a reproduction cost basis.

Of course, in practice obsolescence creeps up on a plant or piece of equipment gradually through time and is usually forecast and taken into account in setting depreciation rates. When the historical cost principle is applied, experience tables can provide an average expectancy of useful life for different types of plant or equipment and these take account of expected obsolescence. But when the reproduction cost principle is applied, it must start from the actual plant and what it is good for, not from an average expectancy. It must take into account not only the cost of constructing a new plant but it must also make an appraisal of its superiority. And to the extent that the new plant would be superior—to the extent that the existing plant is obsolescent—this would reduce the value arrived at on the basis of reproduction cost.

In practice, the adjustment for actual obsolescence would not be easy. In some cases this adjustment could be made by estimating the difference in operating expenses per unit for the old and the modern plant and capitalizing this difference for the expected remaining useful life of the old plant. The figure for the value of the old plant would then be the cost of the modern new plant less the obsolescence adjustment, because the old plant would be less efficient than the new and still less because the old plant is partly worn out. In other cases, where the new plant would also produce a better product, the adjustment would be even more complex. It is sufficient here to recognize that the principle of reproduction cost involves the reproduction cost of the function, not of the physical plant and that in addition to the usual adjustment for depreciation it requires a depreciation adjustment for any inferiority in efficiency or product of the existing plant over a new modern plant.

When the value figures presented by the officials of U. S. Steel are examined in the light of the principle of reproduction cost, it is apparent that little or no attention has been paid to the improvement in technology and the obsolescence factor.

Take first Mr. Reed's figures for the increased cost of blast furnaces. The figures he gives purport to be for furnaces built in the 1940's and 1950's which, according to him were "practically identical" with furnaces built in 1930. We can presumably accept his figures for the relative costs of the earlier and later furnaces but were the earlier and later furnaces "practically identical"? Was there no progress in technology between 1930 and the period when the new furnaces were built?

Another vice-president of U. S. Steel, Mr. R. Conrad Cooper, presented evidence of the great technical progress made by the U. S. Steel from 1929 on.[19] Included in this evidence were the following figures for the *average* rated capacity for all U. S. Steel's blast furnaces for selected years:[20]

Year	Rated Capacity in Tons per Furnace per Day
1929	665
1939	783
1948	902
1956	1,030

Can it be said that a blast furnace capable of producing 1,000 tons of steel a day is "practically identical" with one that is only capable of producing 600 tons a day?

[19] *Hearings*, pp. 1131-1138.
[20] *Hearings*, p. 1134.

The issue is further sharpened by the "case history of No. 6 Blast furnace at Gary Works of U. S. Steel" given in the Copper statement.[21] Number 6 was built in 1910. In 1946 it was completely rebuilt. Between those dates the price level had nearly doubled. And while the first furnace cost $614,000, the new furnace cost $3,441,000, an increase of 460 per cent[22] and a little more than the increase shown by Mr. Reed's figures from 1930 to 1957. On the face of it this looks like a huge inflationary increase in furnace cost. But actually the second furnace was a much larger furnace with nearly double the hearth area and a capacity of 1,509 tons a day instead of 470 tons. This more than tripling of the capacity means that the 1910 version and the 1946 version were in no significant sense "practically identical." And the fact that the large furnace cost 460 per cent more than the small furnace has no bearing at all on the inflation in the cost of that furnace.

When one compares the two furnaces in terms of the cost of the facility *per ton of capacity,* the picture is startlingly different. The cost per ton of annual capacity for the 1910 model was $3.58, that for the 1946 model $6.25.[23] This represents a cost increase of only 75 per cent, not an increase of 460 per cent which the superficial type of calculation would show.

In the light of this information on the changing character and costs of blast furnace capacity, it is difficult to accept Mr. Reed's assertion that the 1930 blast furnace and the blast furnaces constructed thirteen to twenty-seven years later were "practically identical" facilities. The same holds for his figures for rolling mills and other plants. Indeed it is difficult to find any significance for the problem of steel prices in the figures for replacement cost of such facilities as blast furnaces or rolling mills contained in Mr. Reed's statement. In order to give such figures significance, it would have to be shown that the facilities being compared were

[21] *Hearings,* p. 1137.

[22] The BLS consumer price index had increased 105 per cent and its wholesale price had increased 70 per cent.

[23] Derived from Exhibit II, *Hearings,* p. 1137.

practically identical in the technical sense, and this would be a denial of the technical progress which is clearly indicated by other information avalable. As a result, vice-president Reed's evidence on replacement cost is so superficial that the remainder of his table covering other steel facilities is not worth presenting until information is provided on the character and capacities of the facilities being compared, such as has been provided for Gary Number 6.

The concrete information given by Mr. Cooper in the case history of Gary Number 6 also brings out the necessity of adjusting the value of new plants for their technical superiority, if their cost is to be used in estimating the value of an existing plant. The old furnace required a crew of 9½ men on each turn and could produce only 470 tons of pig iron a day. With three crews a day it required 29.1 man-minutes to produce a ton of pig.[24] The replacement furnace required a crew of 7½ men on each turn and could produce 1,509 tons of pig a day. With three crews a day it required only 7.2 man-minutes of labor to produce a ton of pig, or one quarter of the labor input per ton of the old furnace. The saving in labor cost alone could go a long way in paying for the new furnace. Also, it is reasonable to assume that the new new furnace was able to operate with some saving in coke and power consumption per ton and also a saving in relining cost. Clearly an exact replica of an old furnace would not be as valuable per ton of capacity as a new modern furnace, if it required four times as much labor and more raw materials per ton to operate.

When we turn to the U. S. Steel estimates of needed depreciation (Chart XIV) presented by Mr. Tyson, and their implications for capital values, we find the estimates are even more subject to question. Not only do the estimates show no evidence that account has been taken of the more economical design and the operating superiority of "replacement" plants, but they appear to employ an index of construction that is quite inappropriate and imply an exaggerated value for U. S. Steel's fixed plant in 1942.

[24] *Hearings*, p. 1137.

Mr. Tyson does not indicate just how the estimates of needed wear and exhaustion were arrived at but in connection with them he introduced a chart entitled "Inflation in Cost of Facilities," reproduced here as Chart XV, which shows the rise in the *Engineering News-Record* Construction Cost Index from 1903 to 1956. It is a fair inference that either the historical cost of fixed assets acquired in different years was adjusted by the changes in this index and depreciation recalculated, or some essentially similar method of adjustment was used.

The *Engineering News-Record's* Construction Cost Index, though useful for many purposes, would seem to be particularly inappropriate as a measure of the change in the construction cost of steel facilities. This index is a price index representing the combined price of two and a quarter tons of steel, six barrels of cement, approximately 1 million board feet of lumber, and two hundred hours of common labor. The resulting weights represent the relative importance of these four components in the national economy in 1913 and have not been changed since.[25] Now whether or not an index of construction material prices weighted according to the 1913 importance of steel, cement, and lumber is a good guide to the changes in the prices of materials going into the construction of steel facilities, there can not be any question that an index consisting of an initial 38 per cent weight of common labor and no skilled labor bears little relation to the realities of steel facility construction. Whether a significant amount of common labor is used in constructing steel facilities is doubtful. Their construction is essentially a matter for skilled labor, and wage rates for skilled labor have been rising much less rapidly than those for common labor.

Fortunately, the difference which would come from substituting skilled labor for common labor in the index can easily be shown. The *Engineering News-Record* publishes a Building Cost Index

[25] *Historical Statistics of the United States,* U. S. Dept. of Commerce p. 378.

which is identical with its Construction Cost Index so far as the two and a quarter tons of steel, six barrels of cement and 1 million board feet of lumber are concerned, but substitutes an equal 1913 weight of skilled labor (68.38 hours at the average of bricklayer, carpenter, and structural iron worker wage rates) for the two hundred hours of common labor. Between 1913 and 1956, the *News-Record*'s Building Cost Index rose only 331 per cent while its Construction Cost Index rose 592 per cent. Substituting the more realistic price index, which uses skilled labor instead of common labor, would greatly reduce the values found for the unrecovered depreciation of the past and for the value of the capital still remaining to be recovered from future use.

But no index of the prices paid for labor and materials can correctly measure the increase in the cost of constructing steel facilities when technical progress is being made both in the design of the facilities and in the use of labor and materials in their construction. The magnitude of the possible discrepancy is suggested by the data on the Gary blast furnace Number 6 presented by Mr. Cooper. We have already seen that for Gary Number 6 the dollar cost of constructing a ton of steel capacity increased 75 per cent from 1910 to 1946. In the same period, the *Engineering News-Record*'s Index of Construction Costs rose 260 per cent and that for the *News-Record*'s Index of Building Cost, including skilled labor, rose 172 per cent.[26] In this particular case, the increase in construction cost per ton of capacity was significantly less than the 100 per cent increase in price level, not two and a half times the price level increase as the index of construction costs used in the U. S. Steel presentation suggests.

Whatever the exact method used to arrive at the U. S. Steel estimates, it is apparent that they overestimate fixed capital values in 1942. The chart presented indicates that the "needed" wear and

[26] Source: *Engineering News-Record*, March 24, 1960. The ENR Building Cost Index is given only back to 1913 and has been extended back to 1910 by splicing with ENR Construction Cost Index.

depletion charge needed in that year was approximately 80 per cent higher than that arrived at by regular depreciation accounting. But when it is recognized that almost all of the fixed assets on the books in 1942 were acquired before the great depression, and when one takes into account both the inappropriateness of the *Engineering News-Record* Construction Cost Index to measure the actual cost of steel facility construction and the technical superiority of new facilities, it is difficult to believe that there was any such increase in values as this figure implies. Indeed, it seems likely that, with the high average age of steel facilities on the books in 1942, a competent estimate of the reproduction cost of these facilities in 1942, properly adjusted for both the technical superiority of new facilities and for the depreciation of the old, would show a net value smaller than the net book value. Until convincing evidence to the contrary is presented, there is no reason to reject the historical cost less depreciation and depletion as representing the fixed capital employed in steel making. How much a reproduction cost valuation in 1953 would add to book values is a different matter.

We can start toward making such an estimate by applying the *Engineering News-Record* price indexes to net book values of 1953 in the same way that the wholesale and consumer price indexes have been applied. This is done in Appendix B, and the results are given in Table 14 along with the corresponding book values. Even if we disregard actual construction costs and the technical superiority of new plant, we find that adjusting book values for the changes in the building and construction price indexes does not produce great increases in the net figure for fixed capital. This is because such a large proportion of this capital had been acquired after much of the price rise from the war inflations had already occurred. But an increase of 30.4 or of 37.7 per cent in capital values would be appreciably greater than the increase from adjusting to the general buying power of the 1953 dollar. Have these figures any significance?

Table 14—NET FIXED CAPITAL OF THE UNITED STATES
STEEL CORPORATION IN 1953 ADJUSTED FOR
DIFFERENT PRICE INDEXES

	Adjusted Figure (in millions)	Percentage Increase Due to Adjustment
Unadjusted for Prices	$1,994	
Adjusted for Wholesale Price Index	2,341	+17.4%
Adjusted for Consumer Price Index	2,370	+18.8%
Adjusted for *Engineering News-Record* Building Cost Index	2,601	+30.4%
Adjusted for *Engineering News-Record* Construction Cost Index	2,745	+37.7%

Source: Appendix B.

We can immediately drop the 37.7 per cent figure derived with the *Engineering News-Record* Construction Cost Index for the reason already given that it rests so largely on common labor.

The 30.4 per cent figure would have to be adjusted downward for the fact that there had been technical progress, both in the design of facilities and in their operating characteristics. How much less labor and materials were needed in 1953 to construct one ton of blast furnace capacity than were required to construct the blast furnaces on the books in 1953? How much less for a ton of steelmaking capacity? How much less for a ton of rolling mill capacity?

We do not have the necessary facts to say. But if Gary Number 6 is any guide at all, it suggests that the actual cost per ton of "reproduction" capacity would be significantly lower than the index of construction prices would imply. And after account has been taken of a smaller use of labor and materials in constructing a ton of capacity, account must also be taken of the operating superiority of new facilities. We know from the rise in labor productivity that great labor-saving improvements have been made over the years, presumably reflecting the superiority of new over older facilities.

Altogether, it seems doubtful that a competent reproduction cost valuation would show as large an increase in value as that obtained by adjusting book values for the general change in the value of the dollar already examined. In any case, a heavy burden of proof rests on the industry to show that on a reproduction cost basis the value of fixed capital employed was significantly greater than the value arrived at on the basis of general buying power. If this is accepted, it does not make too much difference whether book values are adjusted on the buying-power principle or on the reproduction cost principle but both principles would result in a moderately higher value of fixed capital assets than the historical cost principle of valuation.

CONCLUSION ON THE WAR INFLATIONS

The general conclusion flowing from this prolonged analysis is that the doubling of finished steel prices from 1942 to 1953 was in the general magnitude of the increase which could have been expected in the light of the increase in operating expenses, the increase in taxes, and the increase in capital invested, particularly if the latter is valued on the buying-power principle. Wage payments for production workers increased from 1942 to 1953 only about as much as the increase in consumer prices and the increase in national productivity would lead one to expect, while production worker costs per unit of steel output went up less than steel prices, and total operating expenses per unit of steel went up to about the same extent as steel prices. The great increase in peacetime taxes was passed on to customers. Finally, after the payment of operating expenses and taxes, the amount left over as a recovery of capital and a return on capital increased by about the same magnitude as the increase in capital or perhaps a little more. On the whole, the analysis has disclosed no evidence that the rise in steel prices was either seriously excessive or that steel prices had failed to adjust fully to the war inflation by 1953. Therefore, any rise in steel prices after 1953 cannot be justified on the ground that steel prices had not yet fully adjusted to the war inflations.

CHAPTER VI

STEEL PRICES
AND ADMINISTRATIVE INFLATION

*In our most recent negotiation last year—after a five-week strike—
we signed a labor agreement. It was that labor agreement which fore-
ordained our recent price increase.*

*Under that 3-year labor agreement, we hoped to narrow at least
slightly the inflationary gap between our rapidly mounting wage costs
and our slowly rising output per man-hour. Only time can tell if what
we did represented progress.*

*On July 1 of this year we faced what our recent total wage-cost his-
tory demonstrates was about a 6½ per cent increase in our total costs
per man-hour; and to cover these costs in part, we raised our steel
prices by an average of 4 per cent.*

ROGER M. BLOUGH,

CHAIRMAN OF THE BOARD,

THE UNITED STATES STEEL CORPORATION*

*The industry's leader, United States Steel Corporation, which initiated
the 1957 steel price increase (as it has normally initiated the increases
in prior years), could have put into effect a price cut of $6 a ton, in-
stead of a price increase of $6 a ton, absorbed the cost of the wage
increase that occurred in July, and could still have earned greater net
profits after taxes in 1957 than were ever earned in the history of the
corporation.*

OTIS BRUBAKER, RESEARCH DIRECTOR,

UNITED STEELWORKERS OF AMERICA**

* *Hearings*, p. 211.
** *Ibid.*, p. 428.

The rise of steel prices since 1953 presents a different problem from that of the rise in the war inflations. As we have seen, the bulk of the rise before 1953 can be attributed to the excess demand associated with the monetary expansions of the two wars. But from 1953 on there was no monetary inflation and no general excess of demand. As far as wholesale prices are concerned, the war inflations had come to a halt and the price readjustments following them were in large measure complete by 1953. For two and a half years both the wholesale and the consumer price indexes were remarkably stable, though with considerable shifting of relative prices within this stability. Then in the middle of 1955 the wholesale price index started up, followed by consumer prices in 1956.

Steel prices shared or even spearheaded this rise. As Table 15 and Chart XVI show, the index of finished steel prices rose rapidly from 1953 on so that by mid-1959, before the prolonged steel strike, steel prices were 36 per cent above their 1953 levels. In

Table 15—STEEL AND OTHER WHOLESALE PRICE INDEXES: 1953–FISCAL 1959

	Index of Finished Steel Prices	*Wholesale Price Index*	*Index of Prices of Metals and Metal Manufactures*	*Index of Wholesale Prices Excluding Metals and Metal Manufactures*
1953	100.0	100.0	100.0	100.0
1954	104.3	100.2	101.1	99.8
1955	109.2	100.5	105.9	97.8
1956	118.4	103.8	114.2	98.5
1957	129.7	106.8	118.9	100.5
1958	134.2	108.3	120.4	102.0
Fisical 1959	136.1	108.5	121.6	101.5

Source: BLS. Metal Manufactures combines the BLS "Metal and Metal Products" and "Machines and Motive Products."

the same period, the wholesale price index increased only 8 per cent and a wholesale price index, which excludes steel and other metal manufactures, rose hardly at all.

This chapter considers the extent to which this great increase in steel prices can be justified by increases in operating expenses, by increased taxes and by increased capital employed in steelmaking.

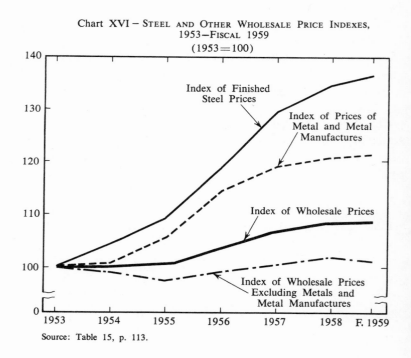

Chart XVI – Steel and Other Wholesale Price Indexes, 1953–Fiscal 1959
(1953 = 100)

Source: Table 15, p. 113.

U. S. STEEL'S PRIMARY JUSTIFICATION FOR PRICE INCREASES

The primary justification which the price leader in the industry, U. S. Steel, has given for this series of price increases has been the increase in labor costs due to "wage inflation" in the steel industry, and the increase in material costs resulting from wage inflation in the production of the materials used in making steel.

Thus, in announcing its July 1, 1957, price increase, U. S. Steel distributed a press release on June 28 which set the pattern for the statement made by its chairman at the Senate hearings that is reproduced at the beginning of this chapter. This release stated:

> Increases in wages and benefits that were provided for in its 3-year labor agreement reached with the United Steelworkers of America last summer will take effect beginning next Monday, July 1, United States Steel Corp. announced today.
>
> The increases occurring on that date will raise United States Steel's employment costs about 6 per cent to an all-time high.
>
> An accompanying increase averaging about 4 per cent in its carbon and alloy steel prices was announced at the same time by United States Steel.[1]

The press release then continued with an extensive discussion of the increase in employment costs and the great increase in both employment and material costs *per employee hour* since 1940 and the much smaller increase in steel prices.

In his famous statement of June 19, 1958, postponing price action,[2] President Hood of United States Steel said: "It must be obvious to anyone that the matter of price adjustment would not even come up under the present economic circumstances if it were not for the very substantial employment cost increase we now face." The same theme was reiterated in the Senate hearings on steel, as we have already seen.

This indictment of labor was made more general by Mr. Tyson, chairman of the finance committee, the United States Steel Corporation. Referring to "employment costs per hour," he said:

> Wartime inflation is traditional, but such persistent peacetime inflation is a new thing in the American economy. We never had anything like it before. Something new has been added.
>
> The wage inflation underlies all other cost and price inflation. Of this there is simple statistical proof. Thus all of 22 available, nonoverlapping, hourly wage series compiled by the Bureau of Labor Sta-

[1] *Hearings*, p. 945.
[2] See Chap. 1.

tistics rose markedly from 1940 to 1956—almost 200 percent on the average. . . . There were, of course, differences in the rate of change, but such differences were not material. This universality and uniformity of employment cost inflation, plus the fact that in consolidated industry employment cost represents three-quarters or more of all costs, explain why costs other than employment costs tend to parallel the inflation in employment costs. The products and services purchased from others, the plant and equipment purchased, the taxes paid—all have embodied in them and parallel wage inflations.[3]

When applied to the monetary inflation generated by the two wars, this indictment of labor is understandable but wrong. To the management in an administered price industry, faced with the problem of meeting payrolls, covering other costs and making a return on capital, a monetary inflation can well appear to stem from the wage pressure from labor in its own and other industries. But labor, like management is only reacting to the monetary pressure. What looks like wage inflation is really a part of the mechanism of monetary inflation where administered prices and wage rates are involved.

This is so important that it is worth spelling out in detail even at the expense of some repetition. We have already seen that in the actual course of a monetary inflation both administered prices and wage rates tend to be insensitive to the rising demand and to lag behind the rise in other prices. In fact, we have described a monetary inflation as one in which an excessive supply of money generates an excess demand for goods; volume of sales moves up for the administered priced industries, while prices rise for the products with flexible prices; as a result of the increases in market prices, the cost of living goes up and the pressure from labor for higher wages becomes intense.

As wage rates are increased by more than the increase in productivity, costs in the administered-price industries go up and administered prices are revised upward. But just as management has to raise prices because of higher costs, so labor has had to force

[3] *Hearings*, p. 244.

up wage rates to meet the higher costs of living. Both actions are forced by the rise in flexible market prices resulting from the monetary expansion. Even where the price of materials, such as iron and steel scrap, are made in the market and respond sensitively to changes in demand, it is easy to disregard the demand factor and imagine that labor costs are also responsible. Thus, the point where monetary inflation has its most direct impact on administered prices is through rising costs, not through rising demand and, to management, labor pressure can look like the source of the inflation when it is not.

The error in blaming labor for the monetary inflations of the war period arises from a failure to look beyond the immediate source of rising costs. Labor was no more a free agent than business in resisting the adjustment to the war-expanded monetary supply. Theoretically, wages could lead the monetary rise of prices, as they did not, or lag behind the general increase, as they in fact did, but no amount of labor restraint could have overcome the rising tide of readjustment to the new price level implicit in the expanded money supply. Thus, neither labor nor business was responsible for the monetary inflations of the war period. And by 1953 these appear to have worked themselves out for the most part.

Our immediate concern is whether this indictment of labor is valid for the steel industry in the period of administrative inflation following 1953. Unlike the monetary inflation, administrative inflation could be caused by too great a pressure for wage increases. It could be caused by an effort of business to widen the margin between operating expenses and revenue. It could be a combination of both. In this chapter we shall try first to answer the question of how much operating expenses contributed to the rise in steel prices. Did labor costs per unit of steel product rise as much as the price of steel? Did material costs per unit of output rise as much as the price of steel? Or did the producer margin between operating expenses per unit of output and the revenue derived from it increase more than the price?

LABOR COSTS IN STEEL AFTER 1953

Our first question is how far the increase in steel prices after 1953 can be explained by the rise in wage rates.

In the Steel Hearings of August, 1957, the prime focus was on the rise in steel prices of 4 per cent on July 1 of that year, which followed the 3 per cent rise in the winter of 1956–1957 and a 7 per cent rise in August, 1956—an increase of over 14 per cent in less than a year. In this chapter we shall cover the whole of the period from 1953 to the start of the steel strike in the middle of 1959.

THE IMPORTANCE OF COMPARABLE RATES OF OPERATION

In order to arrive at estimates of the increase in labor costs per unit of steel output we can proceed as we did in the earlier period to multiply the hours of labor required per ton of steel by the cost of an hour of labor. As before, we have for production workers the index of labor cost per hour introduced in the hearings by labor and the index introduced by management. We also have the index of steel output per production man-hour *paid for* which was relied on by both labor and management in the hearings and also a new index developed by the Department of Labor for the steel output per production man-hour *worked*. These indexes would allow us to appraise the changes in labor costs per ton of steel if it were not for one factor—the variation in the rate of operations during the period.

The leaders in steel management quite rightly insist that in measuring changes in productivity, direct comparison between years of differing rates of operation is misleading. This is so because the output per man-hour varies not only with technical progress through time but also with the rate of operation. An important proportion of the production labor, such as a large part of that employed for repair and maintenance, is in the nature of overhead which does not vary closely with the variation in output. For this reason, a given reduction in the total output of steel does not reduce the production labor employed in the same proportion and an increase in steel output does not require a proportionate increase in production labor. The same is true to an even greater extent for nonproduction workers whose number varies relatively little with short-run variations in output. As a result, the labor used *per ton* of steel is much higher when operations are at 50 per cent of capacity than when they are at 80 or 90 per cent of capacity.

In the analysis of labor costs before 1953, this difficulty has been avoided by focusing the analysis on years of high production— specifically the years 1929, 1942, and 1953. But after 1953 this is not possible. There is no year of high production toward the end of the period and the rate of operation in 1958 was way below that of 1953, while 1959 included the four-months' strike.

This raises the real question of whether we should be comparing the rise in steel prices with the *actual* rise in labor costs per ton or with the rise per ton at *comparable rates of operation.* If labor costs per ton are 15 per cent higher at a low rate of operations than at a high rate, would this greater labor cost justify a *higher* price for steel when demand was low? Or is the relevant relation of prices to labor costs that which would exist at comparable rates of operation? If wage rates rose by just the increase in technical productivity there would be no increase in labor cost per ton of steel so long as we compared costs at equal rates of operation. In asking whether an increase in wage rates has justified an increase in steel prices, should we consider only whether wages have gone up more than this technical productivity, or should we also include the differences in labor cost due to differences in operating rate?

Neither the behavior of steel prices nor the statements by industry leaders suggest that differences in labor costs due to differences in operating rate should enter into the justification for price increases. Steel prices show no tendency to fall with the reduced labor costs accompanying high rates of production or to rise with the higher labor costs at low production. And leaders in the industry have taken the position that the considerable rise in output per man-hour due to an increase in the rate of operation does not provide a basis for absorbing an increase in wage rates. For this reason it will be assumed here that differences in labor costs per ton due to differences in the rate of operation do not call for changes in steel prices. Rather, it is labor costs at comparable rates of operation or labor costs adjusted for difference in rate of operation that are important in justifying price increases.

THE INCREASE IN THE PRODUCTIVITY OF PRODUCTION WORKERS AFTER 1953

There are wide variations in the estimates of increasing productivity in steel in recent years depending partly on the years chosen for comparison and partly on the indexes of productivity employed. For the period 1953 to 1958, the initial year is one of high rate operation—94.9 per cent—and the last year is one of low rate—60.6 per cent. If the long strike in the second half of 1959 had not occurred, we might have been able to extend the period to include the experience with a higher rate of operation, but because of the strike, the rate for the year as a whole was not much greater than that for 1958. We might use the high rate of operation in the first half of 1959, but this would introduce a seasonal factor. The fiscal year 1959, including the last half of 1958 and the first half of 1959, avoids both the strike and the seasonal problem and covers a period of only a little less than average operations—77.5 per cent. This can be compared with the high rate of 1953 and the low rate of 1954.

The results of such comparisons for production labor only are given in Table 16, which shows the average annual rate of increase in output per man-hour according to the two indexes published by

Table 16—UNADJUSTED INDEXES OF INCREASE IN LABOR
PRODUCTIVITY IN THE STEEL INDUSTRY:
1953–FISCAL 1959

	Production Workers Only		
	Output per Man-hour Paid For	*Output per Man-hour Worked*	*Operating Rate (Per cent of Capacity)*
1953	100.0	100.0	94.9
1954	97.6	99.7	71.0
1955	108.9	111.2	93.0
1956	109.8	113.6	89.8
1957	108.5	114.0	84.5
1958	106.6	113.7	60.6
Fiscal 1959	113.5[a]	125.1	77.5

	Cumulative Annual Rate of Increase in		Operating Rate as Per Cent of Capacity		
Period	*Output per Man-hour Paid For*	*Output per Man-hour Worked*	*Initial Year*	*Final Year*	*Points of Difference*
1953–Fiscal 1959	+2.4%	+4.2%	94.9%	77.5%	−17.4
1954–Fiscal 1959	+3.5%	+5.2%	71.0%	77.5%	+ 6.5

Source: BLS Department of Labor.
[a] Average of 1958 and 1959, fiscal year data not available.

the Bureau of Labor Statistics, one for output per man-hour paid
for and one for output per man-hour worked.

Examination of the table shows the wide range of rates of increase in output per man-hour (2.4 per cent a year to 5.2 per cent
a year) which can be obtained from the published data depending
on the exact period covered and the index used. As is to be expected, the rates based on man-hours paid for are lower than those

based on man-hours worked. If the hours in holidays, vacations, and sick leave paid for had maintained a constant relation to hours worked, the two indexes should produce the same results. However, hours in paid vacations and sick leave appear to have been increasing relative to hours worked, so that the regular BLS index of output per man-hour has ceased to be a reliable index of worker productivity. However accurate and useful it may be as an index of output per man-hour paid, it tends to underestimate the growth in productivity. The index for manpower worked is also more useful for the present period because it provides a value for fiscal 1959 while the regular BLS index is only available by calendar years.

The table also brings out the fact that output per man-hour, whether paid for or worked, depends much on the rate of operation. When the annual rate is calculated from 1953 to fiscal 1959, a year with a high rate of operation to a year of lower rate, the values obtained are lower than when calculated from 1954, a year of low operation.

The most significant figures in the table are those calculated from the index of output per man-hour worked from 1953 and 1954 to fiscal 1959. Assuming the accuracy of the index itself, the average rate of 4.2 per cent a year from 1953 to fiscal 1959 understates the technical increase in productivity because it compares a year of high with a year of intermediate operations while the 5.2 per cent figure from 1954 to fiscal 1959 overstates the rate of increase because it compares a year of low operation with one of intermediate operations. Still assuming the reliability of the index, the true average rate of technical increase in productivity must lie between the figure of 4.2 and 5.2 per cent a year.

There is, however, the question of the reliability of the index of output per man-hours worked. In the view of Department of Labor officials this index is not as reliable in measuring output per man-hour worked as the regular index is in measuring output per man-hour paid for.[4] However, in estimating the labor cost of producing steel, the superiority of an index based on hours worked in place of one of hours paid for was sufficient to outweigh its lower reliability and the department used this index in estimating the changes in labor cost per unit of output in its presentation of *Background Statistics Bearing on the Steel Dispute.* On this basis we can say that so far as technical progress is concerned, the rate of increase in output per man-hour worked by production workers increased on the average between 4.2 and 5.2 from 1953 to fiscal 1959.

ADJUSTING PRODUCTIVITY FIGURES FOR RATE OF OPERATION

A second way of approaching this problem is to take the data on output per hour worked and derive from them an adjustment factor for the effect of differences in rate of operation and then adjust the data for each year to a standard operating rate. This has been done in Table 17 and the results are plotted in Chart XVII which shows the actual index of output per man-hour worked, and an index of output per man-hour adjusted to an 83 per cent rate of operation, the average rate for the 1953 to mid-1959 period. This conversion to a standard rate of operation eliminates most of the variation in output per worker due to the rate of operation and reveals the fairly steady rise in technical productivity which could be expected. The adjusted index suggests an average annual increase in productivity of 4.3 per cent a year between 1953 and 1958. It also provides adjusted data for the intermediate years.

[4] The index is based on American Iron and Steel Institute data for steel production, weighed by the BLS for degree of fabrication to yield a weighed index of steel production and on AISI data on hours worked by wage earners for a very large but varying proportion of the industry adjusted by the BLS for coverage to provide an index of hours worked by wage earners for the industry as a whole. While the coverage of wage earners in this index and production workers in the regular BLS index is not identical, there is such a very large overlapping as to make them both in effect indexes for production workers.

Chart XVII – STEEL OUTPUT PER MAN-HOUR AND RATE
OF OPERATION, PRODUCTION WORKERS ONLY
(1953 = 100)

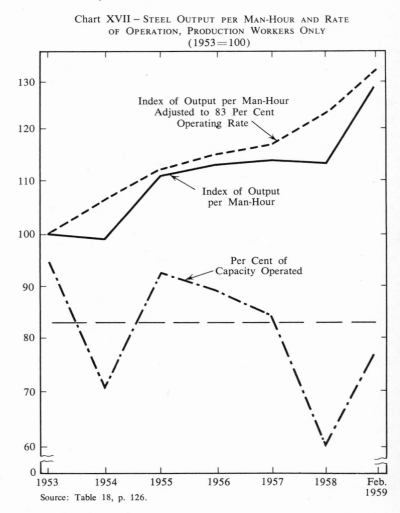

Source: Table 18, p. 126.

PRODUCTION LABOR COST PER UNIT OF OUTPUT

Once we have an acceptable index of output per man-hour, we
can convert this index into an index of the hours required per unit
of output. Then we can multiply this by the indexes of labor cost

Table 17—INDEX OF OUTPUT PER MAN-HOUR FOR
PRODUCTION WORKERS IN THE STEEL INDUSTRY
AT A STANDARD RATE OF OPERATION:
1953–FISCAL 1959

	Reported Index of Output per Man-Hour Worked (1953=100)	*Rate of Operation (Per Cent of Capacity)*	*Index of Output per Man-hour Worked Adjusted to 83% of Capacity*	
			Adjusted Data[a]	*Shifted to 1953=100*
1953	100.0	94.9	96.8	100.0
1954	99.7	71.0	102.9	106.4
1955	111.2	93.0	108.5	112.1
1956	113.6	89.8	111.8	115.5
1957	114.0	84.5	113.6	117.4
1958	113.7	60.6	119.7	123.6
Fiscal 1959	125.1	77.5	126.6	130.8

Source: BLS and AISI.

[a] Actual Index adjusted inversely .27 points for every point in rate of operations above or below 83 per cent. Adjustment factor obtained by attributing the recession difference between average of 1953 and 1955 and actual 1954 to change in rate of operation; doing the same for the 1958 recession using the average of 1957 and fiscal 1959; and taking a rounded average of the two values. The 1954 recession yielded a value of .257, the 1958 recession a value of .285 and the average was .271. An adjustment value of .27 points per point departure from 83 per cent of capacity operation is equivalent to the assumption that at 83 per cent of capacity 22.2 per cent of the production labor is overhead.

per hour used by labor and management respectively to obtain indexes of the production labor cost per unit of product. The results are given in Table 18.

According to Table 18, the cost of labor per ton of steel production dropped between 1953 and 1955 and then rose. If one relies on the index of hourly earnings used by labor, the total increase in production labor costs at a standard rate of operation was only 8 per cent. If one relies on management's figure on employment cost per hour, the total rise for the period would be 15 per cent. Un-

Table 18—INDEX OF LABOR COST PER UNIT OF STEEL
OUTPUT FOR THE STEEL INDUSTRY AT A STANDARD
RATE OF OPERATION, PRODUCTION WORKERS
ONLY: 1953–FISCAL 1959

	Adjusted Index of Man-Hours Worked per Unit of Product (1953=100)	Index of Labor Cost per Man-hour		Index of Labor Cost per Unit of Output	
		Average Hourly Earnings (1953=100)	Total Labor Cost per Hour Worked (1953=100)	Based on Average Hourly Earnings (1953=100)	Based on Total Labor Cost per Hour Worked (1953=100)
1953	100.0	100.0	100.0	100.0	100.0
1954	94.0	101.9	103.0	95.8	96.8
1955	89.2	109.7	111.6	97.9	99.5
1956	86.6	116.6	121.1	101.0	104.9
1957	85.2	124.1	131.8	105.7	113.0
1958	80.9	133.3	144.0	107.9	116.5
Fiscal 1959	76.5	140.3	150.3	107.3	115.0

Source: Calculated from Table 17 and from BLS and AISI series.

doubtedly the true value lies between these two figures, but it must lie much closer to the 15 per cent than the 8 per cent. As we have already seen, the index of hourly earnings used by labor at the hearings differs from the management index in two important respects. It is an index of earnings per hour *paid for,* whereas the appropriate index in this case would be one for hours *worked;* and it does not take full account of the increase in fringe benefits, which was more rapid than that of average hourly earnings. The management index is superior to the labor index in both these respects. But to some extent the estimates of the cost of fringe benefits involve arbitrary allocations by management to which labor takes exception. However, if it is agreed that the appropriate index of production labor costs per hour should be for hours worked and should include the cost of fringe benefits, then the rise in labor costs per hour would be close to the magnitude of the management index and the rise in production labor costs per ton from 1953 to fiscal 1959 would be close to 15 per cent, provided, of course, that costs were adjusted to a standard rate of operation. The significance of this 15 per cent rise in production labor costs per ton will be examined after the rise in nonproduction worker costs has been considered.

LABOR COST FOR NONPRODUCTION WORKERS

In 1953 nearly 15 per cent of the manpower used in steel production consisted of administrative, professional, and clerical workers. For the most part this body of salaried workers constitutes overhead labor which varies only a little with year to year changes in the volume of production. This body of salaried workers increases as new plants are brought into production and as the average volume of steel to be produced and sold increases. Also, technical improvements in management and the electronic computer handling of the vast amounts of information required in operating a big corporation increase the productivity of this overhead labor. The net effect is the reduction in this overhead manpower per ton of output but not at as rapid a rate as in the case of production manpower. And since the salaries of nonproduction workers have gone up in somewhat the same proportion as have wages, the labor cost per ton for nonproduction workers has gone up appreciably more than that for production workers.

An estimate of the increase in nonproduction labor cost per ton after 1953 runs into the same difficulties as those for production labor because of the variation in output. For pricing purposes, it is the overhead labor cost per ton at an *average* rate of operation which is significant, not the actual cost per ton in a particular year of high or low output. For this reason, the nonproduction labor requirements and costs per ton should be calculated at a standard rate of operation. This has been done in Table 19 on the assumption that salaries have risen in the same proportion as wages.

As can be seen from this table, the nonproduction labor per ton adjusted to a standard rate of operation has fluctuated but has tended to go down somewhat. However, because of the rise in salary rates, the nonproduction labor cost per ton has been rising for comparable rates of operation.

TOTAL LABOR COST PER UNIT OF OUTPUT

The total labor cost per ton can be estimated for an average rate of operations by combining the findings for production and for nonproduction workers. If the salary scales were the same per hour

Table 19—INDEX OF LABOR COST PER UNIT OF STEEL
OUTPUT FOR THE STEEL INDUSTRY AT A
STANDARD RATE OF OPERATION
NONPRODUCTION WORKERS ONLY:
1953–FISCAL 1959

	Number of Non-production Workers (in thousands)	Potential Production at 83% of Capacity (in thousand tons)	Index of Non-production Workers per Ton at 83% of Capacity (1953 = 100)	Index of Non-production Worker Salaries[a] (1953 = 100)	Index of Nonproduction Labor Cost per ton at 83% of Capacity (1953 = 100)
1953	93.7	97.5	100.0	100.0	100.0
1954	88.3	103.2	89.0	103.0	91.7
1955	90.7	104.4	90.4	111.6	100.9
1956	97.6	106.6	95.3	121.1	115.4
1957	105.7	110.8	99.3	131.8	130.9
1958	99.8	116.8	89.0	144.0	128.2
Fiscal 1959	102.2	119.6	88.9	150.3	133.6

Source: Calculated from series by AISI and BLS.
   [a] Assumes the same percentage increase in employment cost per unit of salaried labor as for production labor.

of work, the two indexes could be combined with weights in proportion to their number in 1953. But nonproduction workers include a considerable proportion of higher paid workers, so that the average hourly earnings are approximately one-third higher than those of wage earners.[5] This means that a given percentage increase in hourly earnings of salaried workers increases labor costs by more than the same increase in the wage rates for an equal number of wage earners. For this reason the index for nonproduction workers must receive an extra weight in combining the two indexes. This has been done in Table 20 which gives a weight of one and one-third for each salaried worker and a weight of one for each production worker in 1953.

This combined index of labor cost per unit of steel shows more of an increase from 1953 to fiscal 1959 than that for production labor alone. Instead of rising 15 per cent, the combined index rises just over 18 per cent in the six and a half years. While the data available do not allow us to say that this is exactly the per cent increase in the total labor cost which would have occurred between 1953 and fiscal 1959 with comparable rates of operation, this would appear to be approximately the magnitude of increase.

This conclusion is consistent with the cruder figure of 19.4 per cent increase in employment costs per ton for a standard rate of operation, which is obtained by taking the total employment costs reported for the industry by the American Iron and Steel Institute for all steel company activity, dividing by the tons produced and adjusting to a standard rate of operations. It is also consistent with the estimates of total labor cost published by the Department of Labor.[6]

[5] AISI data indicate average hourly wages for wage earners in 1953 as averaging $2.27 and $3.01 for salary cost per hour for salaried workers. The division between the BLS production and nonproduction workers is not exactly the same as the AISI division between wage and salary workers, but in 1953 the categories "production workers" and "wage earners" appear to overlap by more than 97 per cent.

[6] The BLS figures for all-employee employment cost of producing a ton of steel are: 1953 $45, 1954 $50 and Fiscal 1959 $58. The increase from the average of 1953-1954 to Fiscal 1959 is 22 per cent. An adjustment for rate of

Table 20—INDEX OF TOTAL LABOR COSTS PER UNIT OF
STEEL OUTPUT FOR THE STEEL INDUSTRY AT
A STANDARD RATE OF OPERATIONS, ALL
WORKERS: 1953–FISCAL 1959

	Index of Labor Cost per Unit Production Workers	Index of Cost per Unit: Nonproduction Workers	Index of Total Labor Cost per Unit[a]
1953	100.0	100.0	100.0
1954	96.8	91.7	95.9
1955	99.5	100.9	99.8
1956	104.9	115.4	106.8
1957	113.0	130.9	116.2
1958	116.5	128.2	118.6
Fiscal 1959	115.0	133.6	118.3

Source: Tables 18 and 19.

[a] Assumes production workers represent 82 per cent of total labor cost in 1953: Essentially the same index for total labor cost per unit of output at a standard rate of operations would be obtained if total manpower per unit is directly adjusted to a standard rate of operations and then multiplied by the index of employment cost per hour.

Clearly, one can reasonably conclude that for the period as a whole the direct effect of the increase in wage rates was to increase total employment costs per ton at a standard rate of operation by around 18 to 19 per cent, an increase which could justify *some* increase in steel prices but an increase very much less than the 36 per cent increase in the steel price index that actually occurred.

OTHER OPERATING EXPENSES AFTER 1953

The leaders of the steel industry justified the increases in steel prices not only on the direct effects of steel wage increases but

operation would reduce this somewhat. *Background Statistics Bearing on the Steel Dispute* (August 1959), Section 14.

also on the indirect effects which were expected to flow from rising wage rates in other industries and a consequent rise in other operating expenses. The raw materials and services other than labor which are purchased by the steel industry constitute a cost in making steel of the same general magnitude as the cost of labor. Experience in the war inflations had shown an increase in other operating expenses closely parallel to that for labor. And we have seen that this is a reasonable expectation in a general monetary inflation.

But with no general excess in demand since 1953, the principles of a monetary inflation cannot be expected to apply in this later period and the question must be raised whether operating expenses other than labor went up in anything like the same proportion as the increase in labor costs per ton.

To throw light on this question, we have the same two sets of information as for the earlier period, neither of which is completely satisfactory. We have price indexes for some of the major raw materials for steelmaking, but no solid basis for building them into a satisfactory index of steel raw material prices. Also we have the total cost of purchased materials and services charged to operating expenses by the industry as a whole, but an important part of these materials are purchased for operations other than steelmaking and a part of the raw materials for steelmaking are produced by the integrated steel producer and represent in part a labor rather than a material cost to the particular producer.

PRICES OF STEELMAKING MATERIALS AFTER 1953

As we have already seen, for the three major raw materials used in steelmaking—iron ore, iron and steel scrap, and coking coal— we have price indexes that relate directly to the raw materials of the steel industry, but for fuel and power we have to use a more general index, not one directly related to steel. These indexes are given in Table 21. As can be seen, prices for ore, coking coal, and fuel and power were higher at the end of the period and show little tendency to be depressed by the low rates of operation in 1954 and 1958. On the other hand, iron and steel scrap prices were lower at the end of the period than at the beginning. However, scrap prices appear to be made in a classically competitive market and are sensitive to changes in the rate of steel operations, so that the lower prices in 1959 over prices in 1953 presumably reflect in large measure the difference in rate of operation and its effect on the demand for scrap. When a crude adjustment in the price of scrap is made so as to correct for differences in rate of operation, the adjusted index shows some rise in scrap prices.

However, the indexes for these four items which constitute a major proportion of the raw material costs in steelmaking do not show a rise at all comparable to the 18 to 19 per cent increase in labor costs per ton. The largest increases, those in iron ore and coking coal, were only 13 per cent and 11 per cent. Fuel and power went up less than 4 per cent and even after adjustment for the low rate of operations in fiscal 1959, the scrap increase falls between these extremes. A combined index for these four items shows a rise of only 10 per cent. This crude index suggests that material costs per ton could not have risen nearly as much as labor costs per ton from 1953 to fiscal 1959.

This conclusion is confirmed by a more comprehensive but even cruder estimate of material costs per ton, which can be derived from the aggregate data for the whole steel industry compiled by the American Iron and Steel Institute. These estimates show a rise of only 11.9 per cent in material and service expenditures per ton of steel produced from 1953 to 1958.[7] Approximately the same figure would apply to fiscal 1959, since there was no significant difference in the average of prices for the two periods. These estimates are crude because they include all the activities of the steel corporations, not just their steelmaking activity. And

---

[7] The AISI figures show an increase in the cost of materials and supplies per ton of ingot steel produced from $57.70 in 1953 to $64.60 in 1958.

Table 21—PRICE INDEXES FOR MAJOR MATERIALS
REQUIRED FOR STEELMAKING: 1953–FISCAL 1959
(1953=100)

| | Iron Ore | Iron and Steel Scrap | | Coking Coal | Fuel Power and Lighting | Combined Index Using the Adjusted Index of Scrap Prices |
		Unadjusted Index	Adjusted for Rate of Operations[a]			
1953	100.0	100.0	100.0	100.0	100.0	100.0
1954	102.5	77.4	92.8	95.4	98.7	98.4
1955	104.3	101.5	102.2	93.1	98.5	100.5
1956	112.5	128.5	134.6	103.2	101.6	112.9
1957	118.1	113.4	121.9	109.9	107.0	115.0
1958	115.0	91.0	118.7	109.6	102.9	112.3
Fiscal 1959	112.9	95.1	107.7	111.2	103.6	109.7

Source: BLS.

[a] Adjusted for variation rate of steel operation by deducting .75 index points for each point of operation above 83 per cent of capacity, adding an equivalent amount for each point below 83 per cent and recalculating the index to 1953-100.

[b] Calculated with weights of 40-20-20-20 for ore, scrap, coal, and fuel-power.

"other activity" includes such diverse enterprises as railroad operation and cement making as well as the more closely related activities of ore and coal mining. Altogether these other activities represented roughly a quarter of the total.[8] Only if material and services for other activities varied in the same proportion as those used in steelmaking would it be possible to obtain an accurate index of the variation in the actual expenditure per ton. However, if we adopt 10 to 12 per cent as the range of increase in material and service cost per ton of steel we would not be far wrong and

[8] In 1953 man-hours in steel production (including coke) for the reporting companies (constituting 94.5 per cent of steel production in that year) amounted to 1,288 million while 436 million man-hours were engaged in other activity.

this is less than two-thirds of the increase in estimated labor costs per ton.

TOTAL OPERATING EXPENSES AFTER 1953

Between 1953 and fiscal 1959 total operating expenses per ton must have gone up less than the increase in labor costs per ton and more than the increase in other expenses per ton. A rough estimate of the increase can be made by combining the increases, weighting them in proportion to their relative importance in 1953 and 1954. This gives a combined increase of 13 to 15 per cent in total operating expenses per ton of steel at a standard rate of operation.[9] It is the general magnitude of the increase in operating expenses to be attributed to increased wage rates and to increased prices of raw materials and services. And this 13 to 15 per cent figure for the increase in operating expenses per ton is properly to be compared with the 36 per cent increase in steel prices in the same period.

In the preceding analysis we have had to rely, at least for materials and services, on the somewhat heterogeneous figures compiled by the Iron and Steel Institute for the industry as a whole. We also have available the more homogeneous expenditure figures published by the United States Steel Corporation for its own activity. These figures, like those for the industry, include diverse activities, but because they are for a single company the distortions due to a shift in the ratio of steel to other activities are likely to be less. As in the case of the industrywide figures, the expenditures per ton for labor need to be adjusted to a standard rate of operation, while only a negligible adjustment would be needed for material and service expenditures per ton.

[9] In 1953, a year of high production, employment costs amounted to 42.5 per cent of total operating expenses and in 1954, a year of lower production, employment costs amounted to 45.8 per cent. In the above calculation, 44 per cent has been used as the weight for labor, the rounded average of the figures for 1953 and 1954. This leaves 56 per cent as the weight given to materials and services purchased.

The labor expenditure by U. S. Steel for all purposes per ton of steel produced is given in Table 22. As can be seen from the table, total labor cost per ton when adjusted to a standard rate of operation appears to have risen around 17 per cent from 1953 to fiscal 1959, a little less than the 18 to 19 per cent increase for the industry as a whole. The corresponding figures for U. S. Steel expenditures on materials and service per ton show a much smaller and more irregular rise than those for labor as can be seen from Table 23. These figures suggest a rise in material and service costs per ton of about 8 per cent, somewhat lower than the 10 to 12 per cent rise derived from the data for the industry as a whole.

A combined index for the rise in expenses per ton for U. S. Steel

Table 22—INDEX OF LABOR COST PER TON OF STEEL OUT-
PUT FOR THE UNITED STATES STEEL CORPORATION
ADJUSTED TO A STANDARD RATE OF OPERATION:
1953–FISCAL 1959

	Total Labor Cost for All Activities (in millions)	*Total Steel Ingots & Casting Produced (in million tons)*	*Labor Costs for All Activities per Ton of Steel Produced*	*Rate of Operation (per cent of capacity)*	*Labor Cost per Ton Produced Adjusted to an 83% Rate of Operation[a]*	*Index of Labor Costs per Ton Produced at a Standard Rate of Operation*
1953	$1569	35.8	$43.70	98.4	47.40	100.0
1954	1387	28.4	48.90	73.2	46.55	98.2
1955	1615	35.3	45.70	90.8	47.57	100.4
1956	1681	33.4	50.40	85.2	50.71	107.0
1957	1682	33.7	55.20	85.2	55.51	117.1
1958	1489	23.8	62.30	59.2	56.59	119.4
Fiscal 1959	1788	31.3	57.10	76.1	55.44	117.0

Source: U.S. Steel Annual Reports.
[a] Calculated cost per ton adjusted inversely 24 cents for every point in rate of operation above or below 83 per cent of capacity. Adjustment factor is average of (1) change in cost per point of change in rate of operation between 1954 and 1953–1955, which came to 20 cents and (2) the same for 1958 as compared with the average of 1957 and fiscal 1959, which came to 28 cents.

has also been calculated, using the adjusted index of employment costs and the actual index for material and service costs per ton This indicates a rise of 12.8 per cent in total operating expenses between 1953 and fiscal 1959 for a standard rate of operation, a figure just below the 13 to 15 per cent increase arrived at for the industry as a whole.[10] Thus, the more homogeneous figures for U. S. Steel strongly confirm the cruder figures derived for the industry as a whole.

Table 23—MATERIAL AND SERVICE EXPENDITURE PER TON OF STEEL OUTPUT BY THE UNITED STATES STEEL CORPORATION: 1953–FISCAL 1959

	Expenditures per ton of steel produced	
	Dollars	*Index*
1953	39.50	100.0
1954	40.00	101.3
1955	38.40	97.2
1956	44.50	112.7
1957	39.20	99.2
1958	45.50	115.2
Fiscal 1959	42.80	108.3

Source: Computed from U. S. Steel Annual Reports.

In the remainder of this analysis the figure of 14 per cent will be adopted as the general magnitude of the increase in operating expenses per ton of steel at a standard rate of operation between 1953 and fiscal 1959. More relevant data may require a revision of this magnitude but, until the steel industry makes public a segregation of its operating expenses in a manner to allow more accurate estimates, the above estimates will have to serve as a basis

[10] The weights used are the average of the relative importance of labor in 1953 and 1954 which give weights of 54 for employment costs and 46 for material and service expenditures.

for appraising the legitimacy of the 36 per cent increase in steel prices during the period.

PRODUCER MARGINS AFTER 1953

It must be obvious that, if steel prices increased in the magnitude of 36 per cent and operating expenses per ton at a standard rate of operation increased only in the magnitude of 14 per cent, the producer margin at the same standard rate must have increased much more than 36 per cent. Indeed it should have increased by around 120 per cent.[11] Can we check this magnitude by examining the difference between reported total revenue per ton and total operating expenses per ton?

If we had total revenue and total operating expenses from steel-making alone, we could approximate the producer margin per ton shipped or produced. But, as we have already seen, revenue and operating expenses for both the industry as a whole and for U. S. Steel alone include other activities, and there is good reason to expect that the producer margin for these did not increase as much as that for steel. For example, railroad transport—which represented 14 per cent of U. S. Steel's net fixed capital in 1953—is a regulated industry and presumably any increase in producer margin was strictly limited. We could, therefore, expect that the figures for the increase in producer margin covering all activities would be significantly smaller than the increase in the margin for steelmaking alone. Also, to make the figures comparable, adjustments have to be made for the rate of operation and for the fact that costs apply primarily to tons of steel produced while revenue figures are for tons of steel shipped. Finally, we only have semi-

[11] Assuming that operating expense absorbed 80.5 per cent of operating revenue for the industry as a whole (the average of 1953 and 1954), the increase in producer margin would amount to 125 per cent. For U.S. Steel, operating expenses absorbed 77.6 per cent of operating revenue (average 1953 and 1954) giving a figure of 116 per cent as the increase in producer margin from 1953 to fiscal 1959.

annual data for U.S. Steel and so can only derive figures for this third of the industry. As a result, the figures for the increase in producer margin can only be a very rough check against the figures arrived at through the analysis of costs.

When we make the necessary adjustment, the over-all figures for revenue and operating expenses for U.S. Steel do show a very considerable increase in producer margin after 1953, though not an increase of 120 per cent. Combining the figures already arrived at for employment costs and for material and service costs at a standard rate of operations gives a 1953 figure of $87 for the total operating costs per ton at 83 per cent of capacity operation and $98 for fiscal 1959.[12] These figures of cost per ingot ton are equivalent to $123 and $138 per ton of finished steel.[13] In the same period, revenue from the sale of products and services per ton of steel shipped increased from $154 in 1953 to $195 in fiscal 1959.[14] Thus, according to these figures, the producer margin increased from $31 to $57 per ton, an increase of 84 per cent.

The discrepancy between the 84 per cent range and 120 per cent would wholly disappear if the revenue from all sources per ton of steel shipped had risen as much as the index of finished steel prices. From 1953 to fiscal 1959, both the industry's revenue from all sources per ton shipped and that of U. S. Steel increased only 27 per cent compared to the 36 per cent increase in the index of steel prices. The smaller rise in revenue could be explained if the steel price index exaggerated the rise in steel prices, but the index is generally regarded as reliable. Some discrepancy between revenue per ton and a perfect index of steel prices could arise from a shift in product mix, but this is not likely to be large in peace time. The discrepancy would seem to be due primarily to the inclusion of nonsteelmaking activities in the total figures. However, neither

[12] From Tables 22 and 23.

[13] Operating expenses per ingot ton multiplied by the ratio of total finished steel shipped from 1953 to 1958 (135 million tons) to total steel ingots and castings produced (190 million tons) or 1.4.

[14] Source: U.S. Steel annual and quarterly reports.

of the two magnitudes of increase, 120 per cent and 80 per cent, can be regarded as a precise measure of the increase in producer margin. It seems likely that the true figure lies closer to the first. For practical discussion it would seem safe to say that the producer margin came close to doubling between 1953 and fiscal 1959.

Can an increase of this magnitude be justified by increased taxes or by an increase in the capital employed?

With respect to taxes, peacetime corporate income tax rates remained practically the same and other taxes per ton of steel capacity increased by only a small amount. This leaves an increase in capital requirements to be investigated as a possible justification for the big increase in producer margin after 1953.

THE INCREASE IN CAPITAL AFTER 1953

There can be no question that there was an increase in capital investment per ton of capacity from 1953 to fiscal 1959. Even at book value, the net fixed capital per ton reported for the industry increased by nearly 13 per cent and for U.S. Steel by 10 per cent.[15] And these figures clearly understate value on an historical cost basis because of the five-year amortization which has been allowed for tax purposes under certificates of necessity. Also, if the dollars recovered on depreciation and depletion are to have the same general buying power as the dollars invested, account has to be taken of the decline in the value of the dollar. Or if reproduction cost is to be the basis of valuation, consideration must be given to the cost of new plants.

At the minimum, the book values of net fixed capital should be adjusted upward for the over-rapid write-off involved in the five-year amortization program. Unfortunately figures were not presented at the hearings which would allow such an adjustment for

[15] See Appendix C, Table 36, footnote a, and Appendix D, Table 39, footnote a. The above figures are derived from book values without an adjustment.

the industry as a whole. But such an adjustment can be made for the book values reported by U.S. Steel. Between 1951 and 1958, U.S. Steel invested over $800 million in facilities subject to five-year amortization and most of this investment had been charged off or recovered for tax purposes by 1959. If instead of this rapid write-off only regular depreciation had been charged on the basis of a twenty-year useful life, the net book value of these assets in fiscal 1959 would have been $535 million greater, adding 23 per cent to the net book value of U.S. Steel's fixed assets, while the adjustment would add 4 per cent to the 1953 figures. When this adjustment is made, the net fixed capital per ton of capacity employed by U.S. Steel in fiscal 1959 shows an increase of 29 per cent over 1953 instead of the 10 per cent shown by book values.

For the industry as a whole it is difficult to say what the net fixed capital would be if a reliable adjustment could be made for the five year amortization. If the industry figures of depreciation are arbitrarily adjusted in the same proportion as those for U.S. Steel, the net fixed capital per ton of capacity would also show an increase of 29 per cent between 1953 and fiscal 1959.

When the values based on historical cost are adjusted for the change in the general buying power of the dollar, the figures for the increase in net fixed capital per ton of capacity are somewhat lower. For U.S. Steel, the increase from 1953 to fiscal 1959 would only be 25 per cent and the cruder and probably excessive figure for the industry as a whole would be 16 per cent.

The fact that the buying power values show a smaller increase in the fixed capital per ton in this period is easy to explain. In 1953 a significant part of the net fixed capital reflected the lower pre-inflation price level. By 1959 more of the pre-inflation capital had been used up and more capital had been acquired at the post-inflation prices so that revaluations in 1959 dollars increased the average value by a smaller amount. The figures for the net fixed capital per ton are given in Table 24 both for historical cost and

Table 24—ESTIMATED INCREASES IN CAPITAL PER TON OF
STEEL CAPACITY FOR THE UNITED STATES STEEL
CORPORATION AND FOR THE STEEL INDUSTRY:
1953 AND FISCAL 1959

| | *United States Steel Corporation* | | | | | |
| | *Historical Cost Basis* | | | *Buying Power Basis* | | |
	1953	*Fiscal 1959*	*Increase*	*1953 (in 1953 dollars)*	*Fiscal 1959 (in 1959 dollars)*	*Increase*
Net Working Capital per Ton of Capacity	$ 8.99	$16.61	+84.8%	$ 8.99	$16.61	+84.8%
Net Fixed Capital per Ton of Capacity	53.17	68.74	+29.3%	61.79	77.09	+24.8%
Total Capital per Ton of Capacity	62.16	85.35	+37.3%	70.78	93.70	+32.4%
Total Capital per Ton of Capacity if Net Working Capital per Ton had been as Great as in 1942	69.64	85.35	+22.5%	79.26	93.70	+18.2%
	The Steel Industry					
Net Working Capital per Ton of Capacity	$19.97	$25.16	+26.0%	$19.97	$25.16	+26.0%
Net Fixed Capital per Ton of Capacity	50.60	65.41	+29.3%	62.77	72.95	+16.2%
Total Capital per Ton of Capacity	70.57	90.57	+28.3%	82.74	98.11	+18.6%

Source: Appendix C and D.

for the historical cost adjusted for changes in the general value of the dollar.

No attempt has been made to estimate what the increase in capital would be if the reproduction cost principle were applied, but there has been such rapid technical improvement in the designing of steelmaking plant that many of the facilities built since World War II are obsolescent and some are obsolete. The use of low-cost oxygen in furnace operation has spectacularly increased the output possible from a furnace properly designed for its use so that, in spite of high construction costs per furnace, the capital cost per ton of capacity has been substantially reduced. And in other ways technical progress has made a given new investment go further in terms of capacity than would have been true only a few years ago. This rapid technical improvement suggests that an appraisal of the capital value of existing facilities on a reproduction cost basis might easily lead to a lower net value per ton of capacity than that arrived at by either the historical cost or the buying-power principle.[16] In what follows it will be assumed, however, that the reproduction cost principle would result in a value between those reached on a basis of historical cost and buying power.

Whether we adopt an historical cost or a buying-power value, or a value between, we find a substantial increase in the net fixed capital per ton of capacity. This means that, at a standard rate of operation, the recovery of capital per ton and the earnings on capital per ton would have to be higher in 1959 to maintain the same rate of return on capital as in 1953.

Also, working capital required per ton has increased appreciably. For U.S. Steel as we have already seen the working capital was abnormally low in 1953, and in estimating the increase in total capital required from 1942 to 1953, the 1953 figure was adjusted to a more normal figure. Using the same adjusted figures we get an increase of 23 per cent in U.S. Steel's total capital required per ton of capacity on an historical cost basis and 18 per cent on the buying power basis. For the industry as a whole an

[16] For a more extended discussion of this problem, see Appendix E.

increase of 28 per cent is obtained on the historical cost basis and 19 per cent on the buying power basis. The actual figures are given in Table 24. Clearly these increases in capital required additions to the producer margin if the rate of return on capital was to be maintained.

We can estimate the magnitude of the increase in producer margin required to maintain the rate of return on capital by assuming a standard rate of operation and a standard or target rate of return. This has been done on the assumption that after taxes an 8 per cent return on capital is to be made when operating at 83 per cent of capacity and the results are given in Table 25. For U.S. Steel, the calculations suggest that when capital is measured on an historical cost basis a 17 per cent increase in producer margin would have maintained the rate of return, and only 15 per cent would have been necessary when capital is measured on the buying power principle. For the industry as a whole the cruder and probably excessive figures of required increase are 26 per cent on the historical cost basis and 17 per cent on the buying power principle.

For practical discussion, we can adopt the figure of 20 per cent, as the general magnitude of the increase in producer margin that can be justified by the increases in taxes and in capital investment. An increase in producer margin of this magnitude is a far cry from the doubling of producer margin which appears to have taken place and indicates a very considerable increase in profit margins and in the rate of return on capital between 1953 and 1959.

Just how much the increase in profit may have been is hard to determine because of the lack of precision of the published data we have to work with. But from the figures we have developed, it would appear that, at an 83 per cent rate of operation, a doubling of the producer margin would just about double the rate of return on capital. This can be seen by calculating the rate of return in fiscal 1959 if the producer margin in 1953 had been just sufficient to make an 8 per cent return in that year and by 1959 the

Table 25—REQUIRED INCREASE IN PRODUCER MARGINS TO MAINTAIN THE RATE OF RETURN ON CAPITAL FOR THE UNITED STATES STEEL CORPORATION AND FOR THE STEEL INDUSTRY: 1953–FISCAL 1959

(in millions)

United States Steel Corporation

	Historical Cost Basis		Buying-Power Basis	
	1953	Fiscal 1959	1953	Fiscal 1959
Net Working Capital (adjusted)	$ 617	$ 696	$ 617	$ 696
Net Fixed Capital	1994	2,880	2,317	3,230
Total Capital	2,611	3,576	2,934	3,926
State, Local, & Misc. Taxes	$ 89.3	$ 94.3	$ 89.3	$ 94.3
Regular Depreciation & Depletion	152.4[a]	197.4[b]	176.8	221.8
Earnings to Make 8% on Capital	208.9	286.1	234.7	316.6
Federal Income Taxes	208.9	286.1	234.7	316.6
Total Producer Margin Required	$ 659.5	$ 863.9	$ 735.5	$ 949.3
Capacity (in million tons)	37.5	41.9		
Output at 83% of Capacity (in million tons)	31.1	34.8		
Producer Margin Required per ton at 83% of Capacity	$ 21.21	$ 24.82	$ 23.65	$ 27.28
Increase in Producer Margin per Ton		+17.0%		+15.3%

The Steel Industry

Net Working Capital (adjusted)	$2,249	$ 3,518	$2,249	$ 3,518
Net fixed Capital	5,698	9,144	7,068	10,199
Total Capital	7,947	12,662	9,317	13,717
State, Local, & Misc. Taxes	$ 191.3	$ 248.9	$ 191.3	$ 248.9
Regular Depreciation & Depletion	417.9c	668.6	518.2	745.5b
Earnings to Make 8% on Capital	635.8	1,013.0	745.0	1,097.4
Federal Income Taxes	635.8	1,013.0	745.0	1,097.4
Total Producer Margin Required	$1,880.8	$ 2,943.5	$2,199.5	$ 3,189.2
Capacity (in million tons)	112.6	139.8		
Output at 83% of Capacity (in million tons)	93.5	116.0		
Producer Margin Required per ton at 83% of Capacity	$ 20.12	$ 25.37	$ 23.52	$ 27.49
Increase in Producer Margin per Ton		+26.1%		+16.9%

Source: For capital and capacity figures, Appendix C and D.
For state, local, and miscellaneous taxes, and for depreciation and depletion on the historical cost basis, U.S. Steel Annual Reports and AISI, except as noted.
For depreciation and depletion on the buying power basis, the historical cost figures raised in proportion to the rise in fixed capital due to revaluation on the buying power basis.

a Reported depreciation and depletion of 236.6 million adjusted for five-year write-offs.
b Actual figures for Average of 1958 and 1959 since five-year amortization adjustments just about cancelled out.
c Reported depreciation and depletion of 613 million includes large but unknown amount of five-year write-offs. Figure used assumed depletion and depreciation in 1953 bears same ratio to net fixed assets as in fiscal 1959.

margin had doubled. According to this calculation, and using historical cost figures, the rate of return on capital for U.S. Steel would have increased from the assumed figure of 8 per cent in 1953 to 16.5 per cent in 1959, and for the industry as a whole from 8 to 14.8 per cent. If buying power values for capital are used in the calculation, the increase in rate of return for U.S. Steel would be from 8 to 16.6 per cent, and for the industry as a whole from 8 to 16.0 per cent.[17] These figures suggest that if, at a given operation rate, a return of 8 per cent would have been made at 1953 prices and costs, something like a 16 per cent return would have been made at the same operating rate at 1959 prices and costs.

This conclusion is consistent with the actual earnings of U.S. Steel in fiscal 1959. In that period its operation averaged 76 per cent of capacity and its total revenue from all its activities less operating expenses amounted to $1,208 million. When we deduct state and local taxes and depreciation, as shown in Table 25, and divide the remainder equally between income taxes and return to capital it indicates a 12.8 per cent rate on an historical basis and 11.3 per cent on the buying power basis. If these figures were adjusted to an 83 per cent rate of operation, this would add approximately two percentage points. If the 14 per cent of assets employed in railroading are credited with earning only 6 per cent, then the earnings on assets other than railroading would be raised by another 1.3 percentage points. Some further adjustment would have to be made for other nonsteelmaking activities so that the reported earnings on all activities are quite consistent with a return of 16 per cent on steelmaking activities at an 83 per cent rate of operations.[18]

---

[17] Arrived at by doubling the 1953 producer margin per ton at an 83 per cent operating rate shown in Table 25 and calculating the corresponding rate of return under the 1959 conditions of capital, taxes, and depreciation.

[18] A similar analysis for the industry as a whole is not feasible because figures for fiscal 1959 are not available and the calendar years 1958 and 1959 were periods of low operation rates.

Whether in fact an 8 per cent rate of return would have been made in 1953 if operations had been at 83 per cent of capacity, we cannot tell, because earnings from steelmaking are not segregated from those from other sources. But prior to recent years the pricing policy of U.S. Steel does appear to have been "bottomed on the expectation of earning over the years a net return, after taxes of 8 per cent on investment."[19] And our own analysis has led to the conclusion that in 1953 the producer margin made possible returns on capital comparable to those made in other years of equal activity. The evidence thus suggests, but does not prove, that instead of bottoming price policy on an 8 per cent return by 1959 it was based on a target rate of return of closer to 16 per cent.

In arriving at this conclusion, we have had to make many adjustments in the facts on steel as presented at the hearings or subsequently published, and the data are so inadequate to the task of measuring what actually happened that others attempting to make similar estimates may arrive at somewhat different results. But that there was a very sizable widening of profit margins is attested by a quite different approach, that of estimating the change in break-even point.

PROFITS AND THE BREAK-EVEN POINT

The break-even point refers to the level of operations at which the receipts from sales just equal operating expenses and the charges for depreciation and depletion so that there is neither a net profit nor a net loss. At the hearings, estimates of U.S. Steel's break-even point were presented by Mr. Fred V. Gardner, a management consultant who specialized in the problems of break-even points.[20] According to his analysis, U.S. Steel would have just broken even in 1953 with sales of $1,860 million. This is equiv-

[19] See Chapter III, p. 34.
[20] *Hearings*, pp. 713-752.

alent to an output of 17.3 million tons or an operating rate of 47 per cent of capacity. By fiscal 1959 capacity had increased so that a break-even point at 47 per cent of capacity would have meant an output of 19.3 million tons. Yet in fiscal 1959 the figures indicate that U.S. Steel would have been able to break even at an output of 12.3 million tons or at an operating rate of approximately 30 per cent of capacity.[21] Only a very large increase in profit margin could have brought about such a large reduction in the break-even point.

This great reduction in the break-even point achieved by U.S. Steel is confirmed by the data for its operations in the second half of 1960. For the six months as a whole its operating rate averaged 47 per cent of capacity, while its net income after taxes was reported as $111 million or an annual rate of $222 million, nearly as much as it made after peacetime taxes in 1953 when operations were at the rate of 98 per cent of capacity. Of course, the 1960 earnings are on a considerably larger volume of capital, but what is important to notice is that, at the profit margin prevailing in 1953, the break-even calculation suggests that there would have been no net income at a 47 per cent rate of operations.

THE IMPLICATIONS FOR STEEL PRICES

Just what are the implications of this analysis for steel prices? We have arrived at a figure of 14 per cent as the general magnitude of the increase in operating expenses per ton. This alone would justify a price increase of approximately 11 percentage points, 7 points attributable to the rise in labor costs and 4 points to that in materials and services. We have also reached 20 per cent as the general magnitude of the increase in producer margin needed to maintain the rate of return on capital. This would justify a price increase of 4 percentage points. When we combine these figures they suggest that, from 1953 to 1959, a total rise in steel

[21] Estimated by the method described in *Hearings,* pp. 713-752.

prices of approximately 15 per cent would have been a legitimate increase.[22] This leaves more than half of the 36 per cent price increase from 1953 to 1959 unexplained except as an increase in profit rates. Since we found no evidence that the profit margin in 1953 was too low, the conclusion seems reasonable that more than half of the price rise after 1953 cannot be justified by increases in labor costs, in taxes or in the greater amounts of capital used in steelmaking. The unexplained increase is equal to approximately $20 a ton on a standard mix of finished steel products.[23] This would seem to be the magnitude of the increase in price which went directly to increase profit rates.

We can also make a rough allocation between labor and capital of the responsibility for the 36 per cent rise in steel prices. Of the total, 6⅔ percentage points can be directly attributed to increased labor costs per unit of output and 21 percentage points to the widened profit margin.[24] Of the remaining 8⅓ percentage points, some represent increased costs of material and supplies, which in turn reflect returns to labor and capital, and some represent increased capital investment per ton, which also breaks down into returns to capital and labor. Some of the material costs, such as those for ore and coke, are an integral part of the steel industry, while some of the cost of constructing new steel facilities is the cost of steel. Thus, much of the 8⅓ points must divide between labor and capital in about the same proportion as that in steelmaking itself. If the whole 8⅓ points are divided on this basis, the labor responsibility would amount to 8⅔ percentage points or about one quarter of the price rise and capital's responsibility would

[22] This assumes a weight of 80 per cent for operation expenses and 20 per cent for producer margin in 1953.

[23] *The American Metal Market* composite price index for steel rose from $102.60 a ton in 1953 to $139.60 a ton in January, 1959, or a rise of 36.1 per cent. If it had only risen 15 per cent, the average price would have been $117.99, a difference of $21.61.

[24] For labor, the 18 to 19 per cent increase in labor costs per unit of product applied to the 36 per cent of the steel dollar going to labor at an 83 per cent rate of operations.

amount to 27⅓ points or three-quarters of the total price rise. This would seem to be about the proportion which each contributed to the total rise so far as actual costs are concerned.

However, there is a question whether the sizable increase in profit margin is not in some degree responsible for the increases in labor cost. When the steel industry continued to raise prices after the war inflations were over and placed the blame on labor, this would seem to be a clear and present incitement to labor to get its share of the higher revenue per ton. However, because of the complex interrelation between prices, wage rates, and profits, there can be little doubt that abnormally high profit margins offer an inviting target for labor's effort to increase worker income.

On the whole one must conclude that responsibility for the big increase in steel prices after 1953 rests primarily with steel management. It used its pricing power to widen profit margins and increase the profit at any given rate of operation. Only to a much smaller extent does responsibility rest with labor. The crux of the matter is management's power to administer prices and the post-1953 rise in steel prices is a clear example of its use.

CHAPTER VII

THE PRICING ISSUE POSED BY STEEL

In summary, one may conclude that corporate investment decisions are not made in such a way that either the expected or the experienced rates of profit are customarily pushed to the point of equality with the market rate of interest [the competitive cost of capital]. On the contrary, the corporate rate of profit return on investment is ordinarily maintained at more than twice the market rate of interest. . . . The failure to push investment to the point of coincidence with the market rate of interest appears to reside in part in the capability of a corporate economy of large scale production to prevent the erosive effects of unlimited competition from lowering the price of goods and services to the point where the corporate rate of return on investment would equal the market rate of interest.

PROFESSOR CALVIN B. HOOVER
DUKE UNIVERSITY*

Now that we have toiled through the financial facts of steel, let us return to the challenge laid down by Chairman Blough. He cited both the responsibility of management to stockholders and the grave long-range responsibilities to the nation as a whole. The industry must carry out "the replacement of obsolete and worn out equipment to remain efficient and productive"; must discover and develop huge new resources of iron ore; must develop facilities to treat and upgrade iron ores of lower quality; must carry on research to provide new and better steels; and must expand steel-

* "On the Inequality of the Rate of Profit and the Rate of Interest," *The Southern Economic Journal*, Vol. XXVIII, No. 1, July, 1961, p. 12.

making capacity—"so that the economic growth and security of this Nation may never be jeopardized by the lack of steel."[1] As he pointed out: ". . . no one of these responsibilities is possible of fulfillment by a profit-starved industry or by a company suffering from financial malnutrition."[2] And it was in the light of these responsibilties and the facts presented at the hearings that he commended to the thoughtful consideration of the Senate committee the question of whether or not the steel price action had been "responsible and in the public interest."[3]

Our extensive analysis of the facts gives a basis for answering these questions for the inflationary period ending in 1953. Both steel labor and steel management appear to have acted responsibly and in the public interest during that period. Both wage rates and steel prices went up in about the magnitude that would be expected from the general rise in price level, the increase in national productivity and the increase in peacetime income taxes. Furthermore, both wage rates and steel prices lagged well behind in the waves of inflation, helping to slow up the process and only coming into balance with more flexible prices in the readjustment phase of the inflationary process. Within the limits of the type of data supplied at the hearings and our ability to extract its meaning, there would seem to be no clear evidence that wage and price action in the steel industry up to 1953 was not responsible and in the public interest.

It is only in the period after 1953, when there was little or no inflation in the industries not based on steel, that a real issue of responsibility and the public interest arises. Let us take the "facts" of steel as developed in the preceding chapter as valid in their general magnitude—an increase in wage rates in excess of the increase in productivity which could justify 7 points of increase in steel prices; a rise in capital values which could justify 4 points of price

[1] *Hearings*, p. 213.
[2] *Loc. cit.*
[3] *Hearings*, p. 214.

increase; a rise in material costs which could justify another 4 points, a total which would justify a 15 per cent increase in steel prices; and an actual price increase of 36 per cent or more than double the increase justified, by increases in labor, capital, and material costs with the difference going to widen profit margins and increase the rate of return on capital at given rate of operation. It may be that when the industry presents more relevant data, eliminating railroad operation, cement making and other separable activities from those of steelmaking, the picture will look different, though internal evidence suggests that such clarifying data would show a smaller rather than a larger justification for price increase. And there is some room for argument over the appropriate adjustment of the published figures. But few will deny that there was a substantial widening of profit margins at comparable rates of operation between 1953 and 1959. It is this widening of profit margin accounting for more than half of the price increase since 1953 that raises the issue of whether steel's price action was responsible and in the public interest.

Before trying to answer this question, let us clear up one matter which might cause confusion. The issue is not one of whether the steel corporations acted illegally. There was remarkably little suggestion by those conducting the hearings or those criticizing the price actions of the steel companies that illegal action was involved. Some questions were raised as to whether identical bids and the "conversations" through the press prior to the 1958 price increase involve collusion. But no evidence of overt collusion was presented, such as that which was later disclosed in the electrical equipment industry. Rather, it was recognized from the outset that, acting legally, both labor and management had exercised important powers over wage rates and prices. This pricing power, not illegal action, was the focus of the hearings. And the question being raised here was whether this power was in fact used responsibly and in the public interest.

There is difficulty in answering this question because there is no consensus on what constitutes responsible use of pricing power or what constitutes the public interest. We have inherited conceptions of responsible business behavior and the public interest which rest on the absence of pricing power. We have no clear conception of responsible business action or the public interest in the presence of pricing power although there has been a growing realization that the older conceptions do not apply and much groping toward clarification.

THE TRADITIONAL CONCEPTIONS OF RESPONSIBILITY AND INTEREST

Let us start by answering the questions of responsibility and interest in terms of the older tradition. According to the inherited wisdom it is the function of each business enterprise to make as much money as it is able to make within the legal framework laid down by government and consistent with the morals of the community. Traditional wisdom has it that competition will so control the behavior of individual enterprises that the public interest will be served. Under this tradition it would be sufficient for the management of U.S. Steel to show (1) that it had broken no laws or the moral code, and (2) that it had acted in a way to make the most profit possible. This would be sufficient to estabilsh "responsible" behavior so far as prices and production are concerned, and the traditional wisdom argues or presumes that this would serve the public interest. On this basis, the question of responsible behavior would turn on whether a higher or lower price would have made more money for the individual firm. If U.S. Steel could show that it had set the most profitable price, this alone would be sufficient to establish responsible pricing action.

But this conception of responsible behavior and the public interest played no part in the Senate hearings on steel. Those who questioned steel pricing did so on the ground that the rise in steel prices was too great because it increased steel profits too much, while the steel corporations defended their action on the ground that the price increases did not raise profits too much but were for the most part made necessary by increased costs. Basically this is a complete rejection of the idea that it is the function of each business to make as much money as possible.

This general rejection of the traditional wisdom is a remarkable fact that emerged from the hearings. Both those who criticized the steel price increases and those who defended them were in tacit agreement that the public interest would not be served by an all-out drive for corporate profits. Both sides recognized the existence of a substanital degree of pricing power and both sides accepted the need for restraint in the exercise of this pricing power. The whole issue turned on the degree of restraint which should be exercised. But there was no agreement on just how much restraint should be exercised or what criteria should be used to determine the appropriate degree of restraint.

However, certain points of view did emerge. The chairman of the Senate committee urged greater restraint on the ground that lower prices would still yield a return adequate to bring forward as much new capital as the steel industry could effectively use. The spokesman for the industry defended the higher rates of return on the two basic grounds (1) that a higher rate was needed to supply new capital for expansion without the necessity of going into the market for savings, and (2) that the objective was to bring the earnings on steel capital into line with the earnings of other comparable industries.

THE NEW STOCK-OPTION BONUS SYSTEM

The issue was somewhat confused by the new system of bonuses to management adopted by U.S. Steel in 1951, which puts great pressure on management to increase corporate profits. According to Chairman Blough, "The plan was adopted to provide an incentive for the top-management group of United States Steel Corporation."[4] Under this plan key individuals in the management of the corporation were to be given ten-year options to buy the common stock of the corporation at the price which prevailed in the market at the time the options were given. Under present tax laws, if the option were exercised, say, after a couple of years and the stock held for six months, any profits on the transaction would be treated as a capital gain with a maximum income tax of 25 per cent.

The pressure which such a bonus system places on the recipients to increase the corporation's profits must be tremendous. If increased profits brought about a rise in the price of steel shares in the stock market, top management could in turn realize high profits subject to only moderate income taxes. Indeed, under the present tax laws, it is difficult to imagine a bonus system which would go further to intensify the management's desire to increase corporate profits.

This bonus system is consistent with the traditional wisdom. It tells management to make the most profits legally possible and gives management a great personal incentive to carry out this instruction. It identifies the personal interests of management with the personal interest of stockholders in greater corporate profits. By thus intensifying the drive for corporate profit it, in effect, denies that corporate management should exercise any restraint in pricing to make the most profit possible other than that implicit in law and in public morals. In so far as this bonus system is a guide to corporate policy, it directs that the most profitable price should be charged.

Whatever its merit, the new bonus system does seem to have been successful in stimulating U.S. Steel's management to make greater profits. We have seen the statement attributed in the Brookings study to an official of U.S. Steel that its pricing policy was bottomed on the expectation of earning over the years a net return, after taxes, of around 8 per cent on its investment. And

---

[4] *Hearings*, p. 366.

there is much evidence in the rate of earning that this was the basis of the corporation's pricing policy prior to the new bonus system.

It is difficult to believe that the new bonus system did not play an important part both as symbol and incentive in the great widening of the profit margin and the doubling of the target rate of return on capital which appears to have occurred in the period after its adoption. The intensified directive to make more profit was sharp and clear. And equally clear was the existence of the pricing power to widen profit margins and increase the rate of return.

On the other hand, the increase in the rate of return on steel capital was in the nature of a catching up to the high rates of return on capital being made in other concentrated industries such as automobiles, petroleum refining and chemicals. In moving from a target of 8 per cent to a higher target, U.S. Steel was not using its pricing power to exceed the earning rate of other concentrated industries in which there was substantial pricing power but only to bring steel more nearly into line. The issue of restraint is brought into sharp relief by the movement of steel prices because, in the short period of six years, the pricing restraint represented by a target of 8 per cent was replaced by the lesser restraint of a much higher target. The issue itself is of equally great importance in those concentrated industries in which the higher rates of return have been maintained over a longer period.

THE QUESTION OF RESPONSIBILITY AND THE PUBLIC INTEREST
But let us return to the basic question: since 1953 has the pricing action of U.S. Steel been responsible and in the public interest? Here we must divide the question into two parts. Was the price action responsible? And was it in the public interest?

Responsibility implies established and generally accepted principles of behavior. Yet today the only principles of guidance to competitive business are those of the traditional wisdom—that body of theory which explains why the profit drive serves the public interest and the body of clichés with which this body of theory is interpreted to guide daily behavior. According to this wisdom, we must say that the management of U.S. Steel was irresponsible when it was pricing to make only 8 per cent on its capital if it could have priced to make more; that only when the corporation uses its pricing power to the full is it acting responsibly.

But if one rejects the traditional wisdom, as applied to the big concentrated industries, one has no alternative in terms of which to measure responsible action. One can point out that the traditional wisdom did not deal with situations in which both competition and a substantial degree of pricing power existed. One can say that responsibility in such situations cannot be measured in traditional terms. But, until the principles of responsible action for such situations have been spelled out and become widely accepted, there is no basis for saying that a particular pricing action is responsible or not responsible. Because there are no widely accepted guides to the use of pricing power outside the regulated industries, there is no valid basis for saying that U.S. Steel's pricing action since 1953 was not responsible.

The situation is different when we ask whether the pricing action of U.S. Steel was in the public interest. We can reject the traditional wisdom as it applies to profit making in the presence of substantial pricing power and yet find in that wisdom the basis for measuring the public interest. The high value which the traditional wisdom places on the drive for profits rests on the conclusion that, in the absence of pricing power, market forces will direct the use of resources in a way which will serve the public interest and more specifically that this will result in prices for the products of industry which will just cover their economic costs, including a rate of return on capital for an industry which tends to approximate the cost of capital in the market. On this basis one can say that, when capital is readily available at 6 or 8 per cent, prices which yield 12 or 14 or 16 per cent after taxes when an industry is operating at an average rate of capacity are not likely to serve the public interest.

The damage to the public interest from prices that are too high in relation to costs takes four major forms.

Most obvious and perhaps of least importance is that the suppliers of capital receive too high a return for their saving and risk taking, a return which depends not on the supplying of capital for use but on the exercise of substantial pricing power.

A second important damage is that too high a price prevents as extensive use of a product as its economic costs justify. In the case of steel, there is a greater turning to steel substitutes than would occur with a lower steel price, some borderline activities would not be undertaken at all and the high price could be expected to act, and in fact has acted, to stimulate steel imports and reduce steel exports. In these ways, steel-producing resources would be less effectively used than if steel prices were closer to their economic cost, including a more competitive rate of return on capital.

In a third important way, the public interest is damaged by the use of pricing power to create too high a rate of return on capital—the failure to invest new capital in improved techniques or products as rapidly as would be economical. If a corporation has to see an average probability of making 16 per cent on a new and more efficient machine or a new product, it will be less progressive than if it only requires an average probability of 8 per cent. And if capital is available at the latter figure, growth is less rapid than would be economical.

Finally, a high rate of earnings can be expected to work against the public interest by giving labor an inviting target to stimulate its pressure for higher wage rates. If management is under a bonus pressure to price for high profits, why shouldn't labor press for its share? And as long as an industry maintains a high profit margin, resisting labor pressure is more difficult. How much less would have been the wage increases bargained from steel after 1953 if management had not used price increases to widen profit margins and then tried to place the main blame for the price increases on labor?

Management has urged that labor exercise restraint in its wage demands. Labor has urged that management exercise restraint in its pricing policy. Public officials have urged restraint on both. But as long as the drive for corporate profits dominates pricing policy and pricing power makes possible high rates of return on capital, a like policy on the part of labor can be expected and the public interest is not likely to be well served.

The rise of steel price since 1953 thus poses a basic issue that has application to other concentrated industries in which big corporate enterprise predominates. Where both competition and a substantial degree of pricing power exist, can the drive for corporate profits be expected to serve the public interest? And if not, what principles of responsible behavior can be developed and how can action according to those principles be induced? The remainder of this book will be concerned with this problem of pricing power and with a new approach to its solution involving neither government regulation nor the break up of big business to reduce its pricing power.

PART II
APPROACHES TO LEGITIMACY

CHAPTER VIII

THE BASIC PROBLEM

I believe in the main, while once upon a time it could be said that some of our managers had no adequate social conscience, I believe today that the corporate managers of the country are fully aware of, and I think they exercise, an abiding sense of social responsibility.

SENATOR EVERETT MCKINLEY DIRKSEN*

Pricing power in the steel industry is an outstanding example of a basic problem that has been created by modern technology and the modern corporation. Modern technology calls for big producing organizations, each subject to a unified control. The modern corporation makes such organization possible in a free-enterprise economy by bringing together the capital of a great number of investors, also subject to a unified control. At the same time, the very size of the individual enterprise limits the number of producers who can serve a given market efficiently. As a result, competition occurs among a few producers rather than among a great many and pricing power emerges.

Historically, pricing power as such is not new. The pricing power of monopoly has long been recognized, and traditional theory has called for the breakup of monopoly or its regulation. Also, where competition was among a few small enterprises and the entry of new competitors was easy, the resulting pricing power was neglected or regarded as of small social consequence.

But pricing power where production in an industry is dominated

* *Hearings*, p. 7.

by a few big modern corporations is a different matter. Its social importance is increased by the very size of the single enterprise unit. Its impact is altered by the difficulties of entry where the efficient enterprise must be huge and complexly organized. The conditions of its exercise are radically altered, too, by the dispersion of ownership and by the separation of ownership and control implicit in the modern corporation. As a result, the pricing power of big business presents a basic problem for which the wisdom of traditional theory provides no answer. Should we attempt to destroy this pricing power by pulverizing these industries? Should government control this pricing power by regulating prices? Should the management of big business take on the social responsibility of running big business in the public interest? Or can some way be found to make the exercise of pricing power result in economic performance that will serve the public interest without breaking up big business where it is efficient, without government regulation, and without placing on corporate management the burden of exercising social judgment?

It was one of the great beauties of classical competition that under it no one had to exercise social responsibility. As long as each private enterpriser sought only his own interest, the unseen hand of market forces controlled matters so that, acting in his own interest, the enterpriser tended to serve the public interest. Of course, in his personal relations the enterpriser could exercise as much social responsibility as he chose: feeding the poor, voting at elections, and in other ways acting as a socially responsible individual. But as a businessman, his only responsibility was to try to make as much profit as possible within the morals and laws of the society. He could say "the public be damned," and still be serving the public interest through his contribution to production. Competition would not allow him to charge too high a price and shoddy goods would only bring him a lower price. Whatever price resulted from the interaction of supply and demand in the market was in the public interest and therefore legitimate.

Surely something new has been added when it is seriously suggested that big business should be socially responsible and when the head of a great enterprise asks a Senate committee to examine the record and see "whether or not our price action was responsible and in the public interest."[1]

So far as pricing is concerned, the new thing that has been added is the substantial area of private discretion in administering prices. In Part I of this book we have seen the area of discretion in steel pricing and the possibilities that pricing power may be used contrary to the public interest. Such private discretion lies outside the scope of pricing which traditional economic theory has analyzed and approved.

As we have seen, traditional economic theory has placed the seal of approval on prices which are reached under two different sets of conditions. It has shown how extensively business policy can be expected to serve the public interest when business operates under conditions of classical competition. Prices arrived at under such conditions are regarded as legitimate. Also it has supported government regulation where natural monopolies make competition impractical and treats the resulting regulated prices as in the public interest and therefore legitimate.

On the other hand, traditional theory has placed the seal of disapproval on unregulated monopoly prices. Private monopoly prices are all too likely to be greater than is reasonable in relation to costs and in general not in the public interest. Thus, private monopoly prices are regarded as illegitimate and theory supports the antitrust laws which seek to prevent monopoly.

But between the legitimate prices of classical competition and the illegitimate prices of nonlegal monopoly lies a great grey area to which economic theorists have given too little attention. It is, for the most part, the area in which prices are administered so that, obviously, the conditions of classical competition do not prevail. On the other hand, there is recognizable competition so that it is

[1] See p. 45.

equally obvious that the conditions of classical monopoly do not prevail. Perhaps the prices of two-thirds or more of this country's production fall into this grey area. And it is in this area that steel prices and most of the prices of unregulated big business belong.[2]

ECONOMIC THEORY IN THE GREY AREA

Only within the last generation have theoretical economists recognized the importance of this grey area and sought to unravel its complex implications.[3] In recent theoretical analysis, this area has sometimes been designated "competition among the few" in contrast to the classical competition among a forest of enterprises. Sometimes it has been lumped together with monopoly into a single theory of imperfect competition on the principle that even classical monopolies compete with other business for the consumer dollar. And sometimes it has been lumped together with both classical monopoly and classical competition into a theory of monopolistic competition that treats classical competition and classical monopoly as limiting cases within the theory.

So far economic theorists have made a great contribution in delineating and focusing attention on this great grey area to which neither the principles of classical competition nor those of classical monopoly apply. Much new theory has been developed concerning pricing behavior in this area. But theory is still in a state of flux and some of the apparently most logical theories have not stood up under empirical testing.[4]

What is of even greater importance is that the theories so far

---

[2] See, for example, Edwin B. Nourse, *Price Making in a Democracy* (Washington, D.C.: The Brookings Institution, 1944), particularly chapter I.

[3] See the pioneer works by Edward Chamberlin, *The Theory of Monopolistic Competition* (Cambridge: Harvard University Press, 1933), and Joan Robinson, *The Economics of Imperfect Competition* (London: Macmillan and Co., 1933).

[4] See R. A. Gordon, "Short-Period Price Determination," *American Economic Review*, XXXVIII, No. 3 (June, 1945), 265-288; R. F. Lanzillotti, "Pricing Objectives in Large Companies," *American Economic Review*, XLVIII, No. 5 (December, 1958), 921-940.

developed have *not provided a logical basis for determining what conditions could be expected to result in legitimate prices in this grey area.* There has been a tendency to assume that the closer conditions are to those of classical competition, the closer the approximation to legitimacy and the closer conditions are to those of classical monopoly, the further prices are likely to be from legitimate. Thus, one writer says of the concentrated spark plug industry, ". . . in the long run five producers of spark plugs are better than three, and might eliminate the functionless monopoly profits on replacement plugs."[5] But it has not yet been established on the basis of logical theory supported by empirical evidence that five competitors are likely to serve the public interest any better than three or that twenty competitors will serve it better than five. Nor has any other clear basis been established for distinguishing between legitimate and illegitimate pricing where neither classical competition nor classical monopoly prevail.

At the same time, there have been strong feelings among economists that the pricing powers of big corporations that operate in this grey area are not so controlled by competition that the pricing results are reasonably in the public interest. Suggestions have been made that the big companies should be broken up to increase competition or that they should be regulated so as to make their prices more nearly in the public interest. But economic theory has given no solution to this problem.

THE INSTITUTIONAL BASES FOR ECONOMIC THEORY

The great institution, the Modern Corporation, is fundamentally different from the small private enterprise which provides the basis of traditional economic wisdom. Just how different we can see more clearly if we go back to the origins of economic thinking.

[5] Arthur H. Kahn, "Discriminatory Pricing as a Barrier to Entry: The Spark Plug Litigation," *The Journal of Industrial Economics*, VIII, No. 1 (October, 1959), 12.

First, consider the ancient Greek family, the institution which first gave us the term "economic." The typical Greek family was an extended family with aunts and uncles and cousins brought into a single operating household and a household which was largely self-sufficient. Within this household community, food was raised and prepared, cloth and clothing made, and the great bulk of other wants were satisfied. There was little or no buying and selling and no significant market. Rather, the economy was the household, a collective enterprise producing for its own consumption. Within this collective, consumers and workers and owners and managers composed a single entity and control over the instruments of production lay with this entity—the family. The interest of consumer, labor, and owner were served by the household management and there could be no problem of market price or of pricing power.

Next, consider the institutional basis of Adam Smith's economic theory. Adam Smith wrote before the industrial revolution had made much headway, and the enterprise unit with which he was primarily concerned was the one-man enterprise of butcher and baker and candlestick maker. While he recognized the existence of apprentices and hired workers, he was not much concerned with them and when he spoke of labor he was referring, not to employees, but to the work of the owner himself. In his economic model he envisaged a large number of small one-man enterprises competing with each other and so numerous and weak that no one producer had any significant power over price. True, he recognized the existence of government-created monopolies and the tendency of competitors to get together on prices, and inveighed against both. And when he wanted to show the efficiency of the division of labor, he chose the example of a pin factory with a dozen or more workers rather than say the division of labor between the independent individuals who contributed to the making of a pair of shoes such as the butcher, the tanner, and the shoemaker. But his economic model and his theory of classical competition were concerned with competition among a large number of one-man enterprises. Today we have the prototype of his model in the vast number of family farms. And before the recent government intervention, we had the classical competition in farming which made the prices of wheat and cotton adjust so as to equate supply and demand according to the expectations of classical theory.

There are two things to be noted about Adam Smith's model. First, as compared with the Greek household, it involved a separation of the *consumer* from control over the instruments of production. The one-man producer was worker-owner-manager all in one and controlled the enterprise.[6] In contrast, the consumer had no direct control over the instruments of production and could influence production only through the market. He must depend on the influence he and his fellows exercised through the market for the protection of his interest. And second, according to Adam Smith, the unseen hand of market forces would, in most cases, adequately protect the consumers' interest. The drive of individual producers to make personal profits would be controlled by competition to produce an economic performance which would serve the public interest.

The industrial revolution brought the factory system and the separation of the *worker* from control over the instruments of production as the market for products had separated the consumer from control over the enterprise. This control rested with the owner-manager, while the workers, like consumers, could influence production through the market, but had no control over the instruments of production.

It was this separation of workers from control which provided Marx with the basis for his theory of the class struggle. And while we need not accept his labor theory of value, we must recognize that factory enterprise required a reconsideration of the theories

---

[6] It should be noted that Adam Smith was perfectly aware of factory enterprise and joint stock companies. But in his basic economic model he used the one-man enterprise and did not introduce into his theory of ideal economic functioning any implications of factory or corporate behavior not implicit in a one-man enterprise and the treatment of labor as a commodity.

based on Smith's model of one-man enterprises.

However, economic theory was slow to take full account of the factory type of enterprise. The theorists, by treating labor as a commodity and each worker as a one-man enterprise selling labor, were able to retain Adam Smith's model. The only change that had to be made was to include labor as a raw material bought by enterprise like any other raw material. In Adam Smith's analysis the shoemaker bought leather, shoe twine, and shoe pegs, combined them into a pair of shoes and sold the shoes. In the later analysis, the shoe manufacturer bought leather, shoe twine, shoe pegs, and *labor,* combined them into a pair of shoes and sold the shoes. No significant modification of the classical model was made in nineteenth-century theory because of the separation of worker from control. True, labor became a commodity of special interest and the forces influencing its long-run supply and demand were given special attention. But outside the followers of Marx, little attention was given in traditional theory to the implications of the economic fact that labor was not a commodity.

Also, little attention was given in the nineteenth century to the reduction in the number of competing units that was brought about by factory enterprise. The conception of competition as that between a large number of small units continued to be the core of traditional theory. Thus Alfred Marshall built his analysis on the conception of the representative firm and his industry was a "forest" of enterprises. By this assumption he avoided some of the intricate problems of pricing power which arise when competitors are big and few in number.

The modern corporation has provided us with still another institutional form of production, one which separates not only consumers and workers, but also the *owners* from control over the instruments of production. In the typical big corporation, the ownership of stock has become widely dispersed and stockholders have ceased to have significant control over production. This control rests with management and ownership can, as a practical matter, influence production only through the market for capital much as workers can influence production through the market for labor and consumers through the market for products.

The successive separation of consumers, workers, and owners from control over the productive enterprise has made it possible to organize production on a scale and with operational efficiency never before realized. The separation of the consumer from control made it possible for a single enterprise to produce for millions of consumers; the separation of worker from control made it possible for a single enterprise to organize the productive activity of tens or even hundreds of thousands of workers; and the separation of ownership from control made it possible to bring the capital of tens and hundreds of thousands of owners under a single unified control. The result has been the creation of great engines of production of a magnitude, efficiency, and vitality that the Greek family could never envisage, however large it might be, and that would be impossible to one-man enterprise and rarely possible to owner-operated enterprise.

At the same time, in a real sense these modern corporate enterprises have acquired one of the major characteristics of the Greek family, that of collective enterprise. In them a single management interrelates the capital of many thousands of investors and the labor of many thousands of workers and the wants of many thousands of consumers in a great collective undertaking. These collectives differ from the collective of the Greek family, since the same group of people are not both owner and worker and consumer in a single collective. But they are even more different from the private enterprise of Smith's one-man units or Marshall's owner-operated representative firm. It is the external economic power of these great collective enterprises with which we are concerned and, as we shall see, the difference is basic because collective enterprise does not fit into the traditional economic theories which have been built around the concept of competitive private enterprise.

Central to traditional theory of private enterprise is the concept of the owner-operator's drive for profits controlled by competition. But the extensive separation of ownership and control has dissolved out the owner-operator of private enterprise and radically altered the logic of the drive for profits. The fewness of competitors and the difficulty of entry have radically altered the logic of competition. The huge size of the individual collectives and their economic importance raise questions of social policy. Can competition be expected to control the profit drive of collective enterprise in a way to serve the public interest. And if not, what can take its place?

It will be argued here that big collective enterprise has its own logic just as definite as the logic of the one-man enterprise so thoroughly developed in classical theory. It is the aim of this book to outline the logic of collective enterprise and suggest conditions under which the pricing power of big collective enterprise could be expected to produce economic performance that would serve the public interest and thus provide legitimate pricing.

As a preliminary step, the traditional approaches to legitimacy will be examined in the remainder of Part II and it will be suggested that while both can contribute to our understanding of pricing power neither fits the case of such industries as steel. Part III will examine the logic of administrative competition, the particular part of the grey area which applies to most unregulated collective enterprises, and show why administrative competition under the drive for the maximum corporate profits cannot be expected to produce the results to be expected from classical competition or adequately serve the public interest. Then, in Part IV, the logic of collective enterprise will be discussed and a new approach proposed which would establish the conditions likely to produce legitimate pricing and satisfactory economic performance without the necessity of government price regulation, widespread corporate break-up or dependence on the social judgment of corporate management.

CHAPTER IX

THE LOGIC OF CLASSICAL COMPETITION

As every individual . . . endeavors as much as he can both to employ his capital in support of domestic industry, and so to direct that industry that its produce may be of the greatest value; every individual necessarily labours to render the annual revenue of the society as great as he can. He generally, indeed, neither intends to promote the public interest nor knows how much he is promoting it . . . by directing that industry in such a manner as its produce may be of the greatest value, he intends only his own gain, and he is in this, as in many other cases, led by an invisible hand to promote an end which was no part of his intention . . . By pursuing his own interest he frequently promotes that of society more effectively than when he really intends to promote it.

ADAM SMITH[*]

Our starting point is the logic of classical competition for two reasons. First, it is the only logic which has provided a basis for public policy in a free-enterprise system and, second, because the *results* expected from the operation of the classical mechanism provide a set of goals which can serve as appropriate objectives for public policy in a modern, corporate, free-enterprise economy.

The logic of classical competition has been spelled out by a long line of economists. Adam Smith was its first great· expounder and Alfred Marshall its most perfect. We do not need to review it in detail, but certain elements of its logic need to be kept in mind in the search for an answer to the problem of pricing power.

[*] *The Wealth of Nations,* I (Everyman's Library; New York: E. P. Dutton and Co., 1910), p. 400.

173

THE CLASSICAL CONCEPT OF ENTERPRISE

The first step in understanding the logic of classical competition is to be clear on the classical conception of business enterprise. This was the conception of small and numerous private enterprises. The modern corporation with its tens or hundreds of thousands of workers and ten or hundreds of thousands of stockholders lies entirely outside the framework of classical theory.

Its first formulator, Adam Smith, held that the joint stock company could not be a successful mode of carrying on business enterprise except under special conditions such as those of banking, insurance, and canal operation.[1] Alfred Marshall, the last of the great classical economists, still made relatively small enterprises the basic unit of his theory. Compared to our modern giants, his "representative firm" was a small affair with a life cycle very much like that of its owner. The owner starts the enterprise and drives to expand it, but then when his own vigor wanes the enterprise itself weakens and is likely to die, except as sometimes a son or relative picks it up and gives it a new life cycle of rise and fall. Such life-time enterprises were the basis for his development of economic principles. Thus, he thought of each industry as having hundreds or even thousands of such enterprises. In his famous analogy, he likened an industry to a forest with individual trees sprouting, growing, and finally declining but with the whole maintained as new trees replace the old. In his own words, "as with the growth of trees, so it is with the growth of businesses."[2] This is the concept of enterprise which underlies Marshall's *Principles of Economics*.

Marshall himself has made clear that his *Principles* were written around the concept of the representative firm and did not take account of the big corporation. In the sixth edition, published in 1910, twenty years after his principles were formulated, he changed the tree analogy to read "as with the growth of trees, so it *was*

[1] The Smith, *op. cit.*, II, 242.
[2] Alfred Marshall, *Principles of Economics*, 1st ed. (London, 1890), p. 395.

with the growth of business as a general rule before the recent development of vast joint-stock companies."[3] But his *Principles* were not revised to take account of this momentous change.

Even Keynes' *General Theory* rests on the assumption of competition among such a large number of producers that prices are made in the market and are not administered. This is made apparent when he discusses basic economic policy "apart from 'administered' or monopoly prices which are determined by other considerations besides marginal cost."[4]

It is the competition among a forest of firms, each of which is small relative to the market it serves, that we are discussing in this chapter and will refer to as classical competition.

THE CLASSICAL CONCEPTION OF COMPETITION

It is also necessary to understand the classical conception of competition. We have already seen the confusion surrounding the use of the term "competition" as senators envisage one thing and businessmen another.[5] For the present we can disregard both meanings and consider what was envisaged by economic theorists in discussing classical competition.

An essential characteristic of classical competition is the lack of pricing power on the part of any individual producer or purchaser. For classical competition to be present there must be a large enough number of producers, and each must be small enough relative to the market so that no one producer can significantly affect the price by his own decision to produce more or less. In the absence of government intervention, the wheat producer or the cotton farmer does not know what price he will get for his product, but he can be sure when he makes his planting decisions that the price he gets will not be significantly affected by his decision to

[3] *Op. cit.,* 6th ed., p. 316. Emphasis added.
[4] John Maynard Keynes, *The General Theory of Employment Interest and Money* (New York: Harcourt, Brace and Co., 1936), p. 268. See also p. 270.
[5] See pp. 29-45.

plant more or less. In making this decision its effect on price is no part of his calculation. In the same way, there must be enough buyers so that no one buyer can significantly affect the market and each buyer can make his decisions to buy or not buy without considering the effect of his action on price. Under these conditions price is determined by market forces and not by the administrative decision of any buyer or seller.

If the conditions of classical competition are met, an administered price is not possible. Likewise, the presence of an administered price is sufficient evidence that the conditions of classical competition are not currently present.[6]

THE CLASSICAL MODEL OF AN ENTERPRISE SYSTEM

In the familiar classical model of an enterprise system each industry is thus presumed to be made up of a multitude of relatively small enterprises producing for the market and with the price of each product adjusting continuously to equate supply and demand. Also, enterprisers, in their search for gain, expand those activities in which prices are high relative to costs and reduce those in which prices are low. The individual worker is treated as an enterpriser producing and marketing "labor," and wage rates—the prices for "labor"—are assumed to adjust flexibly to equate the supply and the demand for different types of "labor." Capital, too, in the search for gain is expected to flow into those activities in which more

[6] Classical competition should not be confused with the "pure and perfect competition" of later-day classicists. In the pursuit of abstract and theoretical perfection economists have developed the concept of competition among a large number of small producers each of whom has perfect knowledge of market conditions, is perfectly rational, and has resources that are perfectly transferrable from product to product. It has become a cliché among economists that there never has been and never can be "pure and perfect competition." In contrast, classical competition has existed and does exist today. Indeed, if one includes a commercial farm as a business enterprise and looks only at numbers and not at value of product, there may well be as many enterprises in the United States which operate under conditions of classical competition as under any other condition.

than a competitive rate of return can be realized and, in so far as it is mobile, to flow out of those industries in which the prospective return is less than the going rate at which capital is available. By this self-seeking process it was expected that the resources of an economy would be directed into productive uses by the pricing system as each possessor of a resource sought to use it in the way that would yield the highest market value. This classical model not only provides the core of classical thinking on competition and the public image of the free enterprise system but it underlies the traditional wisdom which still dominates so much of the thinking of business and government in the field of price-making and antitrust policy.

THE RESULTS OF A CLASSICALLY COMPETITIVE STATEMENT

The great appeal of the classical system lies in its expected results. The four most important of these have to do with the relation of prices to costs, the determination of incomes, the optimum use of resources, and the pressure for improving technology.

PRICES AND COSTS

The most basic result of competition under the conditions of the classical model is to bring prices into reasonable relation to costs so that profits constitute only a competitive rate of return on capital. The price for each product under classical competition would be determined by costs. For any particular product there would be two major sets of costs which would influence price, the out-of-pocket costs of producing the product with the existing plants and the full costs of producing the product with potential new plants, including both the out-of-pocket costs of operating the plant and the capital costs involved.

So long as only existing plants were required to meet the demand and possible new plants are disregarded, the price of a product, according to the classical model, would be determinate when all the units which could be produced at an out-of-pocket cost of less than the price were being produced and demand at that price was equal to production. Price would correspond closely to the average out-of-pocket costs of the least efficient producer that was required to meet the level of demand. This is presumably what President Homer of Bethlehem Steel referred to when he suggested that the market price of a product "reaches a level slightly above the cost of the marginal producer."[7]

A different situation was presumed to hold when demand was sufficient to require the construction of new capacity. If new investment was constantly being required, prices would have to be high enough to cover both operating and capital costs including a competitive rate of profit for the most efficient modern plant that could be built. The price could not remain for long above the combined operating and capital costs of new plants or new plants would be built to expand the supply and bring the price down. Thus, where competition was among many small enterprises, it would be the full cost of producing with the most efficient mills, not the *out-of-pocket* costs of the *least* efficient or marginal mill which was expected to dominate prices in a stable or growing industry.

Also, where technology was improving so that successively more efficient mills could be built, it would be the full cost of producing with the new or rebuilt efficient mill which could be expected to dominate prices under classical competition.

This dominant role of the full costs of new up-to-date plant in the pricing process is of vital importance. It presupposes that in deciding whether or not to build a new mill, the enterpriser will take account of the rate of obsolescence in the industry. Thus, in

---

[7] *Hearings*, p. 612. It should be noted for the marginal producer—the producer on the ragged edge of not continuing in business—marginal cost and average out-of-pocket costs were presumed to be equal. Also, most classical theory neglects the case where an enterprise is operated at a current out-of-pocket loss in order to achieve some longer run gain such as a better position if demand increases.

calculating his depreciation cost per unit he will be considering, not the physical life of the plant, but its economically useful life, a life which is likely to be shorter than its physical life where technical progress is to be expected. It also presupposes that, with easy entry in the industry, competition among investors and enterprisers will bring about the construction of new plant whenever the prospect of return on capital approximates the competitive rate.

WHO GETS HOW MUCH INCOME

A second important result to be expected under classical competition is that the benefits to labor and capital arising from production will be related to their respective "contributions" to production. For capital, the competitive rates of return would reflect the value of added output which could be expected from added units of investment; for labor, the competitive wage rates would reflect the value of the added output which could be expected from added units of work; for enterprisers, using both their own capital and their own labor, the competitive rate of earning would reflect both the value of the added output which could be expected from the exercise of added skill in management and that of the added output to be expected from added units of capital. In a similar way the income derived from the ownership of limited natural resources, such as land, metal ores, and water power, was treated as reflecting the "contribution" of the owners with the rates of income approximating the value of the additions to output due to additional units of the limited resource made available. In this particular sense, a perfect operation of the classical model would reward each individual according to his "contribution" to production.

Of course, it was never thought that in real life the practical condition of classical competition would actually produce the income results to be expected from the model, but it was regarded as an approximate guide to the way classical competition would work. Also, even if income were distributed to each according to his "contribution" to production, it was recognized that the resulting income distribution was not ideal. Some individuals could not "contribute" to production because of sickness, accident, age, or for other reasons and so would not receive income under the model conditions. Also, the "contribution" to production on the part of the owners of limited natural resources was recognized as qualitatively different from the contribution made by labor and newly created capital. As a result, taxation, "poor relief," and other social payments were advocated even by the exponents of classical competition as a means of modifying the distribution of income. But in spite of such modification, the *basic determinant of income distribution under classical competition was expected to be the "contribution" of labor and capital to production.*

THE OPTIMUM USE OF RESOURCES

A third important result would be a strong tendency toward *the optimum use of resources.* Such optimum use would be related to the particular distribution of income, either that arising from classical competition or that resulting from classical competition modified by taxation and other social action. But whatever the income distribution, classical competition was expected to direct the use of resources in such a way that the best use of resources was made in the light of that particular income distribution while a different use of resources would mean a misdirection of resources and consequent waste.

TECHNICAL IMPROVEMENT

A fourth important expected result is *constant pressure to reduce costs and improve products.* Among the competing producers, those who find improved techniques or superior products have a temporary advantage over competitiors and can make more than competitive profits. This provides an incentive for improvement. Then as the improvement is adopted by the bulk of the industry, the profits of the innovator would return to the competitive level except as further new innovations were developed.

Furthermore, the conditions of classical competition facilitate the spreading of innovations. If the wheat farmer discovers a technique for increasing his yields, his own profits will not be noticeably altered if he passes on this knowledge to his wheat-growing neighbors, since even in combination their output will not significantly affect prices. He does not regard his neighbors as competitors and has no advantage in secrecy. As a result, improved technology can spread as rapidly as communications allow. The gains from improving technology under the conditions of classical competition would thus soon be passed on to the community through lower relative prices and improved products. In this way, classical competition could also be expected to benefit the public through stimulating technical improvement which, in combination with optimum use of resources, would provide the basis for economic growth.

These four results to be expected from classical competition give ample reason for the great popular appeal of this form of competition. What more could be wanted from a free-enterprise system than that prices should just cover costs, including both labor and capital costs; that incomes should be received according to the "contributions" made to production; that resources should be used to the optimum; and that there should be constant pressure for technical improvement with the gains rapidly passed on to the consuming public?

It is no wonder that prices arrived at under the condition of classical competition have been regarded as legitimate.

CLASSICAL COMPETITION AND THE CONCENTRATED INDUSTRIES

But one glance at the steel industry leaves no doubt that modern industry does not, *and cannot be made to,* meet the conditions of classical competition.

Take for example, the production of pig iron. One can try to imagine a forest of small concerns bringing various grades of iron ore, coal, limestone, scrap, and the other ingredients to Pittsburgh and selling them in the open market for what they would bring. Then, harking back to the very small-scale furnaces of 150 years ago, one could imagine a forest of firms operating blast furnaces, buying the raw materials in the open market as cotton mills buy raw cotton, charging their furnaces, and selling the resulting pig iron in the open market for what it would bring. If there were a large enough number of pig producing firms, one could expect that no firm could administer its price. Each firm would only start operating a furnace when the market price was above its out-of-pocket costs and would close it down whenever the price fell below its out-of-pocket costs and appeared likely to remain below for some time. Thus, the supply of steel would fluctuate with the price. With a high demand, the price would rise and higher cost furnaces would be fired. With a lower demand, the higher cost furnaces in operation would be closed down. In this way price would adjust to keep supply and demand in balance. Also, some of the forest of furnaces would become obsolete and new furnaces would be required, particularly with a growing demand for iron and steel. As a result, the total cost of production with the best designed new furnaces would tend to determine which of the existing furnaces were obsolete and control the average around which current prices tended to fluctuate.

But could modern blast furnaces be employed without destroying the conditions necessary for classical competition? An average blast furnace can produce 400,000 to 450,000 tons of pig iron a year. Efficient operation requires that two or more blast furnaces be operated as a unit, and they are usually operated in multiples of four. Thus, the average economical grouping of four furnaces would have an annual capacity of over 1,500,000 million tons. Yet in the whole Pittsburgh region there are only 60 blast furnaces with a combined capacity of around 22 million tons a year. This means that if each company were limited to four blast furnaces there would be room for only 15 pig iron enterprises in the Pittsburgh area. On the same basis, the 220 blast furnaces in the whole United States would allow at most only 55 separate, efficient big iron producing enterprises.[8] This is a long way from the forest of separate firms necessary for the operation of classical competition. Indeed, it is difficult to conceive of classical competition in the making of pig iron without gross inefficiency.

A similar situation applies to steel rolling mills. Today the efficient rolling of ingots into rolled sheets is in continuous hot sheet mills and there are only thirty-eight such mills in the country.[9] If each were owned by a separate firm, this would allow, at a maximum, only thirty-eight competitors. Also, high cost of shipping steel reduces the effectiveness of competition from plants located in different parts of the country. On the basis of the size of efficient blast furnace units and efficient rolling mills alone it is not possible to have the forest of competing units necessary to establish the condition for classical competition in the steel industry even if each efficient unit were separately owned.

Too, there are important economies to be derived from integration beyond the individual functions of making pig iron or rolling steel. In an integrated plant molten iron can go directly from the blast furnace to the steel furnaces without the cost of

[8] Source: Business and Defense Services Administration, U.S. Dept. of Commerce. In 1960, the industry averaged 1182 tons a day per blast furnace operated or at a rate of 431,000 tons a year. Armco Steel Corporation's modern furnace averaged 2500 tons a day or a rate of 912,000 tons a year. *New York Times,* October 1, 1961.
[9] *Ibid.*

reheating, the production flow can be more efficiently controlled; transport costs can be reduced; the back flow of scrap can be more orderly; and in many other ways the costs of production can be kept down. Similarly, the administrative control of ore production, shipment, and storage can add efficiencies in the flow of production, as can the fabrication of steel products. All of this leads to large vertically integrated steel enterprises for maximum efficiency.

Furthermore, there are important economies to be achieved by multiplant operation. Some of these arise from efficiencies in production such as the handling of more diversified production and the application of experience gained from operating one plant in the design of the next. Some arise from efficiencies in marketing, as where advertising expenditure and sales organization cover the output of a number of plants. And some arise from economies associated with size itself such as the ability to spread the costs of research and development over a larger volume of sales. All of these can contribute to make a well-run multiplant enterprise more economical than the same plants independently run and thus to reduce the number of efficient enterprises required to supply the market.

How far the creation of the great steel complexes goes in adding to efficiency is not important at this point. What is important is that, if the big steel companies were broken up into individual steel plants with each plant owned by a separate firm, competition between them would not be likely to produce the market prices of classical competition. There would still not be the forest of independent firms necessary to classical competition. Steel prices, locality by locality, would almost certainly continue to be administered prices and not prices determined by the market forces of supply and demand. Only by an extreme pulverization of the steel corporations and a serious loss of efficiency could the logic of classical competition be made to apply to the steel industry. Some other logic must be applied if we are to have a logical basis for social policy in respect to steel and in respect to other concentrated industries which, like steel, cannot be operated on the basis of classical competition without great loss in efficiency. For such industries technology dictates that, at its greatest, competition can only be among the few.

The problem this poses will be considered after the other major basis for legitimate pricing has been examined—that of government regulation.

CHAPTER X

MONOPOLY AND THE LOGIC
OF GOVERNMENT REGULATION

The price of monopoly is upon every occasion the highest which can be got. The natural price, or the price of free competition, on the contrary, is the lowest which can be taken, not upon every occasion, indeed, but for any considerable time together. The one is upon every occasion the highest which can be squeezed out of the buyers, or which, it is supposed, they will consent to give; the other is the lowest which the sellers can commonly afford to take, and at the same time continue their business.

ADAM SMITH[*]

A second logic which we must consider in our search for legitimate pricing is that of government regulation. It has long been recognized that some economic activities such as railroad transport, power, and communication are natural monopolies and where they are not carried on by government, a system of government regulation has been built up to control them in the public interest.

The reason for government regulation of natural monopolies is the obvious one that private operation of a monopoly for private gain is not likely to serve the public interest. The profit-seeking monopoly, left to itself, could be expected to limit services and charge what the traffic would bear. Under favorable conditions an unregulated monopoly could make much more than a competitive rate of return on its capital. Its prices or rates would

[*] *Op. cit.,* I. 54.

be above a reasonable relation to costs and its services might not be those which the public has a right to expect. And even if conditions turned unfavorable and a natural monopoly were unable to make a competitive rate of return, unregulated operation could be harmful to the public interest.

What makes an activity a "natural" monopoly is the impossibility or great inefficiency of having more than one enterprise supply the service. Different power companies might supply different parts of a city, but if each tried to make power available to every potential customer, there would not only be great waste in duplicate transmission lines but the limited street facilities would be wastefully used. Competing telephone companies might provide a forest of telephone poles but hardly a forest of competing enterprises offering services to the same group of customers. Monopoly is implicit in the efficient operation of such enterprises. And it is because monopoly pricing could not be expected to produce legitimate prices, that public regulation has been adopted.

Here we are concerned not with the great complexities of utility regulation, but with the principles on which such regulation is based and their applicability to the regulation to such industries as steel.

OBJECTIVES OF REGULATION

The main objective in government regulation has been to approximate the results to be expected from classical competition. Regulation seeks to keep rates in reasonable relation to costs. It seeks to keep incomes, particularly those of investors, in reasonable relation to "contribution." It aims at optimum use of resources. And it seeks to encourage technical advance.

The first of these objectives—the maintaining of the prices of service in reasonable relation to costs—has been given shape in a formula whose meaning has been forged over the years by the interaction of the utilities, the regulatory commissions and the courts. According to this formula, rates should be set which will, as far as possible, allow, but only allow, "a fair rate of return on a fair value for the assets used and useful in the public interest." Each of the phrases in this formula has been subject to debate and, though its meaning has been clarified to a greater or lesser extent, its application to a particular situation is not always clear. However, the formula itself is regularly accepted as the basis for rate making and rates or prices which conform to it are regarded as legitimate.

A fair rate of return on capital is not a precise concept, but in practice the utility commissions have gravitated around 6 per cent or a little more. This range may well be considered as approximating a competitive rate of return on capital that involves the risk and regulation of such monopolies. It is higher than the return to be found on such low-risk investments as government bonds and thus takes account of the fact that the rate of return is not a guaranteed rate. The extra is, in effect, an offset to the chances of loss in unsuccessful utility ventures. On the other hand, the rate has been sufficiently high to allow the utilities to obtain great amounts of capital from the public for expansion. It has allowed the sale of bonds at rates well below 6 per cent and stocks with the prospect of appreciably higher rates. Presumably, if experience showed that the rates of return allowed to the utilities did not stimulate public investment to supply capital needed for expansion, the commissions would revise upward their conception of a fair rate of return. Historically, the rates in the vicinity of 6 per cent appear to have served both investors and consumers reasonably well.

Also, there has not been too much trouble with the concept of assets used and useful in the public interest. As we have seen in the case of the steel industry, assets not used or useful in the business should not be included in the rate base in calculating the rate of return made in the productive activity of the business and the courts have so found with respect to utility assets. Also the courts have excluded from the rate base assets used but not actually needed. However, both courts and commissions have been fairly liberal in determining what is "used and useful" when a substantial case for inclusion has been made by the utility.

The greatest difficulty has arisen over the value to be placed on assets. When prices are stable, no great problem arises. But a major change in price level creates the almost insoluble problem of valuation which we have already met in the case of steel assets. In the early days of utility regulation when the price level was falling, the utility companies argued before the courts that the historical cost of plant and equipment (depreciated) was the only sound basis of valuation, while the utility commissions argued that reproduction cost (depreciated) was the only sound basis. Subsequently, with a higher price level after World War I, the two parties changed sides and the commissions gave more emphasis to historical cost while the compaines urged reproduction cost. Clearly, the issue is not one that can be decided on principle.

In practice today some commissions adhere to historical cost partly on the ground of technical simplicity and partly on the ground that since the companies will not accept reproduction cost when prices go down they should not expect reproduction costs when prices rise. Other commissions give a broader interpretation to "fair value" and while giving major emphasis to historical cost, do make some adjustments for change in price level. Also, even the commissions most rigidly adhering to historical cost are likely to temper their actions by being more lenient in control on rates when a rise in general price level has occurred. On the whole it appears that utility regulation keeps the price of services very much closer to costs than if there were no regulation and reasonably close to the relation that could be expected if classical competition were operating.

The second result to be expected from classical competition —making incomes conform to contribution—can also be expected to result from effective regulation. Because utility regulation takes competitive rates for capital and prevailing rates for wages as the basis for arriving at costs and a fair rate of return, there is a presumption that the returns to these factors do fairly relate to the contribution being made.

The third result to be expected from classical competition— optimum use of available resources—is a more complex problem in the case of regulated utilities. It is a responsibility carried partly by the regulatory agency and partly by the utility management. As far as operations are concerned, management is primarily responsible for not using resources wastefully, for adopting improved techniques, and for keeping costs down. On the other hand, questions of expanding or contracting services and the quality of services are usually a prime responsibility of the regulating agency. How far this joint endeavor does, in fact, make optimum use of resources is a matter of debate which will be considered below.

The success of government regulation in achieving the fourth result of classical competition—technical improvement—is also a matter of debate. On the engineering side, there has been great technical progress under regulation. How much this has been the result of competition among the unregulated producers of equipment and how much it has arisen within the utilities is not clear, but the rate of engineering progress compares well with that of unregulated enterprise. On the other hand, there is always pressure not to reduce the value of capital already invested. This can lead to the postponement of improvements which, if available, would have been made sooner under conditions of classical competition.

The conclusion seems justified that while government regulation of monopoly can go a considerable distance in producing the results that could be expected from classical competition, it falls short in important respects. Also, it has certain drawbacks of its own which need to be considered if regulation is to be considered as an alternative to classical competition in such concentrated industries as steel.

DRAWBACKS TO GOVERNMENT REGULATION

There are six major drawbacks to government regulation even as applied to a monopoly.

The first is the cost of regulation. This is not only a cost to government, but also to the enterprises being regulated. And in the last analysis the public pays for both. In most cases the regulated prices are likely to be very much less than if the natural monopolies were free to charge what the traffic would bear so that the costs of regulation can be regarded as a necessary expense. But in considering government regulation for an industry such as steel, these costs must be weighed in the balance.

A second and much more important drawback to government regulation is that it places a premium on fighting the regulating agency of government. If the monopoly can pressure a commission or the courts to raise the rate of return which is treated as fair, or if it can increase the value the commission or courts place on its assets, or if it can include more assets as being "used and useful" in the public interest, it can make more profits without danger of having its rates cut. In fact, under close regulation these may be the only ways that the profits of a utility from its regulated activity can be increased, as reductions in costs will be quickly offset by the requirement of rate reductions. This premium on conflict not only absorbs resources but often diverts management from a concern with efficient operation. Indeed, it often leads to a high proportion of legal executives in management as compared with engineering and business executives. It is difficult to believe that such conflict is a healthy contribution to the maintenance of a free society.

The third drawback is that it greatly weakens the profit pressure for economic efficiency. When reductions in cost are almost immediately followed by enforced cuts in rates, the profit inducement to reduce costs is limited. This does not mean that there are no progressive and efficient utilities, but rather that the profit incentive for efficiency is diminished.

A fourth major drawback to regulation is that it operates to limit venturesomeness. In an unregulated enterprise, it is possible to undertake various risky ventures in the hope that some successful ones will more than offset the losses on the unsuccessful. But such an offset is not feasible under regulation. For a utility that is already making its allowed rate of return, the successful venture will lead to cuts in rates with no significant increase in profits, while the unsuccessful will reduce profits. Thus, the management of a utility is under considerable pressure to be conservative, not venturesome.

A fifth major drawback is that it greatly reduces the flexibility of enterprise. When important decisions have to be taken up with a government commission, delay is inevitable. Often, what appears to be economically sound from management's point of view does not appear sound from that of the commission, and court action can lead to further delay. Adjustment which would be in the public interest may not be undertaken because of the difficulty of persuading a commission that it would be in the public interest.

Finally, there is always the possibility that a regulatory commission will become a political instrument or subservient to the enterprises it regulates. In either case, the result of regulation could be expected to depart even further from these to be expected from classical competition.

GOVERNMENT REGULATION AND STEEL

These serious drawbacks to government regulation do not appear to outweigh the advantages of regulation where natural monopolies are concerned, but it is quite a different matter for an industry like steel. While classical competition is lacking, there is competition of a sort. If one had to choose between atomizing the steel industry so that classical competition could operate or adopting government regulation, the inefficiency of small scale steel production would undoubtedly make regulation preferable to a thorough going breakup of the industry. But it would be too much like Hobson's choice. Before we can discuss this choice seriously, we need to consider just what competition among a few competitors can be expected to accomplish in the public interest and what it is not likely to accomplish.

/

PART III

THE LOGIC OF ADMINISTRATIVE COMPETITION

CHAPTER XI

THE GRAY AREA AND ADMINISTRATIVE COMPETITION

It is my considered opinion that the economic institutions and business practices described as administered pricing grow naturally and properly out of the conditions of modern industrialism and that they may be so used as to promote both economic growth and business stability vigorously and consistently.

DR. EDWIN G. NOURSE

FORMER CHAIRMAN, COUNCIL OF ECONOMICS ADVISORS*

At the time the first antitrust act was adopted—the Sherman Act in 1890—the concepts of classical competition and classical monopoly were well established, but the great gray area of competition among the few which lies between classical competition and classical monopoly was barely recognized and the implications of price administration had received little if any attention. For this reason, the Sherman Act, in seeking to prevent monopoly and maintain competition, drew no distinction between competition among the few and competition among the many. It was frequently assumed that as long as there was competition, essentially the results to be expected from classical competition would be achieved. The same assumption underlies the subsequent legislation. As a result, the antitrust legislation must be regarded as antimonopoly legislation, not as legislation aimed to maintain classical competition. This is reflected in the fact that operations under it have been

* *Hearings*, p. 9.

substantially successful in preventing monopoly but have been quite unsuccessful in maintaining the conditions of classical competition.

Only in the last generation have explorations in the gray area disclosed how different the results of competition among a few can be from those to be expected from competition among the many. These differences arise in part from three important patterns of behavior which an enterprise can adopt when competitors are few and which cannot be employed by an enterprise operating under conditions of classical competition. These three patterns of behavior combine to make competition among the few different in results from those to be expected from competition among the many.

SELLING AT AN ADMINISTERED PRICE

The first of these different patterns of enterprise behavior is the use of administered prices as the basis for selling.

Under the conditions of classical competition the individual producer can accept or reject the prevailing market price, he can withhold his product from the market to speculate on the possibility that the price may rise. But he cannot set a price above the current market price and expect to make current sales. Nor is he likely to set a price below the current market price, since he can sell his whole output at the current market price.

In contrast, where competition is among a few producers selling to many buyers, no one of whom has significant bargaining power, the individual producer can—and in the United States usually does —sell on the basis of an administered price. It is not only that the conditions of pricing are such that an individual producer can expect to sell more at a lower price than at a higher price, but also that he can operate with a price which remains constant over a period of time in spite of changes in demand and cost. It may be that, as in the steel industry, a price leader sets a price and other producers follow this price. Or products may be so differentiated by character or location or promotion that each of the few competitors can set its own price provided it is reasonably in line with those of others. What is immediately important is that each producer is selling at a price which is constant over a period, often an extended period of time, and is insensitive in some degree to changes in demand and cost. The question of just why such prices are likely to be insensitive to changes in demand and cost will be discussed in later chapters.

THE CAPACITY VERSUS THE FLOW PRINCIPLE OF PRODUCTION
The second difference in enterprise behavior where there are only a few producers is concerned with the principle likely to control the rate of operation.

Under the conditions of classical competition, the only principle controlling the rate of operation of an individual enterprise is that of operation at economic capacity.[1] If the price is high enough to justify operation at all, the plant should be operated at economic capacity, that is, to produce all that could be produced at a unit out-of-pocket cost of less than the current price. Since the producer can sell all he can make at the prevailing price, he does not have to consider the possibility of spoiling the market by producing too much. Therefore, if he could produce more at an out-of-pocket cost below the market price, he would be passing up a potential increase in profits. Thus his main decision on the rate of operation is essentially one of whether to operate a plant at economic capacity or not at all. Of course, the price might be so high that it would pay to operate the plant on a double shift in spite of the higher operating cost of a second shift; then the decision would be between operating at one shift capacity or two shift capacity. Also,

---

[1] In technical terms, the individual producer operating under classical competition can be expected to push production to the point where marginal cost approximates price. This defines economic capacity.

even at one shift capacity, the output of a given plant can usually be increased a little by incurring added expense so that the higher the price, the higher the economic capacity. It is in this sense that the producer, operating under classical competition, can be expected to operate at the economic capacity corresponding to the market price or not at all.

One can think of a model of a classically competitive industry as one in which a multitude of enterprises are pouring a particular type of product into the market with each plant in operation working at its economic capacity and taking whatever price the market brings. Fluctuations in demand would be reflected in price changes that would alter the economic capacity of individual plants. Plants already operating would expand or contract their rate of operation as a change in price increased or reduced their economic capacity. Additional plants would be brought into operation or plants would be taken out of production as the price rose or fell. In these circumstances, each enterprise would be controlling its production on the principle of capacity operation.

Where competition is among a few and selling is on the basis of administered prices, the industrial enterprise is likely to adopt quite a different principle for the control of production, one which might be called the "flow" principle. Once the individual enterprise has determined on its prices, it will hold these prices constant and vary the flow of output in the light of the demand at these prices, changing its prices only occasionally as conditions change so greatly as to exceed some threshold.

The pattern of behavior is clearly exemplified by recent developments in the steel industry. During the first half of 1960 demand dropped to such an extent that operation had to be curtailed from around 95 per cent of engineering capacity to 50 per cent. Yet, according to *Business Week,* even by late July there had been only a very mild softening of the mill prices for steel.[2] The steel mills

[2] July 23, 1960, p. 31. It should be noted that, with no substantial change in price there would be no substantial change in economic capacity.

were sticking to their base prices and to most of their standard dealer discounts. In the case of standard pipe, "one of the hardest hit products in the entire steel list," the price was in effect reduced 2 per cent by increasing the dealers' discount, and a few other types of pipe were given similar small reductions. There were rumors of concessions on extras and one can presume an increase in the number of special situations in which some freight was absorbed. Also, there was a greater softening of prices among the warehouses which wholesale steel. But for the steel producers as such one can say that, in spite of a 47 per cent drop in demand, the great bulk of sales must have taken place with no change in prices and such price concessions as did occur were minor. Production was controlled on the flow principle.

A more extended example of the flow principle is to be found in the automobile industry, perhaps as a natural extension of the assembly line. An auto company will set the price to dealers for each new model as it is introduced and usually keeps the same price to dealers throughout most of the model year. And it is likely to make contracts with parts suppliers to furnish parts at prices negotiated in advance, but in quantities to be determined by the auto producer from time to time. These open-end contract prices are also administered prices since the quantity to be purchased is left open. Similarly, the parts maker in turn may subcontract some parts on the same basis. Many supplies such as steel and tires may be available too, at administered prices or on open contract with prices but not quantity specified. Wage rates as well are negotiated on open contract. Thus at the beginning of the model year prices at various stages of production are lined up in whole or in large part and fixed for a period and the process of mass production is ready to begin.

As actual production gets underway, the pipelines of production are filled up. Parts begin to flow toward the assembly line and, as they arrive, the assembly line is started. Cars come off the assembly line and flow to dealers who begin to make sales. And all this occurs with most if not all prices constant.

From this point on, the flow of production is closely articulated to the sales by dealers. While forecasts of expected sales are made and give a basis for general policy and for the adjustment to seasonal norms, the actual rate of production is adjusted to actual sales by dealers. If sales by dealers prove less than expected, the producer sends out messages to its suppliers to slow up the rate of production or delivery and at the same time the company's own production of parts is slowed and the assembly lines are operated for fewer hours. Similarly, if actual sales exceed expectations, the whole process is speeded up. Production is thus controlled on the flow principle with prices fixed and output at each stage controlled in the light of the sales at the final stage.

This does not mean that prices must remain entirely unchanged. If there is gross error in forecasts of demand, or if costs change unexpectedly during the model year, the price may also be changed during the model year. Contracts with suppliers can be renegotiated. The administered prices of such raw materials as steel and aluminum and nickel may be changed by their few producers. Changes in the model may be made during the model year which, while not taking the form of actual price changes, have somewhat the same effect as price changes. And toward the end of the model year, reductions in prices to dealers may be made to clear the market for the next year's model.

But the pattern of price and production changes is fundamentally different from that which could be expected under conditions of classical competition. If classical competition operated in auto production, each of the parts suppliers would operate at economic capacity or shut down and the imbalance in the supply of different parts would have to be corrected by changes in price which might well be fairly violent except as wastefully big inventories were kept on speculation. And even then, changes in model design could make suppliers of specialized parts incur a tremendous risk of inventory loss.

The essential difference between the smoother operation of the flow principle with administered prices and the more jerky operation under the capacity principle where individual flexible prices are the regulator of production can be compared with that between a freight train with air brakes and one with hand brakes. With air brakes, the engineer alone can pull a lever and the brakes go on with just the degree of hardness or softness he pleases. With hand brakes, the engineer has to blow a whistle to signal his brakemen to put on the brakes and each brakeman has to go to the nearest brake and wind it down. Some cars will not be braked at all and go bumping the next. Others will be braked hard and be bumped into. The jerking and uneven braking can slow down the freight train but only with waste and wear as compared with the smooth control of the air brakes.

The great efficiency of the flow principle for a particular company or industry should be clear. Under it, inventories in the filled pipe lines and the stock of finished cars can be kept to a minimum and relatively stable, except for seasonal variations and gross errors in forecasting. Design and quality control can be handled more effectively, and the risks of uncertain prices for supplies and parts are avoided. For a particular model, once the system of administered prices is set, the management can focus on establishing and maintaining a smooth flow of production and promoting sales. That administered prices and the flow principle may increase the instability of the economy as a whole unless countermeasures to maintain demand are taken does not alter their value for the operation of a single enterprise or an industry.

Today most of American industry operates on the basis of the flow principle and this principle applies to most of distribution and to most service industries. It is almost standard for big manufacturing business and it is a major basis for the efficiency of the modern supermarket. On the other hand, for most of agriculture and some raw materials, competition is classical and neither administered prices nor operation on the flow principle is possible. Also there are many situations in which each unit produced differs so much from the next that its production or sale has to be a matter of negotiation between buyer and seller. And there are some situations in which sales could be made at administered prices but bargaining, customer by customer, is preferred. But in spite of these exceptions, the bulk of production in this country is sold at administered prices and its rate is controlled on the flow principle with prices changed only from time to time in the light of changing costs and demand. Indeed, an economic model which assumed that all production was organized on the flow principle with administered prices would not depart as much from the American economy as does the classical model which assumes that all prices are flexible and production is controlled on the economic capacity principle with each producer pouring into the market whatever volume it is economical to produce at the prevailing price.

There is a different principle of control which economists have suggested as the appropriate principle on which a monopolist should control production and have often applied the principle where competition is among the few. According to this principle, the individual producer should push production to the point where the extra revenue to be expected from producing and selling additional output will be just over the out-of-pocket costs of the extra production. This principle, known as equating marginal *revenue* and marginal cost, is very similar to the capacity principle, since it includes the capacity principle as a special case. However, apart from the special case of classical competition, there is little empirical evidence that any significant amount of production is controlled on the principle of marginal revenue and the principle is inconsistent with the flow principle which empirical evidence shows is so widely used. The reasons why the marginal revenue principle is seldom used as the basis for controlling production where competitors are few will become clear in the next two chapters.

COMPETITIVE SALES PROMOTION

The third important behavior pattern open to enterprises where competition is among a few and is not available under classical competition is that of sales promotion.

Under classical competition, the individual producer can gain nothing by advertising his product or promoting it in other ways. Under the classical conditions he can already sell all he can produce at the market price and advertising his particular wheat or cotton would not bring him a higher price.

In contrast, where competitors are few, the individual enterprise can increase its sales by promoting its product through advertising, through sales organization, and through various other techniques which differentiate its products from those of competitors and give it superiority in the eyes of customers because of its qualities, its availability, the services associated with it, or even because of the psychological success of pressure selling.

This promotion operates in part to increase sales of the industry as a whole. But to a considerable extent the expenditure on promotion is likely to be aimed at offsetting the promotion by others of the few competitors. The more some competitors advertise, the more the others must advertise to hold their position in the market. From the point of view of customers, it is difficult to see that this competitive promotion serves a useful purpose commensurate with its cost, and this waste is often recognized by industry. This cost-increasing effect of competitive promotion where only a few competitors are involved is so familiar that it needs no elaboration.

These three patterns of behavior—administered pricing, the use of the flow principle for controlling production, and expenditure on promotion—are all patterns of enterprise behavior that would be impossible or irrational under conditions of classical competition. Indeed, evidence of any one of them would be almost overwhelming proof that the enterprise involved was not producing under conditions of classical competition.

On the other hand, competition among the few does not necessarily make these three patterns of behavior possible or rational. Where there are only a few competitors, prices may or may not be administered. In the case of a few buyers and a few sellers, prices are likely to be arrived at on a basis of bargaining instead of being administered, although this is not a necessary result. Thus in the usual retail market for autos the frequent necessity of putting a value on a specific trade-in car has made it difficult to sell new cars in the local markets on the basis of an administered price and each sale involving a trade-in tends to become in effect a separate bargain. Yet in the steel industry, the few producers of standard steel rails sell to the few railroad buyers at administered and inflexible prices. Also where competition is among a few sellers for the patronage of many buyers and administered prices are feasible, there may be reasons for not using this technique of selling. At one time, there were grocery stores on opposite sides of a street in New York, one selling at administered prices and the other making a bargaining process out of each transaction in order to satisfy the traditional bargaining habits of its Italian customers. In still other cases an enterprise may sell a part of its product on the basis of bargains with powerful customers and the remainder at administered prices to its smaller customers. Thus, in the late 1940's each of the three big spark plug producers supplied one of the big three auto companies with spark plugs for original equipment at low bargained prices and sold at wholesale to the replacement market at administered prices which were around four times as high.[3] However, in the United States, wherever producers are few and buyers are many, selling is likely to be on the basis of administered prices.

---

[3] See Arthur H. Kahn, "Discriminatory Pricing as a Barrier to Entry: The Spark Plug Litigation," *The Journal of Industrial Economics,* VIII, No. 1 (October, 1959), p. 1.

Also, where prices are administered, it does not necessarily follow that production will be controlled on the flow principle. It could be that prices, though administered, were so frequently changed as to be relatively sensitive to changes in cost and demand and production would be controlled by pushing production close to the point where marginal revenue equalled marginal cost. That empirical evidence has not disclosed this type of behavior does not make it impossible.

And finally, competition among the few does not necessitate promotional selling, but it makes it likely, as any survey of the American scene discloses.

THE CONCEPT OF ADMINISTRATIVE COMPETITION

These three patterns of behavior in combination appear so widely where competition is among the few that they can be thought of as presenting a standard mode of operation. The competition among the few when this mode is adopted properly deserves to be singled out and named as a specific kind of competition in order to distinguish it from other types of competition within the broader category of the gray area of competition among the few.

Here, this type of competition will be called *administrative competition*. It can be said to occur wherever prices are administered and production is controlled on the flow principle. Usually it will also involve expenditures for promotion. These conditions are met so widely in this country that administrative competition can be said to be typical of most of American industry and, more important for this book, it is the type of competition which occurs most often where big manufacturing enterprise is involved.

EASY VERSUS DIFFICULT ENTRY

In order to see how administrative competition could be expected to work, we need to examine one more major difference between competition among the many and among the few—that of the ease of entry.

In order for classical competition to be present, there must be such a large number of competitors that each must be relatively small and entry to the industry relatively easy. A new entrant can immediately get his share in the market since, at the market price, he can sell all he can produce. Also, his additional production will not so affect the market price that he needs to take this effect into account in deciding to enter or not. Furthermore, if there are already a large number of small competitors, the capital outlay and the complexity of organization necessary to enter the industry are not likely to be great, at least in comparison to the corporate giants of today.

Where there is administrative competition, there are two quite different situations with respect to entry. In some situations, entry can be so easy that the existing producers have to price in terms of the immediate market situation and can give little or no attention to the longer-run considerations or the effect of price on potential new entrants. In other situations, entry is sufficiently difficult so that prices are likely to be set in terms of long-run considerations and aimed to balance greater current profits against the greater risk that high current profits will induce new entrants or otherwise inhibit the growth of future profits.

Both of these situations can occur under administrative competition. Many examples could be given of administrative competition and easy entry. The local entry into the retail store business, into retail gasoline distribution, into a great many of the service trades, and into some of the manufacturing industries where production is for a small or local market are all cases in point. But where mass production is involved and the really big corporation is more efficient than small-scale enterprise, the usual situation is one of difficult entry. It would take many years to build up a new big enterprise with wholly new capacity to compete with the existing big three or big four on even terms. A big efficient producing organization cannot be built over night. Selling organizations and market reputation only ripen slowly. Research, which has come to be such a valuable tool of big business, is a long-drawn-out affair. The *esprit de corps* which can make a big corporation such a powerful engine of production is in part a product of time. And a big enterprise which is made simply by combining already existing smaller enterprises into a larger unit would not add to the industry's capacity and in this sense would not be a new entrant, even though it might be a stronger competitor to the initial big three than before combining. New entry on a big scale is thus difficult if not impossible in a concentrated industry like automobiles or steel.

This does not mean that smaller companies cannot break into a concentrated industry. In the industries which have the bulk of production in the big three or the big four, there are usually a number of smaller companies which survive under the umbrella of prices set by the leaders and it may not be too difficult for newcomers to break into the industry on a small scale. But usually such smaller enterprises are special in some important respect. Often such small producers specialize in one or a small group of the products or processes of the big companies in such a way as to provide a wider range of the special product and extra services which the big company could not supply efficiently. In the steel industry this is true of the smaller companies that focus on stainless steel or other special alloy steels. In some cases the smaller companies have a special geographical advantage, such as that of Kaiser Steel on the West Coast. And sometimes the smaller enterprise is built around some specialty process which is not available to or is inappropriate to the mass production of the big companies. In such cases the freedom to start new enterprise and the possibility of efficient operation of smaller scale enterprise under special conditions can influence the behavior of the big enterprise but does not constitute the easy entry to their mass production which makes the distinction between easy entry and difficult entry important in analyzing administrative competition.

ADMINISTRATIVE COMPETITION AND ANTITRUST

In this book, our prime concern is administrative competition where entry is difficult. But before we analyze this type of competition, it will be useful to consider administrative competition where entry is easy, not because it is relevant to the actual competition among big businesses but because of the possibilities of antitrust action as a solution to the pricing power of big business.

Few have suggested that it would be possible to break up an industry like steel to such a degree that the conditions of classical competition would prevail. If every separate plant in the steel industry were owned by an independent company, we would still be faced with competition among the relatively few and almost certainly with administrative competition.

But it is often suggested that, by breaking a concentrated industry into a larger number of competing units, entry could be made easy and, though competition would still be among a relatively few competitors, easy entry would cause it to bring about nearly the same results as those to be expected of classical competition and thus the public interest would be served. If this were so, a strong argument could be made for a policy of breakup as the method of dealing with the pricing power of big business. It is this which makes it necessary to examine the effects to be expected from administrative competition where entry is easy as well as where it is difficult.

TWO PRINCIPLES OF ADMINISTRATIVE COMPETITION

Because theory in the area of competition among the few is in a state of flux, there are not dependable and empirically tested theories on which policy can be reliably based. Much of the theory in this area is based on such abstract and unreal assumptions that its conclusions cannot be converted into operational terms and given empirical test. In other cases, the possible conversion into operational terms has not been made and the conclusions remain untested. This means that, to an unfortunate degree, we are forced into the realm of logical exploration and not that of established and generally accepted principles.

However, there appear to be emerging two quite different principles which apply to administrative competition and are of prime importance for our consideration of the pricing power of big business.

The first principle applies only where entry is so easy that any premium profits, that is, profits in excess of the competitive cost of capital, are likely to be wholly or largely eliminated by the entry of new firms into competition with the existing firms and a consequent dividing up of the market. In this situation, pricing policy could be expected to focus on profits in the current pricing period. And the conclusion is implicit in prevailing theory that, if this is done, the effect of competition is likely to be that of establishing prices above the classically competitive level with a resulting waste of resources. For this reason, this emerging principle will be called here *the principle of competitive waste.*

The second principle applies primarily where entry is possible but difficult. In this situation, pricing policy could be expected to focus on profits over a period longer than that for which the prices are being set and with some sacrifice of current profits to discourage entry and so increase the chances of future profits. As a result, current premium profits would be made but would be less than those which could be expected from a monopoly. At the same time the competitive waste of excessive entry would be avoided. The pricing principle applicable in this case appears to be that involving a target rate of return on capital and will be called here *the principle of target pricing.*

The application of two different principles depending on whether entry is easy or difficult raises a question of the dividing line between them. In practice, it is reasonable to suppose that the difficulty or ease of entry in different situation grades from one extreme to the other, so that there is no sharp dividing line which would allow us to classify concrete market situations into easy or difficult entry. However, the price-makers themselves have to choose the kind of pricing policy which they will adopt and the pricing results will differ depending on whether their focus in setting a particular price is on current profits or longer run profits. As a result, the dividing line in practice is drawn by the enterprises themselves.

Also there are some situations in which a current price is set below that which would yield the highest current profits and yet not for the purpose of reducing the likelihood of new entrants. This would be true, for example, in the case of a promotional price where the price of a new product is set low to build up consumer acceptance and with the idea that the current profits sacrificed will be more than made up through the greater volume of sales, once the product is established. Such cases can occur both under easy entry and under difficult entry and, as such, do not necessarily involve the principle of target pricing.

Similarly, where entry is difficult and premium profits are possible, the purpose of discouraging new entrants may not be the only reason for aiming at less than the maximum current profits. Public pressure through the possibility of antitrust action or investigation may be important. Also, greater premium profits could be expected to increase labor's pressure for higher wages. Indeed, it could be that other considerations than keeping out new entrants are the dominant influence in a particular decision to adopt the target pricing principle. But what is immediately important is that these considerations could be expected to operate where difficult entry makes premium profits possible and not where easy entry operates to eliminate premium profits. Thus, the crucial factor leading to two sharply distinct principles of operation is that of easy or difficult entry.

In the following two chapters, the logic of administrative competition will be examined, first on the assumption of easy entry and then under that of difficult entry.

CHAPTER XII

EASY ENTRY AND THE PRINCIPLE OF COMPETITIVE WASTE

Therefore, if competition is our goal, and I repeat that, if competition is our goal, the only real solution, the most effective remedy, is dissolution, divorcement, and divestiture; trustbusting in the literal sense.

PROFESSOR WALTER ADAMS
MICHIGAN STATE UNIVERSITY*

It is often believed by economists that if entry is easy, even under conditions of price administration, competition from new entrants will bring about essentially the same results as those of classical competition and that, therefore, administrative competition with easy entry would serve the public interest in substantially the same degree as classical competition. It is largely on this basis that they advocate the break-up of big business into a somewhat larger number of units even though this would not bring about the condition necessary for classical competition.

The reasoning behind this belief in easy entry involves two major steps. First, it is argued that if entry is easy and particular producers are making premium profits, new producers will come in and their competition will tend to bring profits down to competitive rates. And second, it is argued that since there tend to be no premium profits and prices are in reasonable relation to costs, the public interest is served.

* Hearings, p. 4783.

213

The first of these two steps is quite acceptable and is consistent with the logic of administrative competition and the empirical evidence. But the second step must be questioned.

It does not necessarily follow that because prices are in reasonable relation to costs the public interest will be served. Rather it may be that where competitors are few and entry is easy, administrative competition will eliminate premium profits in whole or in part by increasing costs instead of reducing prices. In some situations, it could be expected that prices would be in the nature of monopoly prices and monopoly profits would be eliminated by a wasteful rise in costs. In other situations it could be expected that prices would be lower than monopoly prices but higher than classical competitive prices, with a part of the difference absorbed by higher costs. Only rarely could administrative competition be expected to eliminate premium profits without some wasteful increase in costs. And insofar as such competition with easy entry operates to eliminate premium profits by raising costs, it results in a waste of resources. It is this wasteful operation of administrative competition under condition of easy entry which is referred to here as *the principle of competitive waste.*

This principle, which appears to be peculiar to conditions of easy entry, should not be confused with the wasteful competitive promotion already discussed. The latter can arise under conditions of difficult entry as well as those of easy entry. Where entry is easy, it may contribute to the rise in costs which eliminates premium profits but is not essential to this rise. Indeed, the principle of competitive waste is just as applicable where the products of different producers are interchangeable so far as buyers are concerned, so that there is no such advantage in promotion as where the products are highly differentiated and promotion is important.

The competitive-waste principle turns on the factors determining prices and the tendency of administered prices to provide a price umbrella to new entrants, whether or not costs are also increased through competitive promotion. It provides a sort of Parkinson's

Law for easy entry. According to Professor Parkinson, bureaucratic work "expands so as to fill the time available for its completion."[1] According to the principle of competitive waste, the number of enterprises expands to the extent necessary to do the work available at a premium price but without premium profits. This principle can be seen at work in the multiplication of gasoline stations.

THE GAS STATION EXAMPLE

The retailing of gasoline is a clear case of administrative competition and easy entry. It is easy to set up a new gas station. Both the land and the equipment can usually be rented and, even if not rented, the capital outlay required is not great. The skills required are not unusual. As a result, unusually high profits will lead to the creation of new stations.

Also, competition in the retailing of gasoline is administrative. The typical buyer of gas at retail is concerned with convenience and perhaps with brand name and perhaps with the service given him by a particular station. He is likely to patronize those stations along his traveled route or close to it. As a result, a given gas station will be competing primarily with a relatively few nearby stations and to a vague and uncertain extent with more distant stations. It will administer its price, keeping it constant over a considerable period of time, usually not changing it except when the tank price charged to it is changed. Stations handling nationally or regionally advertised brands are likely to have identical or close to the same prices for the same grades while other stations make up for the lack of advertising by selling a few cents under the advertised brands, obtaining unadvertised gas at a somewhat lower tank price.

We need not concern ourselves with just how the system of retail prices are arrived at. The retail prices or station margins

[1] See Cyril Northcote Parkinson, *Parkinson's Law and other Studies in Administration* (Boston: Houghton Mifflin Co., 1957).

may be recommended by the gasoline producer, or may be set by a big producer operating a chain of stations, or may be a matter of custom, or may be arrived at as a result of calculations by the separate station operators. What is immediately important is that whatever the station margin, administrative competition is likely to expand the number of stations until the available business is so divided up that the typical station only makes a competitive profit.

Let us suppose that on a given twenty-five-mile stretch of highway there is enough traffic to keep ten efficiently organized stations operating at a reasonable per cent of capacity. Also assume that, at a station margin of say four cents a gallon, these stations would make only a competitive rate of profit. As long as the margin was only four cents, there would be no inducement to set up additional stations. However, if the margin happened to be put at six cents, these stations could be expected to make such high profits that other stations would be set up. For example, five more stations might divide up the business so that each was only able to make competitive profits on its investment. With an eight-cent margin, the same highway might support twenty stations, each operating at only a small proportion of its capacity, but each making a competitive profit.

In practice, it is likely that a high margin will not lead so much to partial use of capacity as it will to the creation of inefficient capacity. Let us say that the efficient station is one with ten or twelve pumps operated at a reasonable per cent of capacity. If the station margin is so wide that twenty stations will divide the business that five efficient stations could easily handle, many of the twenty stations are likely to be small stations which presumably would have higher operating costs per gallon than the larger station if both were adequately utilized, but would have lower capital costs to support than the larger stations whose facilities are only partially operated. Thus, the effect of administrative competition may show up only partly in excess capacity and partly in the rational creation of inefficient capacity.

Here the logic of administrative competition suggests that for gas stations, whatever station margin may prevail, the number of stations will be increased and their average efficiency reduced to the point where profits are kept close to a competitive rate and no one makes unreasonably high profits. In this case, it is easy entry and the inflexibility of an administrative price or, more exactly of an administered margin, which provides an umbrella and makes competition result in a waste of resources rather than lower prices.

This situation was well symbolized in the statement attributed to a former Secretary of Interior in an address to the National Petroleum Institute, "You can talk all you want about the inefficiency of government, but the government never put four post offices on the four corners of a highway intersection."

This waste of resources is overcome on some of our superhighways where the highway authority auctions off the right to operate gas stations and spaces the stations far enough apart so that they can operate efficiently and at a reasonable proportion of capacity. The difference between the prevailing station margin and the margin that is needed to operate efficiently and make a competitive profit then helps to pay for the cost of the highway instead of paying for waste. Here, what would be monopoly profits under conditions of monopoly and would be excessive costs and a waste of resources under administrative competition with easy entry, becomes a sort of tax to support the cost of the highway. The limited entry of the superhighways thus underlines the principle of competitive waste which operates in gasoline distribution where entry is easy.

The logic behind this principle can be given more precision and can be tied directly into the modern theories of competition among the few by examining two type situations which lie at the heart of these theories. The first is that in which products of different producers are interchangeable so far as buyers are concerned and the total market is supplied by a small enough number of competitors to permit each to take into account the effect of his own price action on the prices of the others, and all recognize that whatever the price, it is going to be the same for each. This case will be examined in some detail, not because of its great practical importance but because it brings out so clearly the principle of competitive waste. The second case to be discussed has much greater practical importance but the waste is less obvious. This is the case in which the product of each producer is well differentiated from that of others, so that each has his own product and price.

THE CASE OF INTERCHANGEABLE PRODUCTS

It is generally accepted that under certain circumstances competition among a few could be expected to result in what is essentially a monopoly price. This is where the product being made by each enterprise is interchangeable with that of others so far as buyers are concerned; where each producer knows that the price charged by each will have to be the same; each has the same costs and capacities; and each has accurate knowledge of demand.

In these circumstances, if all the existing producers were to get together to set a price, they could presumably determine the price which would bring each the maximum profit in the immediate pricing period. This would be in the nature of a monopoly price. And if demand were sufficiently high in relation to costs and the number of producers was sufficiently low, each would be able to make premium profits.

However, it would not be necessary for the producers to get together. Each producer could figure out what price would be the most profitable for him *if he had a monopoly of his share of the market.* Under the special condition assumed above, each could arrive individually at the price that would be most profitable for him. Also, since each has the same costs and assumes a constant share in the market, the best price each would arrive at independently would be the same for all. As a result, if any producer announced the price best for himself, it would be just right for each of the others. Each would be content with the price and no one would seek to change it. Thus a monopoly price could be established without any discussion or agreement.

The question then arises, if this monopoly price results in premium profits what could be expected to happen if entry were perfectly easy so that a newcomer could get a share of the market simply by setting up in business?

First, assume that any potential newcomer would have to build a new plant having the same costs and capacities as the existing plants. Would the newcomer set a lower price? With the same costs as the others, the same considerations that led them to set or accept the monopoly price would operate with him. As long as he could get his share of the market at the monopoly price, it would be just as good for him as for the other producers and he could be expected to accept it.[2] The essential change would not be a reduction in price, but a reduction in the total profits of each producer since the volume of sales of each would be reduced.

In these circumstances as long as the producers actually in the industry were making significant premium profits, there would be an inducement tending to bring in newcomers. And so long as entry was easy, the process of new entry would continue until the market was so subdivided that no producer was making significant premium profits. For practical purposes, the end result would be a monopoly price, no premium profits, and the waste of capital tied up in partly idle or excessive plant. In this special case, instead of price coming down to the level of the total cost per unit plus a competitive profit as would be expected under classical competition, total cost per unit could be expected to rise to eliminate premium profits at the monopoly price.

In this special case, we have assumed that all the plants had the same costs and capacities, but this limiting assumption is not necessary to produce essentially the same result. If each producer had

---

[2] This also assumes that marginal costs are not significantly altered by the smaller volume of sales per producer.

different costs, the price might well be the quasi-monopoly price of the low cost producer, i.e., the price it would choose to set if it had a monopoly of its share of the market. But whatever the price reached, if premium profits were being made, easy entry could be expected to multiply producers until profits were brought down to competitive level by the division of the market and the rise in the total cost per unit of each producer.

The introduction of plants with different cost and capacity characteristics does, however, introduce an important additional element. As the subdivision of the market among more producers reduces the percentage of capacity that each producer is able to operate, this opens up the profitable opportunity for the construction of smaller plants even though they are less efficient. If the expansion in the number of enterprises has eliminated premium profits and the larger established plants are only operating at, say, two-thirds of capacity, it still may be profitable to build smaller plants even though their operating costs are higher than those of the larger and more efficient plants when these are fully operating. Indeed, it is not difficult to picture a situation in which, if the capital represented by the efficient plants could be freely withdrawn (say by setting on fire and collecting the insurance), it would pay to replace all the efficient plants by smaller ones even though they were less efficient. Thus, the cost-increasing effect of easy entry in this interchangeable product case could be brought about either by the building of a surplus of plant capacity or by the construction of less efficient plants. Whichever happened, the premium profits would be eliminated. But from the point of view of the consumer the premium profits would have been converted into a waste of resources, not into lower prices.

This monopoly-like price solution might break down in two different ways.

The first is a temporary breakdown as the result of a price war. One producer might try to increase his share of the total market by cutting price and others could be expected to follow suit. But sooner or later the advantage of the monopoly-like price for each could be expected to assert itself and it would be restored. Such temporary price wars give buyers a temporary advantage but there is no reason to expect that they would reduce the waste of resources except in some degree while they lasted.

The likelihood of such temporary price wars could be expected to increase both with the number of competitors and with their inexperience. Indeed, it is usually assumed in modern theory that where the products of different producers are interchangeable, there lies between competition among the few with monopoly-like prices and competition among the many with classical results a range of situations in which competition among the few breaks down and prices become indeterminate even in theory. Thus, as numbers in an industry increase, this point of indeterminacy would be reached, and as they increased still further the indeterminate situation would change to the determinate one of classical competition with a forest of enterprises. But there is no reason to expect that in the indeterminate situation the results of competition would be close to those of classical competition or that the public interest would be effectively served.

The other way in which the monopoly-like situation could break down would be a partial shift from administered prices to bargained prices through the action of big buyers. For example, a big mail order house could work out a bargain with an efficient producer to take all its output at a classically competitive price. If part of the output of an industry was sold on such a bargained basis and the rest was sold to weaker buyers at administered prices, the principle of competitive waste would apply only to that part in which administrative competition prevailed. Also, the effect of the bargained output on the demand of the ultimate buyers could be expected to alter the character of demand for the remainder of the output and result in a lower monopoly-like price. This could reduce the competitive waste in the area of administrative competition, but could not be expected to eliminate it except as all output was sold at prices bargained by strong buyers. Thus, where administrative competition prevails, the products of different producers are interchangeable and entry is easy, modern theory suggests that premium profits would tend to be eliminated by the rise in costs, not by a fall in price.

THE DIFFERENTIATED PRODUCTS CASE

A similar conclusion is reached by the modern theories of competition among the few when entry is easy and the products of different producers are not interchangeable but are differentiated to a greater or less degree by differences in physical characteristics, by geographical location, or by promotional effort. This is undoubtedly the more common case of administrative competition and easy entry. In this case, the determination of price is likely to be a more complex matter than when products are interchangeable but competition with easy entry is just as likely to eliminate premium profits by increasing costs and wasting resources.

There is this important difference, however. In the case of interchangeable products, the whole of the difference between a monopoly-like price and a classically competitive price could be expected to be reflected in a rise in costs. Where products are differentiated, easy entry may result in monopoly-like prices with the whole difference absorbed by cost increases. But it can also result in some lowering of price below the monopoly-like price so that the elimination of premium profits is only partly through a rise in costs and partly through a reduction in prices. This means that the actual situations in which products are differentiated and entry is easy range all the way from those closely akin to the case of interchangeable products to situations in which the reduction of price plays a major role. But even where price reduction plays a part in eliminating premium profits, modern theory suggests that after premium profits have been eliminated the competitive price will be at least in some degree a premium price.

The reasoning involved in reaching this conclusion is complex and need not be given here. But a simple example can give some indication of how easy entry could be expected to raise costs where each producer has a well-differentiated product. Suppose that Producer A is making product A efficiently and reaping premium profits. Then a Producer B could be expected to come into the market with product B, which differs from product A in some degree and appeals to a different clientele but also appeals to some of the buyers of product A. Presumably this would take some of the business away from Producer A and so reduce his premium profits. If both producers A and B were able to make premium profits, there would be inducement for a Producer C to introduce a third product, which might appeal to some of the customers of Producers A and B but also appeal to a new clientele. This would still further reduce the premium profits of A and reduce those of B. With entry easy of similar products, this process could be expected to continue until premium profits were substantially eliminated.

Whether this process of competitive entry would also reduce prices is another matter. It might easily be that if A's initial price was the most profitable under the initial conditions, the same price would also be the most profitable under the new conditions in which premium profits have been eliminated. It could even be that in the new conditions a higher price would be more profitable. And in still other situations a lower price would be more profitable. But it is difficult, if not impossible, to design a situation in which the most profitable price would not be in some degree a premium price. Thus even where products are differentiated, modern theory suggests that the principle of competitive waste is likely to operate, resulting in premium prices while premium profits are converted into a waste of resources.

This principle of competitive waste is not only inherent in modern price theory where competition is among the few and entry is easy, but the practical considerations in price administering appear likely to increase its effect.

PRACTICAL PRICING AND THE ZONE OF PRICE INDIFFERENCE

Modern price theory, like classical monopoly theory, rests in large measure on the use of the profit-maximizing calculus of a monopolist. This in turn rests on the assumption that the individual producer has a clear idea of the quantity of product that can be sold at different prices. The theorist recognizes that the producer is almost necessarily uncertain as to the actual demand for his product and assumes that in arriving at the most profitable price he will create something in the nature of a demand schedule representing his best estimate of the amount he can sell at different prices. But then modern theory treats the producer's best estimates of demand as the equivalent of certain knowledge and gives no further attention to the implications of this uncertainty. It is sufficient that, if demand and costs are known, the profit-maximizing calculus can indicate the most profitable price.

In practice, however, the producer seeking high profit in the current period is likely to be concerned with other implications of this uncertainty. The prices above or below the price most likely to be most profitable in the current pricing period became significant for his pricing problem. If he does not guess right as to the most profitable price, how much profit is he sacrificing?

A little investigation of the possible relations between demand, cost and profits shows that, where all other prices are given, the price significantly above or below the most profitable price is likely to give almost as great profits in the period covered as the most profitable price. This is because, if the price is somewhat higher than the most profitable, the loss in sales will be almost made up for by a larger profit per sale; if the price is somewhat less than the most profitable, the greater quantity sold will almost make up for the lower profit per sale. For example, in one plausible case to be discussed directly, a price 5 per cent above or below the monopoly price would yield 98 per cent of the profits to be expected from the most profitable price.

In such a case, if the price-maker were certain as to demand and costs, he would presumably price to make the extra 2 per cent. But if he is uncertain as to demand, then he is likely to be satisfied if he can pick a price which lies within the zone of the more profitable prices. Because of his uncertainty, he is not too much concerned with picking *the* most profitable price. If he knew that a certain price would yield him 98 per cent of the maximum profits he could make and did not know whether a higher or lower price would yield 100 per cent, why should he seek further? For the practical purpose of setting an administered price in the presence of considerable uncertainty as to demand, the rational objective of the price-maker would not be to arrive at the price which would maximize profit but to arrive at a price which lies in the zone which surrounds the most profitable price. Thus, however logical it would be to *calculate* the most profitable price if he were certain of demand and costs, in the presence of uncertainty a guess which lands in the zone surrounding the most profitable price is, for practical purposes, as good as the most profitable price itself. This zone represents what I have elsewhere called the zone of relative price indifference or, more shortly, the *zone of price indifference*.[3]

Just how wide this zone of indifference may be will vary from situation to situation and with the psychology of the price-maker. But that it could be quite wide can be seen if one arbitrarily assumes that, in the light of the uncertainty of demand, the difference between making 98 per cent and 100 per cent of the potential profits in a given situation is unimportant and then calculates the range of prices this would allow in different possible situations of demand and cost.

For example, take the case in which those costs per unit which

[3] *Hearings,* p. 77.

vary with the volume of output, such as operating labor and raw materials, are the same for each additional unit of output and absorb half of the revenue that can be expected at the most profitable price, leaving an equal remainder to cover overhead labor and materials and other overhead costs including depreciation, and provide for income taxes and a return on capital. Also, assume that, at the monopoly price, half of this remainder would go to income taxes and net income. Finally, assume that demand is the most simple function of price. This is a situation which could easily occur.[4] And, in this situation, a price 5 per cent above or below *the* most profitable price would produce all but 2 per cent of the return to capital before income taxes produced by the most profitable price.

As will be apparent in the next chapter, this zone of price indifference does not occur where the focus in pricing is on long-run considerations. Then, a price is likely to be set significantly below the most profitable price in the *current* pricing period. If that

---

[4] In more technical terms, this is the situation in which marginal cost is constant and equal to half the monopoly price, income before income taxes at the monopoly price would be equal to fixed costs, and demand is a straight-line function of price. It also applies if marginal cost is constant only in the range of production relevant to pricing and any excess of average variable cost over marginal cost in this relevant range is treated as part of fixed costs, a procedure often implicit in business pricing behavior. It can be stated as follows:

$$\text{Let} \quad \text{Demand} = K_1 - K_2 p$$
$$\text{Marginal Cost} = K_3$$
$$\text{Monopoly Price} = 2K_3$$
$$\text{Fixed Costs} = \text{Gross Profits when } p = 2K_3$$
$$\text{Then} \quad K_1 = 3K_2K_3$$
$$\text{Demand} = 3K_2K_3 - K_2 p$$
$$\text{Total Variable Cost} = K_2K_3(3K_3 - p)$$
$$\text{Total Fixed Cost} = .5K_2K_3^2$$
$$\text{When} \quad p = 2K_3 \text{ Gross Profits} = .50K_2K_3^2$$
$$p = 1.9K_3 \text{ Gross Profits} = .49K_2K_3^2$$
$$p = 2.1K_3 \text{ Gross Profits} = .49K_2K_3^2$$

Effect of 5% Departure from Monopoly Price:

$$1 - \frac{.49K_2K_3^2}{.50K_2K_3^2} = 1 - .98 = 2\%$$

were done, then it follows that a higher current price would bring in significantly more profit in the current period, a potential current profit which is surrendered in favor of long-run objectives.

But the zone of price indifference does have importance where the objective is high profits in the current period and it has particular importance for the operation of the principle of competitive waste, both where products are interchangeable and where they are differentiated.

In the case of interchangeable products, the existence of a zone of price indifference makes it easier for a number of competitors to arrive at and maintain the same prices. It is not necessary that the profit-maximizing price of each should be the same or that the price be attuned to the monopoly price of the lowest cost producer. Where each producer has a zone of price indifference, there will be a range of prices any one of which will satisfy him. Therefore, if one producer sets a price, other producers might be satisfied with it even though it was not the price each would have set in the circumstances. It would be enough if it lay within the zone of indifference of each. This means that the price to which all adhere may be significantly above that which would be set by the lowest cost producer, and that the pressure for a revision of price which might start a price war would be less.

In the case of differentiated products, the zone of price indifference could be expected to have a similar stabilizing effect with even more important results. If each producer knew just what the demand for his particular product would be, he could be expected to adjust his price quickly to the new situation created as the entrance of new competitors altered his own most profitable price. However, with a zone of price indifference, the individual producer could be expected to keep his price unchanged until conditions had so altered that the most profitable price lay outside his zone of price indifference.

Such behavior would provide a temporary price umbrella giving greater opportunity for new entrants. With easy entry, the inflow of new producers might quickly subdivide the market to such an extent that costs per unit are pushed up until premium profits disappear. Thus, the presence of a zone of indifference increases the likelihood that where entry is easy, the competitive adjustment to premium prices will be to eliminate premium profits by increasing costs instead of reducing prices.

The zone of price indifference also provides a general explanation for the insensitivity of administered prices where price policy is focused on profits in the current pricing period. If prices were set to maximize current profits, they should be sensitive to changes in demand and costs. A change in costs would usually alter the price which would maximize profits if demand remained unchanged. In the same way, a change in demand would usually change the profit-maximizing price. There could be special cases in which the effect of a change in demand and a change in costs just offset each other or in which a change in demand was of such a special character that it did not alter the profit-maximizing price. Also, there could be costs involved in making a price change, such as the cost of printing new catalogues or the less in customer good will if a price cut had to be subsequently cancelled. But in general a change in demand or cost could be expected to be quickly reflected in a change in price if the price-makers had no zone of price indifference. However, with a zone of price indifference the price administrator who focuses on current profits could be expected to change his price only when some threshold of significance is exceeded. In such situations, prices could be expected to be relatively insensitive to changes in demand or cost and there is ample empirical evidence that this is the case.

Finally, the zone of price indifference gives an explanation of why, even where the pricing focus is on current profits, production is likely to be controlled on the flow principle rather than on the principle of equating marginal cost and marginal revenue. When a producer operates with a zone of price indifference, the price he charges may be significantly different from the profit-maximizing price, and this difference would not be due to an error in his appraisal of demand but to his indifference to the *exact* point of maximum profit. His zone of price indifference must contain prices in which marginal revenue would be above marginal cost and others in which it would be below. And these discrepancies could be considerable. In the plausible case already given, a price which yielded 98 per cent of the maximum profit would result in a marginal revenue either 20 per cent above or 20 per cent below marginal cost. As a result, the equating of marginal revenue and marginal costs becomes a poor guide to production policy.

THE LOGIC VERSUS THE EVIDENCE

The foregoing analysis has attempted to outline the logic of administrative competition where entry is easy. In the main this logic is derived directly from the modern theories of competition among the few, which assume that the uncertainties as to demand can be disregarded. It adds some of the implications of this uncertainty for pricing policy. And whether or not one includes the practical effects of uncertainty, the logical conclusion flows that, where the pricing focus is on current profits and entry is easy, administrative competition could be expected to result in prices above the classically competitive level, but with premium profits dissipated through increased costs according to the principle of competitive waste.

However, it should be recognized that this analysis lies in the realm of theory. While it has been couched in operational terms and thus is capable of being empirically tested, it has not been thoroughly tested and no attempt will be made to do that here. For the purposes of this book, it is sufficient to set forth the logic and suggest certain of its implications for policy. Whether in fact administrative competition produces the wastes suggested by theory, how great these wastes are, and how much they may be compensated for by other gains, such as the greater efficiency of the flow principle of production control and the variety of products resulting from product differentiation, can only be determined through empirical investigation. And such testing cannot be accomplished through specific examples.

Specific examples, such as that of gasoline already given, can show that in particular situations of easy entry administrative competition does lead to waste of resources. Various other examples could be given. In manufacturing, most industries operate under conditions of relatively difficult entry. And where entry is easy, the bargaining power of a few big chain-store and mail-order buyers, or other large buyers, is likely to confine the scope of administrative competition. As a result, the manufacturing examples showing the effect of the principle of competitive waste where entry is easy are likely to be for unimportant products or products made for local use. More important examples are to be found in the fields of distribution and the service industries. In these, a few firms often supply a given local market, administrative competition prevails and entry is easy.

EASY ENTRY AND BIG BUSINESS

The point has already been made that most big business operates under conditions of difficult entry. Here the easy entry conditions are important only because the breakup of big business to create the conditions of easy entry is often proposed as a method for controlling pricing power in the public interest. The logic of administrative competition supports the conclusion that a breakup sufficient to make entry easy would tend to eliminate premium profits, even though it did not go far enough to bring about classical competition. On the other hand, this logic suggests that the elimination of premium profits would be achieved wholly or in part by increasing costs, not by eliminating premium prices.

At the present time, this logical conclusion arises from a body of theory which is in a state of flux and has not been adequately tested. It does not provide a solid basis for *rejecting* the intermediate break-up solution to the pricing power of big business. However, it would seem to place on those who advocate this solution a burden of proof to show that the principle of competitive waste would not operate or that the waste would be small or that more effective methods for dealing with the problem are not available.

CHAPTER XIII

DIFFICULT ENTRY AND THE PRINCIPLE OF TARGET PRICING

Target return on investment was perhaps the most frequently mentioned of pricing goals.

Pricing officials of these large corporations feel they do not need to have precise estimates of the price sensitivity of demand nor detailed information on current costs. They vastly prefer to use standard cost methods. . . .

My position, in brief, is that whatever profits maximization may be construed to mean, it does not prove helpful in understanding pricing policies of large corporations.

PROFESSOR ROBERT F. LANZILLOTTI,
WASHINGTON STATE UNIVERSITY*

Most of the really big manufacturing companies in the United States operate under conditions in which entry is not easy. They tend to be in industries which, for purely technical reasons, require both large aggregates of capital and large amounts of capital per worker. They are likely to be industries in which a large producing organization has both economic and business advantages over and above the efficiencies of a single plant and in which organized marketing plays an important role. Each of these

* "Pricing Objectives of Large Companies," *American Economic Review,* XLVIII, No. 5 (December, 1958), 923, and "Pricing Objectives in Large Corporations: Reply," *American Economic Review,* XLIX, No. 4 (September, 1959), 682, 685; respectively.

conditions can create an impediment to the entry of new firms on a scale and with the efficiency comparable to that of the giants. On the other hand, entry is by no means impossible, except in the special case of patents. The possibility and difficulty of entry create quite · a different pricing situation from that which exists where entry is easy and one which is also quite different from monopoly.

Where entry is easy, there is no advantage to the individual producer in pricing so as to discourage new entrants. If he can price to make monopoly profits, the immediate period is the time to make them before newcomers capture a share of the market. As a profit-seeker his pricing should logically conform to the classical goal of the profit-maximizing price except as that goal is broadened by his zone of indifference. Setting a price below the monopoly price in order to discourage new competition would only be effective if it were so low that there were practically no monopoly profits. Ease of entry gives the producer no choice but to price for immediate profits.

In contrast, difficult but possible entry gives the producer a choice between (1) pricing high so as to make high current profits, while stimulating new entrants so that future profits are likely to be lower, or (2) setting a price lower than the full monopoly price and making less than the full monopoly profits in the current period, so that new entrants will not be unduly encouraged and the somewhat lower level of premium profits can be maintained over a long period.

Where entry is difficult there is what might be thought of as a stone wall around the market so that the existing producers must be making much more than competitive profits before there is an inducement for newcomers to climb over. Therefore, prices do not need to be so low that they eliminate premium profits in order to keep out new entrants. Prices can be higher than the no-premium-profit level by just the effect of the stone wall impediment-to-entry without stimulating new entry. And the higher the stone wall, the greater the premium profits that can be made without being subject to the attrition of new entrants. Thus, the price-maker has something to gain by setting a price below the monopoly price yet above the price which would eliminate premium profit. It is this which makes the logic of administrative competition with difficult entry fundamentally different from the logic where entry is easy.

For the big corporations, there are two further conditions calling for an intermediate pricing policy and reinforcing the effect of difficult entry. These are the threat of government action and the difficulties of administering a huge enterprise.[1]

Antitrust and other government actions have been reasonably successful in preventing or eliminating classical monopoly in manufacturing. For most industries, the big three or big four have been prevented from combining into the one big monopoly and where such a combination has taken place, it has been broken up. And where a single company developed into a big monopoly, as in the case of aluminum, government has facilitated new entries. As a result, administrative competition, though not classical competition, has been preserved. But big companies are in the public eye and vulnerable, so that very great profits may stimulate government intervention. How much this threat would serve to hold down profit aims in the absence of the threat of new entrants is not clear, but it is fair to assume that it reinforces the effects of the latter.

The second reinforcing factor involves the complexity of managing a big corporate enterprise. By tradition the economist has been taught to analyze price-making in terms of a small owner-operated enterprise in which a single person sits down and figures the most profitable price. But in a big corporation price is likely to be an organization decision. It may be a group decision, not

---

[1] There are still other considerations that can lead to pricing below the current most profitable price. For a discussion of the various factors, see Joel Dean, *Managerial Economics* (New York, 1951), pp. 29-33.

that of a single person, and even a single price may not involve a single decision but a series of decisions at different levels of the organization.

The complexity of pricing decision in the big corporation is well stated in a report published for the National Bureau of Economic Research.[2] According to this report, pricing decisions in the large firms are customarily "made by a group of officials who seek to balance the diverse, and often conflicting, interests of various departments of the company. . . . In conferences on pricing policy, the sales representative may stress the importance of lower prices and attractive products, the sales credit department the desirability of favorable discounts and terms of credit to customers, the legal department the dangers of larger discounts to different types of customers and the general importance of relationships to the public and to governmental agencies and departments in particular, the manufacturing department the technical difficulties of producing the quantity and quality specified for the desired dates of delivery, the accounting department the need for larger profit margins. . . ."[3] This can lead to prices which are less than the most profitable price.

While the possibility of government intervention and the administrative needs of big business have played a part in big business pricing, the important factor has been the possibility of *continuing* to make more than a competitive rate of return by setting prices below those which would be most profitable in any current pricing period.

Pricing to achieve this objective presents quite a different problem and calls for quite a different calculus from that envisaged in classical monopoly theory and in the modern theories of competition among the few. Instead of starting with estimates of cost and demand and then determining from them the most

[2] *Cost Behavior and Price Policy*, a study prepared by the Committee on Price Determination for the Conference on Price Research (New York, 1943), p. 43.
[3] *Ibid.*

profitable price, the price-maker starts with an estimate of the highest rate of profits which will not induce new entrants and then works back to determine the prices which will just yield this rate of profit when operating at a reasonable proportion of capacity. This procedure has come to be known as pricing for a target rate of return on investment or, more simply, as *target pricing*.

THE TARGET-PRICING CALCULUS

The first logical presentation of this pricing calculus appears to have been made, not by an economist, but by a management engineer. In 1924 Donaldson Brown, then of DuPont and later a vice-president of General Motors, outlined the calculus in five major steps.[4]

1. *Decide upon a target rate of return.* This target rate is "the highest rate of return which can be obtained on capital, consistent with a healthy growth of the business . . ." and with adequate regard to the economic consequence of fluctuating volume. The rate of return must not be so high as to threaten growth by stimulating either new entrants to the industry or the growth of small producers, either of which would take business away from the price maker and limit its healthy growth. Also, the target rate of return must be thought of not as a rate to be achieved in a particular year or shorter period, but as a rate to be approximated as an average over a period of years in which business activity can be expected to fluctuate.

It is important to notice that the crucial factor in determining the target rate is not a consideration of demand and cost but a consideration of what rate of profits on capital will bring new com-

[4] "Price Policy in Relation to Financial Control," *Management and Administration* (February, March, and April 1924), pp. 195-198, 283-286, 417-422. The order in which the steps are given here differ from the order in which Brown first set forth the procedure, but appears to be more consistent with current practice. Also current terms are used.

petition in the particular industry; what rate will keep it out. Because this is the problem, it can be considered without even knowing exactly what products will be made or what their respective costs and demand may be. A target rate can be and is often decided upon and retained for years at a time and for a wide range of products.

2. *Decide upon a rate of operation to be used as a standard.* Total costs per unit usually vary greatly with the rate of operation. To overcome this variability in cost, a standard rate of operation is adopted for estimating costs. This may be the actual average rate of operation over a period of years or a rounded figure close to the actual experience. Thus, if an enterprise finds that in the past, with the ups and downs of business activity, it has operated its plant at close to 80 per cent of rated capacity, it is likely to use 80 per cent as its standard rate for pricing purposes.

Final decision in these first two steps is appropriately taken by top management and the target rates of return and the standard operating rates to be used for pricing purposes can remain unchanged for years and even decades at a time and provide the basis for price decisions at lower levels of management.

3. *Estimate the total cost of production per unit at the standard rate of operation.* This estimate of cost per unit includes both variable costs per unit and fixed costs apportioned over the number of units which would be produced at the standard rate of operation. For example, if the standard rate decided on was 80 per cent of capacity and this represented 10,000 units of output, then an estimate would be made of the fixed costs including depreciation and also of the variable costs involved in producing 10,000 units. The sum of the two costs divided by the 10,000 output would give the cost per unit at the standard rate of operation.

4. *Calculate the price which would yield the target rate of return on investment at the volume of sales necessary to operate at the standard rate.* The resulting price would be the target price

and could be calculated on the basis of the preceding steps plus an estimate of the capital involved. For example, if profits of $20,000 a year were required to provide the target rate of return on the capital involved, and 10,000 units a year would be produced at the standard rate of operation, then a profit of $2 per unit would be required to make the target rate of return at the standard operating rate.[5] Thus, the target price would be $2 more than the standard cost per unit. Up to this point, demand would not enter into the calculus.

5. *Consider the target price in the light of actual market conditions and adopt it as the actual price or modify it.* This final step brings demand into the calculus for the first time. It requires an estimate of what the demand would be if the target price were adopted as the actual price. If it seems likely that under average business conditions, the target price would result in a sales just about sufficient to support the standard rate of operations, then the target price is likely to be adopted as the actual price. Likewise, if sales are likely to be greater, the target price will usually be adopted and capacity will be expanded as quickly as possible to allow the standard operating rate under average conditions. On the other hand, if the volume of sales at the target price seems likely to be significantly less than the standard requires because competitors are setting lower prices or for some other reason, then either the product would not be made or a lower price would be set and a major drive be made to reduce costs so that, at the lower price, the target rate of return would be made at the standard rate of operations.

These last three steps are primarily the responsibility of the lower levels of management. On important products, the decisions are likely to be carefully reviewed by top management and final decisions made there. Also, where the target price is not adopted,

---

[5] Target rates of return are usually stated *after income taxes.* If, in the above example, 50 per cent of profits would go for income taxes, it could be deduced that $10,000 of profit net of income taxes would provide the target rate of return.

there is good reason for higher review and final decision. But on less important items where the target price is adopted as the actual price, final decision can often be left to executives below the top management.

This calculus for arriving at price is a highly logical procedure where new entry is possible but difficult. It focuses on the rate of return which properly balances current profits and the risk to growth. Too high current profits would impair the chances of growth by bringing in new competitors. Too low current profits would be lower than necessary to keep out new entrants and preserve the market. It is quite different from the classical profit-maximizing calculus and different from the monopoly calculus described earlier which results in a zone of price indifference. By balancing the risk of loss of market against profit it does not even attempt to maximize profit but rather to maximize values.[6]

THE ROLE OF TARGET PRICING

That target pricing plays an important role among the concentrated manufacturing industries is clearly brought out in the recent Brookings study, *Pricing in Big Business*. This study included

[6] There has been a tendency among economists to confuse profit maximizing with value maximizing. Profit maximizing is the special case of value maximizing which occurs when the calculus does not involve a balancing of greater profits against greater risk. The calculus of classical monopoly pricing was concerned with this special case of profit maximizing. Target pricing is quite different because it involves the risk-of-entry factor. Technically the various factors in target pricing could be related in equation form, but when this is done the equation could not be differentiated to maximize profit but only to maximize value, i.e., to maximize the combination of profit and a risk factor. In the classical calculus, since no factor of risk is involved in the equations representing cost and revenue, the latter can be differentiated to maximize profit. This also maximizes value in the special case. This confusion of profit maximizing and value maximizing is evident in the National Bureau of Economic Research publication, *Cost Behavior and Price Policy* (New York, 1943), which shifts from a discussion of profit-maximizing to value maximizing without making clear that this shift involves a *departure* from profit maximizing except as a special case (pp. 274 and 275). See also Joel Dean, *op. cit.*, p. 29.

sixteen giant manufacturing companies, nine of which were found to be the price leader in its particular industry. And in *every* case of price leadership, price policy was found to center around target pricing. These corporations are listed below with their target rates (where known) and with the actual rate which they averaged in the nine years from 1947 to 1955.

Table 26—PRICE LEADERS IN MANUFACTURING INDUSTRY AND TARGET RATES OF RETURN

Price Leader	Target Rate of Return on Investment After Taxes	Actual Rate of Return on Investment After Taxes 1947–1955	
		Average	*Range*
General Motors	20%	26.0%	19.9–37.0%
DuPont	20% [a]	25.9%	19.6–34.1%
General Electric	20%	21.4%	18.4–26.6%
Union Carbide	18% [b]	19.2%	13.5–24.3%
Esso (Standard Oil Co., N.J.)	— [c]	16.0%	12.0–18.9%
Johns-Manville	15%	14.9%	10.7–19.6%
Alcoa	10%	13.8%	7.8–18.7%
International Harvester	10%	8.9%	4.9–11.9%
United States Steel	8% [d]	10.3%	7.6–14.8%

Source: R. F. Lanzillotti, "Pricing Objectives of Large Companies," *American Economic Review,* XLVIII, No. 5 (December, 1958), 921–940.

[a] While DuPont is known to be one of the pioneers of target pricing, its management was not willing to give Lanzillotti a specific target rate. The figure given above is consistent with actual profits and is believed to be correct for the period 1947 to 1955.

[b] An average given by Lanzillotti of rates employed by different divisions.

[c] Target rate not known.

[d] Presumably target rate in early part of period before the management decision to price for a larger rate of return. Target rate now appears to be closer to 16%.

It can be seen from the table that, with one exception, these price leaders in their respective industries managed to earn their target rates of return or better for the nine-year period.

The differences in target rate presumably reflect for the most part a greater or less fear that high prices and profit will interfere with healthy growth of the company, either by bringing new entrants into the market or by stimulating other changes which will limit future profits. In the case of United States Steel, the low target rate, since revised upward, may have been an outgrowth of the early decision to limit the growth and profits of U.S. Steel in order to avoid government intervention.[7]

PROFITS UNDER TARGET PRICING

Considerable variations in rates of return around the respective target rates are a natural result of the target pricing technique itself. The target rate is not a target for any particular year (unless that year turns out to be one of average demand). In years of business depression it is expected that successful target pricing will bring an actual rate of return on capital below the target rate, while years of boom are expected to produce actual rates of return above the target rate. It is only on the average with the ups and downs of business activity that actual earnings are expected to approximate the target rate.

Discrepancies between the target rate and the average rate of return actually realized could arise from several sources and would not indicate a failure of target pricing. For example, if national policy brought about a reduction in the depth of business recessions, a corporation's average rate of operation might turn out to be higher than the standard rate decided on. This would result in a higher average rate of return than the target rate. Also, inflation might create inventory profits which would be in addition to the profits aimed at in the target pricing. Nor is there reason to expect that the estimates involved in target pricing are so accurate that a very close approximation to the target is to be expected even when demand just supports the standard operating rate.

[7] See *Hearings*, p. 337.

THE ADAPTABILITY OF TARGET PRICING

So far the target pricing procedure has been described in rather rigid terms, but actually it is a very adaptable technique. A given price leader can establish different target rates for different product lines, as appears to be the case with the different divisions of Union Carbide. New products can be given a higher target rate than old and the latter may be given rather low target rates prior to discontinuance. Also, the target pricing technique does not prevent a corporation from pricing to meet competition.

At the same time target pricing provides management with a powerful tool of administration. The target rate of return and the standard rate of operation to be used in target pricing can be decided upon at the top level of management. This can be done for all the output of a company or separate rates can be decided on for different lines or for new and old. Once these decisions have been made at the top level, the detail of the remainder of the target pricing procedure can be carried out at lower levels. Then only when the market analysis at the lower level indicates a price different from the target price, does the proposed price decision need to be reviewed at higher levels. This helps to decentralize the detail of pricing where a large number of separate items have to be priced.

Also, this procedure can be of great aid to top management in checking on the operation of separate divisions or sections. If, under conditions of average business activity, a particular division fails to make its target rate of return on that part of the corporation's capital which it is using, the top management is put on notice and can investigate and determine whether this failure is due to abnormal conditions; a product that should be discontinued; poor management; or some other factor. In the same way, when average business conditions prevail and a division makes more than the target rate, top management can investigate to see whether the higher rate reflects unusually able management, abnor mal conditions, a market which could be more effectively exploited at a lower price, or what.

Even when business conditions are not average, target pricing can be an aid to management. In a depression, a division cannot be expected to make a rate of return equal to the target rate but it should be making a certain calculable proportion of the target rate so that doing better or worse than this proportion would be a signal to higher management. Similarily, in a boom, a division should make more than the target rate but in a certain ratio to that rate so that profits above or below the appropriate ratio to the target would provide a management signal.

Thus, for a price leader, target pricing provides both an effective technique for pricing to get the most profits consistent with long run growth and an effective instrument for simultaneously decentralizing the administration of prices and centralizing management control. It appears to be a common procedure for the price leaders of big business when operating under the conditions of administrative competition and possible but difficult entry.

PRICE FOLLOWING

Under administrative competition and difficult entry, the big price follower usually has little control over price. Ordinarily, whatever price is set by the price leader will be accepted by the price follower with standard differentials for geographical and quality differences. If the follower's costs are less than those of the leader, the follower can average a higher rate of return than the target rate of the leader. The less efficient or less well located follower can be expected to make a lower rate. But so long as the other big companies in an industry follow the leader, employ substantially the same techniques of production and draw from similar supplies of raw materials and have to pay substantially the same prices for labor, their profits are likely to fall in the same general magnitude.

Occasionally a sharp break in technology, such as the continuous strip rolling mill or the use of oxygen in steel furnaces, can so cut costs that profits of the producer introducing the technique are high relative to others. But when the improved technique becomes general, it will be reflected in the target price of the price leader. Also, such a cost reduction can sometimes convert a price follower into a price leader for a particular product. Sometimes a big habitual price follower may conclude that the prices set by the leader are too high and refuse to follow. Then the leader is likely to reduce his prices "to meet competition" and the habitual follower sets the pattern of prices for the time being. But usually the big price follower has little choice but to adopt or adjust to the prices set by the price leader.

The small producer in an industry of giants is likely to be in quite a different position. Geography or specialization may yield him an advantage over the giants while their prices provide an umbrella for his operation. If he cuts price to obtain business in his own locality or specialty, particularly when demand is slack, the giants may not alter their prices. Similarly, in periods of high demand the small producer may raise his prices above those of the giants. But so long as the production of the small companies does not cut too seriously into the share of the market served by the big companies, the latter may take little or no account of the price action of small and local producers. Advertising and other forms of nonprice competition and a steady improvement in product may be relied on by the big companies to hold their share of the market.

THE PRICE-STABILIZING EFFECT OF TARGET PRICING

Because target prices are dominated by longer-run considerations and do not seek to maximize profits in the current pricing period, they tend to be more stable in the presence of business fluctuations. The pricing objective is not even to make a specified rate of return in each year but only to make the target rate of return *on the average* over a period of years.

Under a perfect operation of target pricing, prices would not be influenced by short-run fluctuations in demand. If operating expenses per unit remained constant and the volume of capital required was unchanged, a fall in demand would not call for a reduction in price. Nor would a rise in demand call for an increase in price. Only as a boom increased the prices paid for materials and labor, or a recession reduced their prices, would business fluctuations as such call for changes in price. With wage rates relatively insensitive to changes in the volume of employment and many raw material prices selling at administered prices and relatively insensitive to business fluctuations, target pricing can lead to prices which are quite insensitive to boom and recession.

In practice, other factors enter into pricing than the target rate of return at a standard rate of operation and the *principle* of target pricing is only approximated. But the relative insensitivity of prices to business fluctuations is apparent where target pricing is employed. Thus in the case of steel, it is not possible from the index of steel prices since 1945 to determine which years were years of recession and which were years of higher demand.

THE TARGET-PRICING SHORT CUT AND BUILT-IN INFLATION

Closely associated with target pricing is a short-cut formula for taking target prices and adjusting them for changes in operating costs. This short-cut formula may be an outgrowth of a statement by Donaldson Brown in his 1924 presentation of the logic of target pricing. In his own words: "Prices of products should change, in the absence of extraneous considerations, with changes in raw material and labor prices."[8] Presumably with this dictum in mind and perhaps misinterpreting it, a formula has been developed for

[8] Quoted in *Price Practices and Price Policies: Selected Writings,* Jules Backman (New York: Ronald Press, 1953), p. 361.

revising the target price when there is a change in material and labor prices. The formula is simple and calls for a change in price from time to time related solely to the price changes of materials and labor. At the time of arriving at a target price, estimates of the material costs per unit and estimates of the labor cost per unit are made. Let us say that 30 per cent of the target price would go to cover material costs and 40 per cent to cover labor costs. Then, if an index of material prices goes up 10 per cent, add 10 per cent of the 30 per cent, or 3 per cent, to the target price in order to get the new target price. Likewise, if the price of labor goes up 10 per cent, add 10 per cent of 40 per cent, or 4 per cent, to the target price. If both of these happened the target price would be raised by the sum of the 3 and the 4 per cent, or 7 per cent. With an initial target price of $1.00, the new target price would be $1.07.

This is a simple formula to apply and on its face it would seem to be a proper way to follow the principles of target pricing so as to adjust for changes in the prices of materials and labor. Indeed, this would be an appropriate procedure if there were no changes in the efficiency with which materials or labor were used.

But if increased efficiency in the use of materials or labor reduces real costs, a formula which adjusts the target price for changes in material and labor *prices* without adjusting for such increase in efficiency becomes an instrument of administrative inflation. It provides a built-in source of inflation that bears no relation to changes in demand and no relation to changes in actual costs per unit of product.

This built-in inflation effect arises because the adjustment formula is in terms of the *prices* of material and of labor, not the *costs* of materials and labor per unit of output. For example, suppose that, in a period, the price of labor per hour goes up 5 per cent and output per hour of labor also goes up 5 per cent. Obviously, the labor cost per unit has not changed. If the regular target pricing procedure were employed there would be no reason to increase the price of the product because of the increase in wage rates. Yet the short-cut adjustment formula would indicate a price increase. The same would be true if the increase in efficiency took the form of using less material per unit of product. Thus, if redesigning a product saved 5 per cent of the steel used in making it and the price of steel went up 5 per cent, there would be no significant change in the cost of steel in the product, and the 5 per cent increase in steel price would not justify the increase in price which the short-cut formula would call for. Thus, the application of the short-cut formula would create a steady rise in price as long as there was increasing efficiency in the use of materials and labor.

How extensively the short-cut formula is used is not clear. It is certainly used for some more routine pricing tasks and for some short-run purposes. Even in the steel hearings, the argument of the steel companies in defense of their price increases ran in terms of the short-cut formula with no attention to increasing efficiency. In Part I, this has been treated as an effort to confuse the issues, on the assumption that the leaders in the steel industry have the business acumen to distinguish between changes in the *prices* of materials and labor on the one hand and, on the other, the *cost* of materials and labor per unit of output. But where big business requires the delegation of decision making and the use of simplified formulas, it would not be surprising if the short-cut formula was extensively used.

ADMINISTRATIVE COMPETITION WITHOUT TARGET PRICING

Target pricing would seem to be the most logical pricing procedure when competition is between a few producers and entry is possible but difficult. However, it is a relatively new procedure. Though its use has been expanding since it was first adopted by DuPont and General Motors, there are undoubtedly many cases of administrative competition in which it is the appropriate procedure for pricing but a cruder procedure is actually employed. And there may be other situations of administrative competition and difficult entry where target pricing is not appropriate. Thus, where a particular producer has to set prices on a large number of individual and relatively inexpensive items, a standard markup over costs may be employed because of the labor saving involved and even though the target rate of return procedure, if applied to each item separately, might, in theory, produce a somewhat different and more satisfactory result.[9]

On the whole, however, target pricing is so logically sound from the point of view of the profit seeking enterprise, that even where it is not actually employed the methods that are employed must tend to approximate those of target pricing where the price leader or price maker aims at prices which will strike a successful balance between greater current profits and greater risk of new entry. For this reason, target pricing will be treated in the remainder of this book as the principle which is appropriate in the price determination of manufacturing industry where conditions of administrative competition prevail and entry is possible but difficult.

[9] The difference would result primarily from the fact that in the standard markup an average capital charge would be made to each category of product without consideration of the amount of capital involved in its production, whereas in the target-pricing procedure the capital involved would have to be calculated for each category of product separately. The same material and labor costs per unit would presumably be used in either case.

PART IV

THE LOGIC OF COLLECTIVE ENTERPRISE

CHAPTER XIV

THE BIG BUSINESS DILEMMA

And the fact is—and this is a very important fact, even if it is a fact in the realm of philosophy—the only fully and systematically articulated doctrine of economics, indeed, one which is widely accepted—holds that big business is monopolistic. In the realms of theory and ideology, the big corporation is still a deviant from the ideal minute atom of classical doctrine. One of the ironies of our time— and this may come as a shock to many administrators of big business —is that still, at this late date, there does not exist a fully developed logic which reconciles and integrates the big corporation with the very basic, traditional justification of laissez-faire capitalism. Nor, has there been developed a new philosophy of laissez-faire capitalism that does provide positively for big business. Men who are practical men of affairs should not underestimate the importance of that fact of the realm of ideas.

PROFESSOR JOHN D. GLOVER,

HARVARD BUSINESS SCHOOL*

In a stirring defense of bigness in business, David E. Lilienthal, an outstanding liberal, has said:

> The argument about what is big enough and what is too big, I regard, generally, as not the central issue. My concern here is with establishing to the fullest of a *climate of opportunity for growth and attainment of size,* as a means of greater productivity, better distribution of goods and income, and greater well-being for the country.[1]

---

* *The Attack on Big Business* (Boston: Division of Research, Graduate School of Business Administration, Harvard University, 1954), p. 13.

[1] *Big Business: A New Era* (New York: Harper & Brothers, 1953), p. 36. Emphasis in the original.

He reached this conclusion on the basis of his own experience as chairman of the Tennessee Valley Authority, then the largest integrated power system in the world, and on his experience as chairman of the Atomic Energy Commission, the largest industrial monopoly in the country. In both experiences, he saw the productivity possible with bigness. And in both instances what he saw was efficiency not coupled with a drive for profits. The likelihood that the pricing power which goes with bigness would be used contrary to the public interest was small.

In big business as it has developed we have the potentials of high productivity coupled with the profit drive. This creates the possibility, indeed the probability, that pricing power will be used contrary to the public interest.

Faced with this situation, those who, like the present author, seek the maintenance and improvement of the free-enterprise system have developed two opposing creeds, neither wholly satisfactory.[2] It is said that American management must choose between the classical profit creed on the one hand or a new creed of social responsibility on the other.

The private profit creed focuses on the big corporation as a private enterprise. It says to business management: your function in society is to make profits for your corporation. Profits provide your measuring stick and goal. If market forces do not wholly guide your actions to serve the public interest and the drive for profits leads to exploitation, the advantages of a clear, familiar, and simply defined goal more than outweigh the departure from the public interest.

The social responsibility creed focuses on the big corporation as a social institution. It says to business management: your function in society is to run your corporation in the public interest, serving the welfare of the owners, employees, suppliers, customers,

---

[2] For a discussion of these two creeds, see Gerhard Andlinger, "The Crucible of Our Business Creeds," *Business Horizons,* Indiana University, II, No. 3 (Fall, 1959).

and the public. This is your measuring stick and goal. If, within the guidance of market forces, the goal is vague and difficult to measure, these disadvantages are more than outweighed by the superiority of the goal.

Obviously, neither of these two creeds is wholly satisfactory. If we did have to choose between them in order to preserve free enterprise there would be a difficult choice to make. But are these the only alternatives? Can we not find in the logic of collective enterprise itself a third alternative which has neither the danger of exploitation involved in the private profit creed nor the vagueness and complexity involved in the creed of social responsibility?

Let us follow the logic of collective enterprise and see where it takes us.

CHAPTER XV

PROPERTY AND PROFIT

To Adam Smith and to his followers, private property was a unity involving possession. He assumed that ownership and control were combined. Today, in the modern corporation, this unity has been broken. Passive property,—*specifically shares of stock or bonds,— gives its possessors an interest in an enterprise but gives them practically no control over it, and involves no responsibility.* Active property, *—plant, good will, organization, and so forth which make up the actual enterprise,—is controlled by individuals who, almost invariably, have only minor ownership interests in it.*

The explosion of the atom of property destroys the basis of the old assumption that the quest for profits will spur the owner of industrial property to its effective use.

A. A. BERLE, JR., and

G. C. MEANS*

One characteristic of collective enterprise which makes it fundamentally different from the private enterprise of traditional theory is the separation of ownership and control. As is well known, the widespread dispersion of stock ownership, and the development of the proxy machinery have operated to remove the stockholder from significant control over the corporate enterprise. At the same time it has, as a practical matter, placed ultimate control over the enterprise in the hands of a management which owns only a small fraction of the outstanding stock.

* *The Modern Corporation and Private Property* (New York: The Macmillan Company, 1932), pp. 347 and 9.

This separation is clearly evident, for example, in the case of the United States Steel Corporation. In 1958 there were 311,000 stockholders, no person owning as much as two-tenths of 1 per cent of the total stock.[1] In May, 1957, the combined holdings of the management, including the board of directors and the chief officers, amounted to about one-fifth of one per cent of the outstanding stock.[2]

In this situation, the management becomes a self-perpetuating body so long as it runs the corporation reasonably well. As a routine matter, new directors are nominated by the board of directors or a committee created by it and elected by the proxies collected from stockholders almost automatically and at company expense.

Only occasionally do the stockholders have a choice of approving slates. A strong group of stockholders outside management may seek to wrest control from the existing management and a proxy fight ensues. But a proxy fight in a big corporation is expensive and the management can use the corporation treasury to finance its side of the fight. Livingstone in his study, *The American Stockholder,* finds among 3000 corporations an average of eighteen such fights a year.[3] For a single corporation this would average out to a fight every 167 years. And for corporations with stock as widely dispersed as that of United States Steel, the likelihood of such a fight would be even more remote. For the immediate analysis the possibility of such "palace revolutions" can be disregarded, although we shall return to it later.

We shall also disregard for the immediate analysis that small proportion of the corporate stock which is owned by management. This holding, though small in proportion, may be large in absolute magnitude and can influence management behavior. Thus, in 1957,

[1] As of December 31, 1958. *Annual Report of United States Steel Corporation,* 1958, p. 21.
[2] *Hearings,* p. 1030.
[3] Joseph A. Livingstone, *The American Stockholder* (Philadelphia: J. B. Lippincott, 1958), pp. 46-47.

the one-fifth of 1 per cent of United States Steel's stock had a market value of $8 million. The largest holding by any one member of management, that of the president, had a market value of just over $2 million.[4] These holdings must be considered later in examining motivation. For the moment, let us carry the separation to the extreme.

THE PURE CASE OF COMPLETE SEPARATION OF OWNERSHIP AND CONTROL

Suppose then that we have a complete separation of ownership and control—a corporation in which stockholders have no control over the board of directors and in which the directors and other members of top management own no stock except the single share that may be required to qualify a person for the position of director. How would this situation relate to the traditional logic of private enterprise?

The great economic justification for protecting property rights in private enterprise is the serving of the public interest. This service arises from two main sources. By protecting the enterpriser in the profits he can make, he is induced to risk his capital in productive enterprise. And by protecting the enterpriser in the profits he can make, he is under inducement to manage his enterprise economically so as to increase his profits. With both capital and economical management induced by the drive for profits and with classical competition to control the level of profits, it was expected that the public interest would be served.

But this dual driving power of profit-seeking required that substantially the same persons provide the risk-taking capital and the ultimate management. In small private enterprise these two usually go together. The owner not only risks his capital but he dominates the enterprise. It is his initiative that finds new products to make. It is his initiative that seeks out new markets. And it is his

---

[4] *Hearings,* pp. 1030, 1032.

initiative that squeezes down costs. The owner may delegate particular functions to others but he controls the enterprise. He is typically the fountainhead of the drive for profits and his profits are rewards for supplying both the risk taking capital and the initiating drive of management. It is to such private enterprises that the traditional logics of property and profits apply.[5]

Collective enterprise divides this double role. Where ownership and control are completely separate, one group supplies capital and has the ownership interest in the enterprise; another group supplies the initiating management and has the actual power over the enterprise. Ownership and control have been separated and rest in different hands. This raises the basic question: In whose interest should such a collective enterprise be run and who should get the profits?

THE TRADITIONAL LOGIC OF PROPERTY

The traditional logic of property derives from the law and according to this logic, a corporation should be run for the benefit of its owners, the stockholders. In the eyes of the law, the corporate enterprise is a machine for making profit and this profit belongs to the owners. "From earliest time the owner of property has been entitled to the full use or disposal of his property and in these rights the owner has been protected by law.[6] Since to its owner, the use of industrial property consists primarily of an effort to increase its value—to make a profit—the owner in being entitled to its full use, has been entitled to all accretions to its value—to all profits it could be made to earn. In so far as he had to pay for the services of other men or other property in order to accomplish this increase in value, these payments operated as deductions; the profit remaining to him was the difference between the added value

[5] For a more extended discussion of the traditional logics of property and profits see Book IV of Berle and Means, *op. cit.*

[6] Except as impaired by the exercise of police power by the state. (Footnote in original.)

and the cost of receiving these services. To this difference, the owner was traditionally entitled. The state and the law have sought to protect him in this right.[7]

Also according to the traditional logic of property, it is clear that the powers of management are powers in trust. Under this logic, the function of the controlling management is to manage a corporation for the benefit of the owners.

"The result accordingly is that the profits of the enterprise, so far as the law is concerned, belong to the security holders *in toto.* Division of these profits among the various groups of security holders is a matter of private agreement, but they, between them, have the complete right to all the profits which the corporation has made. Not only that; they are entitled to those profits which the management in reasonable exercise of its powers ought to make. They have a further right that no one shall become a security holder except upon a suitable contribution to the corporate assets —that is, that the security holding group shall be a group of persons who have committed actual property to the administration of the management and control of the corporation."[8] This is the conclusion which results when the logic of property, based on private enterprise, is applied to collective enterprises in which the two essential attributes of private enterprise are divided through the separation of ownership and control.

But are we justified in applying the old logic to the new situation? Because an owner who exercises control over his wealth is fully protected, does it *necessarily* follow that an owner who has surrendered control of his wealth should likewise be protected to the full. May not this surrender of control have so essentially changed his relation to the wealth in enterprise as to have changed the logic applicable to his interest in that wealth? Does it serve the public interest to have the great collective enterprise operated by trustees who have only a minor proportion of the ownership

---

[7] Berle and Means, *op. cit.,* p. 334.
[8] *Ibid.,* pp. 337, 338.

interest and are in only a minor degree or not at all subject to control by the "owners"?

THE TRADITIONAL LOGIC OF PROFIT

The economist, considering this same problem starts from a different background and with a set of interests essentially different from those of the law. His interest is not primarily in the protection of man in his own, but in the production and distribution of what man desires. He is concerned, not with property but with the production of wealth and the distribution of income. To him property rights are attributes which may be attached to wealth by society, and he regards them and their protection, not as the inalienable right of the individual or as an end in themselves, but as a means to a socially desirable end—"a plentiful revenue and subsistence" for the people.

With this more basic approach, a long line of economists has developed the justification for private enterprise in what can be called the traditional logic of profits. As we have already seen, economic justification for protecting the profits of private enterprise rests on the power of profit seeking (1) to induce the individual to risk his wealth in profit-seeking enterprise, and (2) to spur the individual to exercise his utmost skill in making his enterprise profitable. Thus, when ownership and control are combined, the logic of profit reinforces the logic of property.

But when ownership and control are separated, the logic of profit does not coincide with that of property. While the logic of property assigns all the profits to owners, the logic of profit says that both the risking of capital and the exercise of good management need to be stimulated and that any profits over and above those necessary to induce the supplying of capital should go to the controlling management.

In order to bring out this logic let us compare two situations in one of which a big collective enterprise is run for the benefit of stockholders and the other in which the same enterprise is run for the benefit of the controlling managers. For simplicity, let us say that the stock held by the public is all nonvoting and that the directors of the corporation each own a single share of voting stock, thus control the corporation and have no fear of a proxy fight by public stockholders.

In this situation we can expect that the directors who run the enterprise as trustees for the benefit of stockholders would seek to run it profitably, and to this end would presumably set up a system of profit sharing for the top officers in order to provide them with an incentive to operate economically and thereby make high profits for the stockholders. If the directors were skillful, they would adjust the management share in profits to that level which could be expected to produce the largest net profit to stockholders *after* the payment of management's share. Let us say that in these circumstances, profits would average 10 per cent on the investment out of which one-half a percentage point would go to management and 9.5 percentage points would remain for stockholders.

Contrast this with the situation in which the management runs the enterprise to maximize its own profits, not those of the stockholders. In this case they could be expected to adopt a bonus system in which all profits over some minimum amount for stockholders would go to management. The courts would undoubtedly find such a bonus system inconsistent with the trustee responsibility of management. But here we are concerned not with the law but with the economic effect. Presumably the minimum amount to stockholders would be whatever return on their investment was necessary in order to make it possible to raise additional capital from time to time. In a very real sense this return would be the wages of capital. The *safety* of the limited return to stockholders would be greatly increased, both by its preferred position over the profits going to management and by the fact that management would be under great incentive to make profits more than enough to meet the stockholder requirements. In fact, the common stock would become more like a preferred stock. At the same time, to the extent that profits would be an incentive to good management, as the logic of profit implies, the greater prospects of profits to management could be expected to lead to better management and larger profits. Let us say, following this logic, that because of the greater profit incentive the rate of profits earned would be 14 per cent instead of 10 per cent, half of which would go to management and half remain for stockholders.

Comparison of these two alternatives makes it clear that if the classical logic of profits applies to the new situation of separate ownership and control, i.e., *if* (1) the public interest is best served when corporate management is under the heaviest inducement to make profit, and *if* (2) the prospect of additional profits provides additional inducement to manage well, then the public interest would be better served if profits over and above those necessary to assure new capital were to go to management instead of stockholders. Greater profits to stockholders would not provide *more* capital *if all the capital needed* were already available when the profits to stockholders were less. They would serve no more economic purpose than, say, paying above the market price for cotton or wheat. On the other hand greater profits to management could, *at least in classical logic,* be some stimulus to better management.

THE CASE OF INCOMPLETE SEPARATION OF OWNERSHIP AND CONTROL

Before examining this somewhat shocking conclusion reached from applying the traditional logic of profits to collective enterprise, we must clear up one matter. This logic has been applied to a situation in which separation of ownership and control is complete. Does it apply equally where management owns a small proportion of the outstanding stock and where stockholders can bring about a palace revolution through supporting outsiders in a proxy fight?

First, it is clear that if the management owns only a small proportion of the outstanding stock the conclusion still holds. If management operates a collective enterprise as trustee for the stockholders and owns a small proportion of the outstanding stock, this could be expected to reinforce a profit-sharing arrangement in giving management an incentive to make the enterprise profitable. But such reinforcing would be small compared to the incentive from profit sharing. For example, if management owned one-tenth of 1 per cent of the outstanding stock and received 5 per cent of the profits as bonuses, the bonus incentive would be fifty times that of the ownership incentive. Extra profits to *all* stockholders in order to give the management this small extra incentive would be a wasteful way of obtaining the extra incentive. On the other hand, if the enterprise were run for the benefit of management, the ownership of stock would be irrelevant. All the possible incentive to management to maximize profits would already be provided. Thus, unless management holdings are a fairly large proportion of the total outstanding, the traditional logic of profits leads to the conclusion that only the wages of capital should go to the shareholders and any additional profits should go to provide incentives to management.

The same conclusion applies, even when stockholders have some residual powers over the corporation, though the practical outcome might be different under present conditions. If stockholders had full voting rights, a management which explicitly adopted a profit-sharing arrangement giving it all profits over the necessary minimum for stockholders would quickly find itself in a proxy fight which it was likely to lose. And even without power to vote, an explicit profit-sharing plan of this sort might well be outlawed by the courts as a breach of trust.[9] But neither of these

[9] It should be recognized that a management that sought its own maximum profit would not in present circumstances, employ the overt profit

possible developments would alter the basic conclusion reached when the traditional logic of profits is applied to the new situation. It simply helps to underline the fact that the traditional logic of property and that of profits produce conflicting results when applied to collective enterprise.

THE NEED FOR A NEW APPROACH

Faced with these conflicting conclusions, we need to re-examine the foundations of each logic.

Fundamental to the logic of property is the fact that it was developed to apply to property in which ownership and control are in the same hands. But in the collective enterprise, the owners by surrendering control and responsibility over the enterprise have surrendered the right that the enterprise should be operated in their sole interest—they have released the community from the obligation to protect them to the full extent implied in the doctrine of strict property rights.

But equally suspect is the logic of profits. Fundamental to this logic is the fact that it was developed to apply to enterprises whose profits were controlled by classical competition. Yet it is a characteristic of big collective enterprise that it is too big to allow classical competition to operate. As we shall see, this fact undermines the application of the logic of profits just as effectively as the separation of ownership and control undermines the logic of property. The next chapter will examine the failure of the unregulated profit drive to serve the public interest where big collective enterprise is concerned.

---

plan suggested above but would use many possible devices to increase its share in profits which would be more difficult to attack in the courts or use as the basis of a proxy fight.

CHAPTER XVI

THE PROFIT DRIVE AND THE PUBLIC INTEREST

The public be damned.

CORNELIUS VANDERBILT,
CHAIRMAN OF THE BOARD,
NEW YORK CENTRAL RAILROAD*

We of management are responsible to manage the business in accordance with our judgment as to what will best serve the long-term interests of: the employees whose livelihood is dependent upon the Corporation; the stockholders whose invested money provides the tools of production and jobs; the customers who buy our products and thus provide employment; and the people of the consuming public who depend upon steel as one of the basic commodities of modern life.

WALTER F. MUNFORD,
PRESIDENT,
UNITED STATES STEEL CORPORATION**

While the size of the collective enterprise and the dispersion of its stock have raised the fundamental issue of who should receive the residual profits, an even more fundamental issue is that of whether the drive for corporate profits is itself an effective social instrument where collective enterprise is concerned. We have already seen why it could be expected that, under the conditions of classical competition, the public interest would be served if each enterprise were operated to make as much profit as possible. Also, we have seen that where there is difficult entry, it is logical for pricing power to be used according to the principle

* Reply to a newspaper reporter, *circa* 1883.
** *The United States Steel Quarterly,* August, 1959, p. 3.

of target pricing. It is the purpose of this chapter to consider to what extent target pricing under the drive for corporate profits could be expected to serve the public interest.

In our analysis of classical competition we singled out four major ways in which the profit drive when controlled by classical competition could be expected to serve the public interest. It could be expected to result in:

1. Prices in reasonable relation to costs
2. The division of income according to contribution
3. Optimum use of resources
4. Pressure for improving technology

Let us take up each of these in turn and consider whether this result could be expected with target pricing under the drive for corporate profits.

PRICES AND COSTS

It must be clear that where entry is difficult, as it must be if a single big enterprise is more efficient than a number of small units, target pricing under the drive for profits can be expected to result in prices that are above a reasonable relation to costs. In these circumstances, it is the purpose of target pricing both to provide a rate of return higher than the competitive cost of capital and to preserve such a higher rate from attrition by new entrants. How much higher prices are likely to be will depend on the height of the stone-wall impediment to entry and on the particular circumstances. But that it can be considerable is easily shown.

Take, for example, a product requiring $1.00 of capital per unit of output and requiring $1.00 per unit at a standard rate of operation to cover all costs including labor, materials, overhead and depreciation. Then, with federal income taxes taking approximately half of corporate income, a price of $1.16 would be required to yield a 16 per cent return on capital before taxes and provide an 8 per cent return on capital after taxes at the standard rate of operation. However, if a target rate of return of 20 per cent after taxes were the objective a price of $1.40 would be required. In this particular case, if the competitive cost of capital were 8 per cent, a target rate of 20 per cent would require a price 24 cents higher than that necessary to yield a competitive rate of return. This would mean a 20 per cent premium over the economical price.

The premium would, of course, vary with the ratio of costs per unit and capital per unit at the standard rate of operation. If only 50 cents of capital were required for every $1.00 of costs, then an 8 per cent return after taxes would be achieved at a price of $1.08 and a 20 per cent return at a price of $1.20, or a premium of 11 per cent.

It will be found that many if not most of the big manufacturing corporations fall between these two situations so far as the ratio of capital to cost is concerned. Thus, in 1957 when it operated at 85 per cent of capacity, the United States Steel Corporation had over 80 cents of capital per $1.00 of its total costs.[1]

Of course, half of any price premium goes to the federal government in taxes and this is sometimes used to justify premium prices and profits. But one can hardly justify charging customers a premium, only half of which goes to the government, as a means of collecting taxes. It is too much like adding a sales tax and paying half of the proceeds to the tax collector.

If the corporate income tax were entirely eliminated, the difference in price arising from a premium target rate of return would not be so spectacular. But even then a 20 per cent target rate would call for an 11 per cent price premium if $1.00 of capital investment was required for each $1.00 of costs at a standard rate of operation and capital were readily available at a competitive return of 8 per cent.

How great the price premiums are in practice could only be discovered by extensive empirical studies and a clarification of

[1] U.S. Steel Corp., *Annual Report,* 1958.

the disputed issues involved in measurement, but some light can be thrown on the question by considering what a competitive rate of return on capital might be.

First, it should be clear that neither the actual rates of return on capital now being earned by the big corporations nor the value placed on their earnings by the stock market is a good guide to the competitive cost of capital. Actual earning rates are inappropriate because our aim is to test whether or not they are competitive. The stock market valuation of earnings is inappropriate because other factors than the rate of current earnings affect market values. The fact that a particular stock sells for twenty times earnings is likely to reflect expected growth almost as much as the current rate of earnings.

Some light can be thrown on the question of a competitive rate by the experience of the regulated public utilities. As we have seen, the commissions have regulated prices and thereby limited profits in the public interest. The commissions have recognized that any business involves risk and that the prospective rate of return on capital must be enough higher than the riskless rate of interest to induce capital to take this risk. Over a period of years, the commissions have gravitated toward a 6 to 6.5 per cent return (after taxes) on the capital "used and useful in the public interest." And when utilities have been able to make this return on investment they have had no serious difficulty in raising new capital for expansion. Indeed, in spite of the fact that some utilities such as the traction companies and some of the railroads have lost money, the investment of private savings in the public utilities subject to this regulation has been very great since the war. From 1946 to 1956 thirty-six utilities raised more than $17 billion in the capital markets, more than half of it through the sale of stocks.[2] The probabilities of a return greater than that on virtually

[2] Source: *Financial Data for 300 Large Corporations* (mimeo.), Board of Governors of the Federal Reserve System, October, 1953, and subsequent compilations.

riskless investments has more than made up for the extra risk.

It may well be that the risks involved in such well established collective enterprises as those in electric equipment, steel and other concentrated manufacturing industries, are greater than those of the utility industry. Perhaps the expectation of an average return of 8 per cent (after taxes) would be sufficient to bring forward new capital to be invested in such enterprises.[3] Perhaps a lower rate would be sufficient or perhaps a higher rate would be necessary to bring forth the needed capital. The appropriate rates could only be determined by experience as the market cost of capital became established. But what few will question is that the after-tax target rates of 16 and 20 per cent and the actual earnings in excess of these targets are well above a competitive rate of return. Prices set to achieve these targets must involve substantial premiums over costs, taxes and a legitimate rate of return. To this extent, the public interest is not served by the profit drive as the guiding force in the big collective enterprise, however well the profit drive may serve where enterprise is small and competition is classical.

The conclusion seems justified that where entry is difficult and the rates aimed at under target pricing are set under the drive for corporate profit, not only are prices likely to be set above the level which is in the public interest but the discrepancy can be substantial.

THE DIVISION OF INCOME

It also follows that target pricing under the profit drive can be expected to distort the distribution of income. A premium price

[3] It should be noted that the 8 per cent referred to above would be an average rate on the total investment, not the rate on equity investment. If part of the capital of a collective enterprise were borrowed at lower rates, then more risky equity capital could yield higher rates and still have the average return on capital "used and useful in the public interest" at a competitive average comparable to the 6 to 6.5 per cent of the public utilities.

and profit mean that the income to investors exceeds their contribution as measured by the competitive cost of capital. If, in fact, capital is available that will take commensurate risks at an 8 per cent return and the pricing power of big business is used to set prices which yield 16 per cent, the investors are getting through dividends and appreciation much more than is commensurate with their contribution to production. If the price premium were eliminated by a price reduction, the real income of all users would be increased to a small extent. But as long as the premium income is being made it results in an inequitable division of income.

It is sometimes argued that premium profits are justified because they provide capital for expansion and for research and development. There is no question that retained earnings do provide an easy way to obtain capital.

To the extent that earnings are legitimate, their retention in the enterprise may be an economical way to raise capital. Studies by the statisticians of the New York Stock Exchange show that it costs the listed big companies $2.60 per hundred of capital to raise it through the open sale of common stocks.[4] It is likely to be even more expensive for a corporation to offer securities to existing shareholders at a discount through rights than to sell in the open market.[5] These costs are saved if capital is obtained by not distributing all of a corporation's earnings in dividends. This is usually acceptable to stockholders since earnings that are plowed back into the business provide a basis for future earnings and dividends. And to this extent the public interest is served.

However it is quite another matter to overcharge customers in order to obtain capital. If premium profits are made and *all* the premium is added to capital, this is, in effect getting the customers to supply the capital and giving the stockholders the benefit of the future earnings. If the customers are overcharged to supply capital and given an equivalent amount of stock to

---

[4] Economic Research Memorandum of June, 1957.
[5] See J. A. Livingstone, *op. cit.*, p. 211.

represent their interest, this might be reasonable. In fact it is often done in cooperatives which withhold the patronage savings of customers and give stock certificates in lieu of patronage dividends. But it is difficult to see how the need for capital can justify charging a premium to customers and crediting this capital to the account of stockholders. Even less can a premium price be justified as a source of capital when only part of the premium profits are kept as capital and a part are distributed to stockholders as dividends.

Yet unregulated big business has almost ceased to draw on the capital market for capital through the sale of stocks. In the seven-year period, 1950 to 1956 two-hundred large manufacturing corporations added $19 billion to their net capital, but $17 billion was by the reinvestment of earnings and by net borrowing while only $2 billion was by the sale of stocks, or less than 7 per cent.[6] In contrast thirty-six large public utilities made a net addition to their capital of $14 billion, of which $7.5 billion or more than half was from the sale of preferred and common stocks. The big manufacturing corporations have simply not used the stock market as a significant source of capital in spite of the large number of willing buyers of corporate stock. This defeats the will to save in equities and thus fails to make use of this important source of capital.

Moreover the premium income to investors is likely to aggravate labor-management relations. It is one of the myths of traditional economic theory that before the formation of unions, wage rates were *determined* by the supply and demand for labor. This grows out of the traditional treatment of labor as a commodity and the failure to recognize that under the factory system and even more under the system of collective enterprise, wage rates tend to be

---

[6] Source: *Financial Data for 300 Large Corporations, op. cit.* The compilation of large manufacturing corporations includes 202 corporations from 1950 to 1952 and 196 from 1953 to 1956. Net capital is measured as total assets less current liabilities. The thirty-six public utilities include one communication corporation.

administered. In the absence of labor organization, the wage rates are set by management and are likely to be only very crudely related to the equating of the supply and the demand for labor. Labor organization makes the administration of wage rates bilateral; it does not convert classically competitive prices for labor into administered prices.

For the present purposes, the most important modification introduced by the presence of strong labor organization is in the power struggle which develops between union and management. If managemnt operates under the profit drive and uses its pricing power to make premium profits, why should not unions use their power to make premium wages? The demand from a profit-driving management that labor be "reasonable" in its demands can be regarded as either part of the sound effects of collective bargaining or as self-serving. And the presence of premium profits not only justifies the demand for premium wages but as has already been suggested, it provides a very specific target. That wage increases can be passed on in higher prices so that the premium profits are not reduced makes the premium profits no less a source of labor pressure. Thus the profit drive combined with target pricing can not only produce significant inequity but, perhaps even more important, it can contribute to the disruption of industrial relations. Both conflict with the public interest.

THE OPTIMUM USE OF RESOURCES

The third major result to be expected from classical competition is the optimum use of resources. Within the framework of income distribution and use of resources established by government, classically competitive prices were expected to guide the profit-driven enterprises into making the best possible use of resources. Within the enterprise, the effort to make more profit would lead the individual producer to combine the resources available to him in the most economical manner. And between enterprises, relative prices would guide both producers and consumers to direct their activities in ways to obtain the most from the available resources. Can these results be expected to flow from the profit drive in the presence of the pricing power of big business?

Let us first consider the use of resources within the collective enterprise.

So far as wasting resources in the operation of a given plant or set of plants is concerned, the profit drive can be a reasonably effective incentive, though perhaps not as effective as under classical competition. Where an enterprise is easily able to make a high target rate of return, a reduction in costs could be expected to lead, not to higher profits, but to a lower price. However, a lower price can be expected to expand the market and so give opportunity for a greater amount of profitable investment. Thus the profit drive would provide an inducement to reduce costs. Also where it is not initially possible to make the target rate, either because of low demand or because of the prices of competitors, there will be great pressure to reduce costs. Thus the profit drive can be expected to stimulate economical use of resources within the given plants.

In addition, the profit drive can be expected to keep new entrants to a minimum and so avoid the competitive wastes of overbuilding capacity and fractionation of the market that could be expected with administrative competition and easy entry.

On the other hand the effect of target pricing under the profit drive beyond the individual enterprise is likely to be less than optimum use of resources. In the free-enterprise system, relative prices are expected to guide both producers and consumers in the use of resources. If some prices are out of line with costs and others are not, the best use of resources would not be made. Too little would go into the high-priced production and too much into the low. For example, if steel prices were too high in relation, say, to lumber, there would tend to be an overuse of lumber in construction and less than optimum use of steel.

Thus, where big collective enterprise is concerned, the profit drive could not be expected to produce the optimum use of resources even though it did operate to keep down waste within the enterprise.

PRESSURE FOR IMPROVING TECHNOLOGY

The fourth result to be expected from classical competition is the pressure for improving technology. Economic growth in an economy that maintains reasonably full employment can be expected to come in part from the growth in the labor force and the accumulation of capital. But the greatest source of growth is improvement in technology.

There is little question that the big corporations have done a great deal to advance technology, particularly through their research and development programs. The costs of such research can be spread over a large volume of output and the value of organized research has become clear. It results both in new products and in more efficient ways to produce old products. And a strong case could undoubtedly be made that improvements in technology tend to be more rapid when competition is between a few big enterprises than when competition is among a forest of small enterprises. Indeed, the rapid technical developments in agriculture in the last thirty years appears to have come much more from the organized research of government and industry than from the action of individual farmers in working out new techniques or new products.

On the other hand, the profit drive which results in high target rates of return can be expected to slow up the *adoption* of new techniques because of the higher rate of return they must yield before they are introduced.

Consider first the case where an improved machine is available and the question arises whether to buy and install it, or continue to use a machine that is not yet worn out but is less efficient. The answer should turn largely on whether the saving in operating expenses by the new machine would earn enough to yield the target rate of return on the new capital that would have to be invested. And obviously it would make a difference whether the new equipment had to earn a target rate of 8 per cent or the target rate of 20 per cent. Yet from the public point of view, improved equipment when it can save enough to earn a competitive rate of return should replace less efficient equipment. The failure to replace less efficient plant and equipment when it is economical *from the public point of view* means a waste of resources and a less rapid growth in national output than would be most economical.

The same failure to use resources effectively arises when new products are developed but are put on the market only when they promise to make a high target rate of return.

If the big collective enterprise will only expand the use of its skills and technical knowledge and strategic position when it can expect to make a 20 per cent return on its capital and capital is available at an expected return of 8 per cent, then the resources available to it are not being effectively used so far as the public interest is concerned and it is not providing the public with the gains from technical progress which its power and position make economically possible.

THE INADEQUACY OF THE PROFIT DRIVE

Thus the general conclusion one can reach is that when a big business enterprise has a substantial degree of pricing power, the profit drive itself cannot be expected to be an effective instrument for achieving the public interest. Under this drive, prices are likely to be in excess of a reasonable relation to costs; income division is likely to be inequitable and the conflicts between labor and management intensified; optimum use of resources is not likely to be approximated; and economic growth is likely to be delayed because a premium rate of return must be in prospect before the capital outlay required for new products and improved techniques will be undertaken.

If these great engines of production are to perform their essential function as social institutions, the logic of collective enterprise suggests that an alternative must be found to the drive for corporate profits.

CHAPTER XVII

FROM CORPORATE PROFITS TO
ECONOMIC PERFORMANCE

In all of these endeavors we seek to make it crystal clear that:
1. It is in the interest of the stockholders that there be equitable compensation for the employees.
2. It is in the interest of the employees that there be equitable return for the stockholders.
3. It is in the interest of the customers, the employees, the stockholders, and the public that, after payment of employee compensation and other costs, and stockholders dividends, there be a remaining profit to maintain United States Steel in a healthy financial condition to meet the new and ever-expanding needs of this Nation.
4. Anything that operates against these objectives is contrary to the best interest of all concerned.

CLIFFORD F. HOOD,
PRESIDENT, THE UNITED STATES STEEL CORPORATION*

If the unregulated drive for corporate profits is not to be the guiding force in the big collective enterprise, what can take its place?

We have suggested that it is impractical to break up big enterprises to such a degree that the forces of classical competition can control the profit drive in the public interest and that an intermediate break-up is unlikely to be a satisfactory general solution. Thus, we accept the continued existence of big business.

Also we have considered the serious drawbacks of govern-

* *Hearings*, p. 361.

ment price regulation and have tentatively rejected such regulation as a satisfactory method of controlling the power of management where at least a few competing enterprises can be efficiently maintained.

A third approach has been suggested: that in the big collective enterprise, the management should operate, not as trustees for the stockholders, but as trustees for the public.[1] The corporate management is expected to have a social conscience and this, plus the force of public opinion, plus the threat of political action, plus the competition among the few, would be relied on to enforce the trust. Such a solution places great reliance on the public spirit of management and calls on management to judge the public interest. Certainly a corporate management with breadth of viewpoint and a concern with the public interest is a desirable thing. But to place major reliance for the operation of collective enterprise on an "abiding sense of social responsibility" is to run counter to both the teachings of history and our knowledge of human nature.

The logic of collective enterprise suggests a different approach. It would reject the principle of trusteeship and would regard management as neither a trustee for the stockholders nor as a trustee for the public. Instead, it would seek the public interest by applying two basic principles.

First, *it would start with the principle that management will and should run a collective enterprise in its own interest.* Management has power and to assume that it will not use its power in its own interest as it sees that interest is to run counter to experience.

Second, *it would operate on the principle that conditions can and should be established, so that when management operates a collective enterprise in management's own interest, the public interest will also be served.* This is the underlying principle of

[1] See A. A. Berle, Jr., *The 20th Century Capitalist Revolution* (New York: Harcourt, Brace and Company, 1954), especially chapter III.

classical competition where such competition is feasible. And there is no reason why the same principle should not be made to operate in the case of collective enterprise. Under this principle, it would not be necessary for management to feel a sense of social responsibility or even to consider the public interest. To the extent that management also took a broad point of view and found its own interest in serving the public interest, this could be a gain. But the basic reliance would be on those conditions which make management's action in its own narrower interest also serve the public interest.

This chapter will be concerned with developing such a new approach. This approach will not apply to small corporations or medium sized corporations which might have widely dispersed stock ownership, but whose individual actions have no great public significance. It would apply only to the enterprise whose activity is clearly vested with a public interest and not subject to the public utility type of regulation. Thus, it applies primarily to the hundred or so biggest manufacturing enterprises. It is for these collective enterprises that a new approach is most needed. Whether the approach to be outlined here has relevance for big nonmanufacturing enterprise is a matter lying outside the scope of this book.

MANAGEMENT INTERESTS AND CORPORATE PROFITS

The first step toward a new approach is to register the small extent to which management's interests are necessarily served by maximum corporate profits.

Just what are the motivations of management and how are they served now by corporate profits? Motives are likely to be complex and it is not the purpose here to make an exhaustive analysis but it is possible to list and consider five of the more important:

1. The drive for power

2. The drive for prestige
3. Satisfaction with a job well done
4. Concern with the public welfare
5. The drive for personal profit

There are other management interests such as the desire to be part of a successful team and the satisfaction of solving challenging problems. Also, the five listed are not listed in the order of their importance since their relative importance is likely to vary from management to management and from situation to situation and often a single action or decision will be motivated by a complex of interests. The immediate question is how these interests are served by the drive for corporate profits.

First it should be recognized that, in order to be healthy, a collective enterprise must make an adequate return on the capital invested in it. Only then will it be able to obtain capital for expansion. And profits to the extent necessary for healthy operation clearly serve all five of the specific interests of corporate management. Neither power nor prestige can be derived from managing a sick corporation. Both satisfaction with a job well done and with serving the public interest can be derived from running a healthy collective enterprise. And personal profit, too, can accrue from a well-done job. The making of profits as such is not at issue.

What is at issue is the exercise of the pricing power to make premium profits—profits more than enough to make a corporation healthy and able to obtain new capital in the competitive market. To what extent are the five major interests of management served by operating the corporation to make premium profits—profits in excess of a competitive rate of return on capital?

A little consideration will show that the first four of these five management interests do not depend on the making of premium corporate profits. The drive for power does not depend on maximum profits. A big, successful collective enterprise gives its management power, whether success is measured by profits or by some other criteria and whether its growth comes wholly from reinvested earnings or in part from the sale of securities to the public. High profits are useful for expansion of power but not necessary so long as new funds can be obtained in the public market.

The same applies to the desire for prestige. Today, particularly in the business community, prestige accrues to the more profitable companies and to their managements. But again this is not a necessary condition. If the larger community came to redefine success for the big collective enterprise in other terms than maximum profits, the desire for prestige would not depend on such profits.

Satisfaction with a job well done must depend on the definition of the job itself. If the job is *defined* as one of making the highest profits possible, then, of course, satisfaction depends on making such profits. But if the job to be done is defined in terms that do not involve maximum profits, then such profits are not essential to the serving of this management interest. And finally, to the extent that management interest lies in service to the public, this interest does not depend at all on premium profits. Thus, the first four interests of management can be served without a drive for greater profits.

To the extent that management owns stock in the company it manages, greater profits for the corporation mean greater personal profit. But when management's stock holdings are small this incentive is weak. As Joel Dean has said in *Managerial Economics*:

Management's financial interest in the modern corporation is typically small, and only one of the many motives that keep executives going. Other motives which are just as important often run counter to the corporate financial interests, and thus distinguish management clearly from stockholders, in whose eyes the company is essentially a financial, as opposed to a social organization.[2]

Indeed, the ownership of stock has become such an inadequate incentive in the biggest corporations that bonus systems have been

[2] *Op. cit.*, p. 29.

extensively adopted to bring higher personal profits to management when corporate profits are higher and so bind management to a drive for corporate profits which its individual ownership of stock would not give. As a result, management's drive for corporate profits is primarily the drive which arises from the profit-related bonuses and from the symbolic role of profits as the job of management is now defined. In only a minor degree does it come from the direct effect of that share of corporate profits which management obtains through ownership.

This means that the drive for corporate profits is not essential to the operation of the collective enterprise. A redefinition of management's job which did not define it in terms of a drive for maximum corporate profits but in some other terms closer to the public interest could satisfy four of these major interests of management, while a bonus system that provided rewards to management in terms of the new definition of the job to be done could serve management's drive for personal profit. This suggests the possibility of reorienting the role of management through a change in the bonus system. A reoriented bonus system could not only provide the personal profit incentive to management but, even more important, it could redefine the character of the job to be done by management and so provide the basis for other motivations.

EXISTING BONUS SYSTEMS

The second step toward the new approach is to examine the bonus systems now being used to stimulate management.

At the present time two different bonus systems are widely used in the big corporations, one related to corporate profits and the other related to individual or group performance. The first usually applies to top management, while the performance bonus applies to management levels below the top. Both can throw light on the problems and possibilities of the new approach.

Until recently the most common type of management bonus

was a cash bonus directly related to corporate dividends or corporate profits. For example, in 1936 the Bethlehem Steel Corporation adopted a "special incentive compensation plan" to stimulate the profit drive of its management. Under this plan a cash bonus equal to 6⅔ per cent of cash dividends paid on its common stock was set aside each year for top management.[3] In 1956 this cash bonus to the fifteen top officers amounted to $5.5 million.[4] Similar bonus plans were adopted by many other big corporations. It is reasonable to suppose that such bonus plans greatly stimulate management's drive for corporate profits. Indeed from the point of view of the stockholder it is reasonable to assume that such bonuses have had the effect of increasing profits more than the cost of the bonuses. Also, from the public point of view, *if the profit drive really served the public interest,* $5.5 million of bonuses would not be a great price to pay for the efficient operation of an enterprise having more than $2 billion dollars worth of sales.[5] It would amount to less than one-quarter cent for each dollar of sales.

In actual practice, the effectiveness of cash bonuses as incentives have been much impaired in recent years by the high personal income tax rates. Under present tax rates, once an individual's take-home pay reaches $90,000, federal income taxes take 91 per cent of any addition so that a corporation bonus of $100,000 is necessary to add $9,000 to take-home pay.[6] This is clearly shown in the testimony of the president of Bethlehem

[3] *Hearings,* p. 1352. This replaced a bonus plan already in existence.
[4] *Hearings,* p. 1354.
[5] A large part of this $5.5 million in bonuses must have gone to federal and state governments in income taxes to support public activities. Therefore the economic cost of the bonus to the public may have been less than a million, the rest being a tax on the public collected by the corporation, paid out as part of the bonus and collected by government from the bonus recipient in personal income taxes.
[6] It should be noted that these figures apply to recent years and assume five exemptions and a standard reduction but no contributions in excess of the standard deduction. They also disregard the possibility of income from other sources. Other income would lower the level at which the added income from an additional bonus would be only 9 per cent of the bonus.

Steel and in Table 27, which shows that most of his high income from salary and bonus went in federal taxes.

Because the high tax rates in the upper brackets have greatly reduced the financial potency of bonuses to top management in the biggest companies, increasing emphasis has recently been placed on another powerful stimulus to the profit drive—stock purchase options, already mentioned. In 1950 Congress amended the federal income tax laws to make it possible for a corporation to grant "restricted stock options" to employees under conditions which would allow capital-gains treatment of profits made from the exercise of such options and the subsequent sale of the stock.[7]

Obviously the distribution of such stock options to management can place it under considerable pressure to increase profits so as to increase the market value of the stock. In the stock option, the executive has an interest in the future earnings of the company which he obtained without any cost and without taking any risk and the tax provisions give him a way to cash in on the value of this interest as a low-taxed capital gain and not as high-taxed income. We have already seen that such a stock-option incentive plan was introduced by U.S. Steel in 1951. A similar plan was later adopted by the Bethlehem Steel Corporation. In 1957 it reduced the rate in its cash incentive plan and set aside 2,500,000 shares of unissued common stock equal to approximately 5.5 per cent of the shares outstanding, against stock purchase options to be distributed to management at the rate of half a million share options a year.[8] The top twenty members of management were to get approximately 140,000 share options a year for five years. Given our present tax laws, it is difficult to imagine a more effective stimulus to the profit drive.

Many other leading American corporations have adopted stock

---

[7] *Hearings*, pp. 1348-1351. There is the additional condition that the sale of shares acquired under this plan must not occur within two years of the gift of the stock option if the benefits of capital gain treatment are to be obtained.

[8] *Hearings*, p. 1348.

Table 27—SALARY, BONUS, AND TAKE-HOME PAY OF THE PRESIDENT OF BETHLEHEM STEEL CORPORATION

	Salary	Bonus	Total	Federal Income Tax	Take-Home Pay	Estimated Take-Home Bonus
1950	$120,000	$ 262,000	$ 382,000	$ 270,000	$112,000	$25,000
1951	120,000	255,000	375,000	290,000	85,000	24,000
1952	120,000	255,000	375,000	296,000	79,000	24,000
1953	120,000	255,000	375,000	296,000	79,000	24,000
1954	120,000	367,000	487,000	391,000	96,000	34,000
1955	120,000	463,000	583,000	478,000	105,000	43,000
1956	120,000	549,000	669,000	556,000	113,000	51,000
	$840,000	$2,406,000	$3,246,000	$2,577,000	$669,000	$225,000

Out of the $2.4 million in bonuses received by the president of Bethlehem Steel in the seven-year period from 1950 to 1956, only $225,000 remained after federal taxes for his personal expenditure or investment, or an average net bonus of $32,000 a year.[a] The income figures before taxes may look large but the take-home figures are not large when one considers the size of the enterprise being run and the opportunities open elsewhere to top management skills. The average income after taxes amounted to less than $100,000 a year.

[a] The figure of little more than $225,000 is arrived at by assuming 11 per cent take-home on the first $30,000 of bonus, 10 per cent on the next $50,000, and 9 per cent on the remainder. Of course, if there was income from other sources the take-home bonuses would be slightly less.

option plans for their key employees and these plans, like the bonus plans tied more directly to profits, provide an active stimulus to the drive for corporate profits and can thus serve the interest of stockholders.

The widespread use of these various profit-related bonus plans points to both the effectiveness of the bonus principle and to the impediment placed on the effectiveness of cash bonuses by personal income taxes where incomes are large. Bonuses to stimulate the profit drive are, of course, consistent with the traditional logic of private enterprise and the traditional legal assumption that the corporate enterprise "belongs" to the stockholders. But here, for big collective enterprise, we are seeking an alternative to the drive for corporate profits.

A different type of management bonus system is also extensively used by big business, but is usually applied to key men below the top management. In this case, the job to be done is made specific in terms of cost reduction, product improvement, and other goals set by top management, and bonuses are paid for specific performance in achieving or surpassing such goals. As far back as 1931 one authority on management incentives recommended that "all key men other than (the highest executives and those just under the highest) should derive their incentives from bonus funds created by setting aside a portion of savings made by bettering fixed performances," and regards such performance bonuses as a form of incentive superior to profit-related bonuses for all but the highest levels of management.[9] Since then great progress has been made by management engineers in the development of measures of specific performance. Nearly all aspects of lower-level management can now be covered by such measures. They provide a basis for performance bonuses as an alternative to profit bonuses.

This suggests the possibility that something like the performance

[9] J. P. Jordan, *Handbook of Business Administration* (New York: Mc-Graw-Hill Book Co., 1931), published for the American Management Association, p. 1654.

bonuses for lower management could be applied to top management instead of profit bonuses. In some degree the principles applied to lower management would also apply to higher management performance. To a considerable extent they would have to be different. Because such bonus systems would have to be broad in scope the bonuses under them can be thought of as bonuses for economic performance. The real question is whether the job to be done by the top management of a collective enterprise can be redefined to focus on economic performance and thereby bring it more nearly in line with the public interest. Can such economic performance be defined in measurable terms to provide the basis for performance bonuses to top management?

THE FUNCTIONS OF MANAGEMENT

This brings us to the third step in the new approach: the delineation of the functions of management in a collective enterprise.

From the public point of view, the big collective enterprise is an engine of production. It uses the community's resources of labor and capital to meet the community's wants. It is in the public interest that these engines be run with economic efficiency and with fairness to all the parties involved. Each of these requirements needs to be considered.

For the guide to what constitutes economic efficiency we can go to the logic of classical competition and the results such competition could be expected to produce. Though the big collective enterprise is a far cry from the forest of small enterprises belonging to the classical model, the criteria which made the *results* to be expected of classical competition so acceptable in the public interest still hold, so that the classical results can be used as a goal of collective enterprise even though the method of organizing production is fundamentally different and the productivity is vastly greater.

This takes us back to the four major public interests which classical competition could be expected to serve where such com-

petition is feasible. If collective enterprise is to produce comparable end results, the public interest requires its operation so
that:

1. Prices are in reasonable relation to costs.
2. The benefits to labor and to capital arising from production
   are reasonably related to their respective contributions to
   production.
3. As nearly as possible, optimum use of resources is made
   so that no more of a given resource is used than is necessary
   for the end product and that combination of resources is
   used which involves the least cost.
4. There is technical progress to reduce costs, improve product and introduce new products.

In addition to economic efficiency, the public interest requires
that management should operate with economic fairness as
among the parties directly at interest—the investors, the workers,
the suppliers, and the customers. If the goals of economic efficiency could be perfectly determined and perfectly achieved, this
would take care of the problem of economic fairness.[10] But, in
practice, it is not easy to determine just what constitutes economic
efficiency. And almost any major decision made by management
can be bent in greater or lesser degree in favor of or against one
or more of the interested parties, with little recourse by a losing
party. As a result, management, by the very nature of its power,
is in the position of an arbiter.

The fact of this arbitral role is well brought out in the statement
(already quoted) by a recent president of the United States Steel
Corporation, to the effect that:

We of management are responsible to manage the business in accordance with our judgment as to what will best serve the long-term
interests of: the employees whose livelihood is dependent upon the

[10] It should be noted that economic fairness relates only to the operation of production and the distribution of the benefits in the process.
It may involve social unfairness, as when people are unable to work. The
latter requires nonbusiness measures such as a social security system to
correct the social unfairness.

Corporation; the stockholders whose invested money provides the tools of production and jobs; the customers who buy our products and thus provide employment; and the people of the consuming public who depend upon steel as one of the basic commodities of modern life.[11]

The public interest requires that this arbitral role be played without bias in favor of any of the parties at interest. One of the major drawbacks to the profit bonus is that it introduces a biasing factor in arbitrating the conflicts of interest involved in the collective enterprise. Whoever heard of giving an arbitrator a bonus if he will favor one side? Whether stock ownership constitutes a seriously biasing factor is open to question. Where it is weak as an incentive to make more profits, it is presumably weak as a biasing factor. Whatever the case, the need for unbiased arbitration is clear.

The four objectives constituting economically efficient operation plus unbiased arbitration are by no means all the requirements of the public interest. Stability of operation, safety of operation, integrity of operation—these and other considerations are also important from the public point of view. But the central core of the public interest is covered by the five requirements listed. If management could achieve the four objectives of economic performance and arbitrate the conflict of interests without bias, it would deserve well from the community and the community could afford to pay management well for such achievement.

THE ECONOMIC PERFORMANCE BONUS AND TOP MANAGEMENT
The fourth and crucial step in the new approach is to set up conditions under which management will act in its own interest in ways that will tend to meet these objectives and without having to think specifically about the public interest. This could be brought about if two important changes were made:

[11] Walter F. Munford, president, the United States Steel Corporation in a letter to every U.S. Steel employee at the start of the 1959 steel strike. (Quoted in the *U.S. Steel Quarterly*, August, 1959 p. 3.)

1. If management could be induced to price in terms of target rates of return which approximated the cost of capital rather than in terms of premium profits, and
2. If the bonuses to top management were a reward for improving economic performance and not for greater corporate profits.

How these changes might be brought about will be made the subject of the final chapter. What is important here is to see that these changes would tend to make management actions serve the public interest.

REASONABLE TARGET RATES OF RETURN

The first requirement in considering these changes is to recognize that it must be a responsibility of management to run the collective enterprise at a profit. It is as important to the public as it is to the security holders that the corporation make profits. A collective enterprise that fails, over a period of years, to make a legitimate return on its investment is not using resources effectively. Also, unless a fair return is made on capital, the collective enterprise will have difficulty raising new capital for expansion. The conflict between the public interest and that of the security-holder arises only when more than a legitimate rate of return is made.

Here the technique of target pricing, already extensively employed by big business, provides us with a tool which can be made to serve the public interest. As the technique is now employed, it is a device for achieving the highest rate of return on capital consistent with corporate growth, i.e., the highest rate just short of inducing new competitors to climb into the market over the "stone wall" of difficult entry. But the pricing *procedure,* once the target rate of return on capital has been adopted, is the same regardless of whether the target rate is 20 per cent or 10 per cent or 8 per cent. If a corporate management found that it could obtain over a period all the capital it could use effectively by earning an average of 8 per cent on its capital, and adopted this as its target rate, the rest of the process of pricing would follow the present target pricing procedure.

Also, and most important, if the target rate truly reflected the cost of capital and other costs were legitimate, the prices that resulted from this target pricing technique would be in general those which would serve the public interest and could properly be called legitimate prices. Up to the amount of profits necessary to make a competitive rate of return, the interests of security holders and the public interest run parallel.

In the practical application of this part of the new approach it would not be expected that the target rate would be achieved in each year. If the general level of business activity was very high, a well-run collective enterprise should earn more than the target rate, while in periods of low general demand less than the target rate could be expected, with no difference in the skill or diligence of management.

The principle of setting a reasonable target rate for pricing would not be new. It is essentially the principle employed by U.S. Steel when its pricing policy was bottomed on the expectation of earning over the years a net return after taxes of around 8 percent on investment. And it is the principle underlying the setting of public utility rates. Whether it could be applied effectively and without government regulation in the case of big manufacturing enterprise will be considered in the next chapter.

PERFORMANCE BONUSES FOR TOP MANAGEMENT

The second change suggested by the logic of collective enterprise is the replacement of profit-oriented bonuses by bonuses based on performance. This would involve an extension of the performance bonus systems already developed for lower management. It would cover the more specific goals of management such as reducing costs, improving product, expanding the enterprise, and conducting research to improve technology. It would apply the same bonus principles to top management which are now applied to lower management.

The general character of specific performance has been clearly indicated by a management engineer, Ernest C. Miller, in describing the process for reviewing the performance of lower management:

> The performance review process for each position is designed to measure, within the context of the responsibilities for the position, the specific results that must be accomplished by the position if the company's marketing, manufacturing, financial, personnel and research plans are to be achieved. In preparing the performance review process, the company's overall business plans must be reviewed, translated into specific statements of results required if the plans are to be achieved, and the responsibility for specific results assigned to the different positions that constitute the company's organization.[12]

To apply the same type of performance measures to top management should not be too difficult. For both low-level and high-level performance bonuses, the company's marketing, manufacturing, financial, personnel, and research plans would have to be worked out in concrete detail. The measure of specific performance for top management would then be the extent to which the goals of the plan as a whole were achieved or surpassed. Different weights would have to be given for the over-all success in cost reduction, in product improvement, in stability of operation, and in the other operations representing good management. The working out of measures of specific performance for top management seems well within the economic, accounting, and engineering skills already available.

WHO APPROVES THE BONUS SYSTEM FOR TOP MANAGEMENT?

A performance bonus system for top management would create one new problem which does not occur with management below

[12] Performance Review and Management, *Advanced Management*, 25, No. 3 (March, 1960), p. 26.

the top level. Where top management is designing a plan for subordinate officials, its own bonus plan is not involved and the balance between bonus payments and improved performance can be worked out on an economical basis. But if top management designs its own bonus plan, there would presumably be an incentive to make the bonuses overlarge or the goals of performance overeasy. Some restraining influence would be needed. This restraint might take various forms or a combination of forms. The bonus system might be determined by directors outside of active management and be subject to a bona fide stockholder vote. More important, management engineering firms outside the specific collective enterprises could be expected to develop both methods and criteria for legitimate performance bonus systems and they in turn could be called in to design specific systems for specific corporations. Finally, if a performance bonus system for top management is to be effective, special tax provisions would be necessary and the privilege of lower taxes on such bonuses for collective enterprises could undoubtedly set limits on abuse. This problem will also be considered in the next chapter.

BONUS SYSTEM DEPENDS ON ALL MANAGEMENT INTERESTS

The effectiveness of the performance bonus system would depend not only on management's desire for personal profits but also on management's other interests. Its main value would be to establish a new objective for corporate management. Achieving this objective would bring to management power and prestige, satisfaction with a job well done and service to the public. The bonus system would be the means for setting the new objective, giving it definition and making it precise in terms of monetary reward. Whether personal profit plays a large or a small part in the motivation of a particular management, the performance bonus system would tend to stimulate action in the public interest.

Satisfaction of top management's desire for power would

seem to be inherent in big collective enterprise. The very size of the enterprise requires that management have great power. In some degree, the logic of collective enterprise suggests a need for limiting certain management powers. Thus, the power to collect capital from customers by charging more than a legitimate price is contrary to the public interest. And limiting profits to a target rate based on the cost of capital would in some degree limit the power of management over growth since management would have to go to the financial markets for extra capital, beyond that arising from the retention of legitimate earnings. However, legitimate profits would provide access to the public market and if bonus plans were developed which brought the use of management power close to the public interest, the power held by management would still be great and would be given legitimacy as it approximated the public interest.

The shift in the definition of the job to be done would also shift the effect of the prestige incentive. Considerable prestige will attach to the top management of a big corporation that is successful, whether success is measured in terms of profits or economic performance. Very likely greater prestige would attach to successful economic performance than to high profits, once the public had redefined the job to be done and recognized its closer approximation to the public interest.

Similarly, the redefinition of the job to be done could produce an important change in the satisfaction to be derived from doing a job well. To feel that a job is significant adds to its satisfaction, and a job defined in terms of economic performance is likely to induce a greater effort to do well than one defined in terms of corporate profits.

Concern with the public welfare can be a valuable motivation in the operation of collective enterprise. No matter how well worked out a performance bonus plan may be, the results to be expected can only be approximately in the public interest. At some points it may, in fact, offer rewards for action in conflict with the public interest and a modification of such actions in the public interest would improve the results. A system that *depended* for its substantial success on concern with the public welfare would be unlikely to succeed. But one which depended for substantial success on financial incentives and for greater success on management concern with the public welfare is likely to be more than substantially successful.

It should also be recognized that those who urge corporate managements to operate as trustees for the public, not for the stockholders, are also calling for a redefinition of the job to be done. However, to redefine the job as one of serving the public interest, places on management the responsibility for determining the public interest. This is a responsibility which management is not in the best possible position to carry out. What is required is that management have the more specific goals such as cost reduction and product improvement spelled out in specific terms, so that as far as management is concerned the character of the job to be done is not that of being a trustee for the public, but of running an enterprise with fairly explicit lines of economic performance established.

As the management of collective enterprise becomes increasingly a profession, and as the character and logic of collective enterprise becomes more clearly established, these nonfinancial interests of management should come to play a larger role provided a good economic performance bonus system is in operation. Then the combination of financial and nonfinancial incentives could be expected to go a long way in making the operation of big collective enterprise in the interest of management also serve the public interest and without the drawbacks of government regulation.

CONCLUSION TO THE LOGIC OF COLLECTIVE ENTERPRISE

The logic of collective enterprise thus points to the need for a major shift from profits to economic performance as the basic criterion in the operation of big collective enterprise. Such a shift would replace the drive for corporate profits with a drive for economic performance including adequate profits as the basis of management incentives. It would reward management in terms of performance closely related to the public interest. It would make economic performance the measure of success in doing the management job well and the basis for achieving prestige. It would give a basis for legitimate power.

It could be expected to go much further then this in serving the public interest. It would reduce the basis of friction between labor and management and justify both management and the public in calling on labor to act responsibly instead of aiming at the maximum "profits" to labor that labor's power is able to extract. And equally important, it would justify labor in acting responsibly and in demanding that management also use its power responsibly. At the same time, it would protect the stockholders in the making of legitimate profits. It would avoid the inefficiencies that would come if efficient big business were broken up in order to increase competition or make entry easier. It would avoid the costs and the hampering effect of government regulation. And it would rely on competition among a few efficient big enterprises to keep each on the alert to continue the technical progress and the service to consumers that big business is capable of providing. Adequate incentives to economic performance should thus make the self-interest of management serve the public interest as effectively through collective enterprise as classical competition made the self-interests of the forest of small enterprisers serve the public interest, and would at the same time encourage management to develop to the full the technical potentials of big collective enterprise.

This would seem to be the logic of collective enterprise. Can it be given practical application?

CHAPTER XVIII

CANALIZING CORPORATE ACTION

Almost everyone now agrees that in the large corporation, the owner is, in general, a passive recipient; that, typically, control is in the hands of management; and that management normally selects its own replacements. It is, furthermore, generally recognized that, in the United States, the large corporation undertakes a substantial part of total economic activity, however measured; that the power of corporations to act is by no means so thoroughly circumscribed by the market as was generally thought to be true of nineteenth-century enterprise; and that, in addition to market power, the large corporation exercises a considerable degree of control over nonmarket activities of various sorts. What all this seems to add up to is the existence of important centers of private power in the hands of men whose authority is real but whose responsibilities are vague.

PROFESSOR EDWARD S. MASON,
HARVARD UNIVERSITY*

The development of mechanisms which will change the internal organization of the corporation, and define more closely and represent more presently the interests to which corporate management should respond and the goals toward which they should strive is yet to begin, if it is to come at all.

PROFESSOR CARL KAYSEN,
HARVARD UNIVERSITY**

Given the logic of collective enterprise which dictates that, in the collective enterprise, a drive for economic performance

* Introduction to *The Corporation in Modern Society* (Cambridge: Harvard University Press, 1959), p. 4.
** *The Corporation in Modern Society,* p. 105.

should replace the drive for corporate profits, what can be done to facilitate this shift? What mechanisms can be introduced to stimulate the change in internal organization and bring about both a clarification of the legitimate goals of the big corporate collective and provide inducements toward their achievement?

This chapter aims to outline a program which, if carried out, would go a long way toward reorienting the corporate action of big business so as to bring it closer to the public interest and without the drawbacks of government regulation or the inefficiencies of corporate break-up. It applies only to the big manufacturing corporations and, of course, should not be regarded as an alternative to corporate breakup where smaller enterprises would be equally or more efficient.

THE MAIN ELEMENTS IN THE PROGRAM

In its broadest outline the program proposed here consists of three main elements:

1. The creation of a new legal category *for tax purposes* including only those collective manufacturing corporations whose pricing power is found to be vested with a substantial public interest.

2. The granting of especially favorable income tax treatment for performance bonuses received by management from corporations in this category, provided that

3. Pricing in the corporation is done in terms of target rates of return on capital that are reasonably related to the cost of capital.

The key step in the program would be Congressional legislation to establish the new legal category of collective enterprise. This category would stand midway between the legal category of public utility—where it is presumed that monopoly is in the public interest and needs to be regulated—and the legal category of private enterprise—where it is presumed that competition is an adequate regulator in the public interest. To facilitate discussion, the new legislation will be referred to as an Economic Performance Act and the proposal will be outlined in terms of such an act. The proposal is tentative and is outlined to stimulate discussion. Its adoption would involve a major shift in orientation with respect to big business and such a shift should not, and probably could not, be made suddenly or without careful and extensive examination, modification, and elaboration by the many experts who could contribute to the creation of a final program and contribute to its success.

DETERMINING COLLECTIVE STATUS

The first section of the Economic Performance Act would set up the new *legal* category—that of corporations with the legal status of collective enterprise—and would institute a mechanism for determining, with the public interest in view, which corporations should be entitled to this legal status. Presumably it would indicate, as the basic criterion for legal collective status, *the existence of unregulated pricing power of sufficient magnitude to affect the corporation with a substantial public interest.* This very general criterion would have to be given more concrete meaning in terms of a combination of such factors as the absolute size of enterprise, the size in relation to the market, the importance of the products to the public welfare, the dispersion of stock ownership, the making of profits significantly greater than a competitive rate of return on capital, and similar considerations.

A semijudicial commission to apply these criteria to the specific corporations would be needed. The legislation might designate any manufacturing corporation controlling assets of say half a billion dollars or more as *presumptively* a collective enterprise, leaving the burden of proof before the commission and courts to the specific corporation wishing to avoid such status. Then, for corporations smaller than the designated figure, the burden of proof could rest with the commission to establish that the pricing power was so important from the public viewpoint that the corporation was vested with a substantial public interest. The legislation also could place a lower limit of size, say $100 million or $200 million worth of assets, below which the commission could not designate a corporation as a legal collective enterprise.

At the present time the application of such criteria might give the collective enterprise status to around 100 industrial corporations. In 1957 there were 62 industrial corporations controlling assets over half a billion and 200 with assets between $100 and $500 million.[1] Most of the first group and some of the second would presumably rate the legal status of collective enterprise. In total, the corporations given legal collective status might control two-thirds of the instruments of manufacturing production and account for half of manufacturing output.

Some corporations might voluntarily seek the status of collective enterprise because of the prestige and privileges to be attached to that status. The tax privileges that will be proposed should make the new status most desirable from the point of view of management. And in some situations it might be so attractive to management that the latter would persuade the stockholders to make the change. However, the criterion for such status would still be the presence of a substantial public interest in the corporation's pricing power, and a corporation voluntarily seeking the legal privileges and prestige associated with collective status would have the burden of proving to the commission the public importance of its pricing power.

It could be expected that over a period of years the criteria for granting or enforcing the legal status of collective enterprise would be clarified by the combined effect of Congressional legislation, commission application, and judicial review. In principle, the dividing line between collective enterprise and private enter-

[1] *Hearings,* pp. 100-916.

prise is indicated by the presence or absence of a substantial public interest because of pricing power. But in practice, there is a continuum and any dividing line would be arbitrary. If the dividing line were initially set fairly high, it could subsequently be lowered as experience indicated the need.

A more difficult question arises where a big corporation has pricing power of a magnitude to create a substantial public interest, but its stock is closely held and the owners manage the enterprise. Whether sheer size and significant pricing power without a significant degree of separation of ownership and control should also entail collective status is a matter for debate. From the public point of view, it is pricing power which requires the new status, while it is the separation of ownership and control which provides a basis for the legal shift from the status of private enterprise and size which tends to increase the magnitude of the public concern. It may well be that, initially, big closely held corporations should be excluded from the new legal status in order to simplify the legal problems in making the shift, postponing until later the question of dealing with the pricing power of big owner-controlled-and-operated enterprises. Such enterprises are few, and it may well be that the shift to an economic performance basis by the big corporations having dispersed ownership would so reduce the range of pricing power of closely held corporations as to make their power no longer a matter of substantial public concern. The important problem is to raise the level of economic performance of the hundred or more manufacturing corporations which have both important pricing power and a significant degree of separation between ownership and control.

PROVIDING MANAGEMENT INCENTIVES FOR ECONOMIC PERFORMANCE

A second section of the act would provide management with incentives to favor the shift from profits to economic performance and incentives to drive for economic performance by granting the privilege of special tax treatment for bonuses based on economic performance. Where a corporation, entitled to the legal status of a collective enterprise, adopts a bona fide economic performance bonus system for its top management and employs no other bonus system for the latter, bonus payments under the system would be given preferential tax treatment. The simplest procedure would be to give such bonus payments the same treatment that capital gains now have so that at most only 25 per cent could be taken in federal income taxes. Where adopted, such a performance bonus system could provide as powerful a drive for economic performance as the older bonus systems have given to the drive for corporate profits.

This section of the Economic Performance Act would also aim to clarify the role of management implicit in collective enterprise by establishing the meaning of economic performance. Presumably the preamble to the act would state its aim as that of improving economic performance where the unregulated pricing power of big collective enterprise creates a substantial public interest. A section of the act would have to give general content to the concept of economic performance by citing the end result which classical competition could be expected to bring about: the optimum use of resources in the satisfaction of wants. More specific meaning could be spelled out in such terms as the efficient and economical use of resources, prices which just covered the total economic costs (including the competitive costs of capital), production pushed in each direction within the chosen sphere of the enterprise to the point where demand at the legitimate prices is fully satisfied and the optimum use of capital is made to expand capacity and improve technology. Beyond such general statements of performance the act would not have to go since, as will be seen, the program leaves the determination of the *substance* of economic performance to management and to professional experts.

This section would also introduce the new legal concept of an economic performance bonus. Such a bonus would presumably be defined as one received under a bonus system designed to reward superior economic performance, and evidence of such a system would be that it had been designed or approved by professionals and that it met the canons of practice in measuring superior economic performance. This would leave the design of a performance bonus system for a particular corporation to its own management, presumably with the aid of professionals. And the Treasury would accept such a bonus system as bona fide provided it appeared to be designed in good faith and was certified by an independent professional agency.

The professionals who would be most directly concerned would be the accountants, engineers, and economists. Their combined talents could contribute to the design of a practical performance bonus system for a particular collective enterprise. It can be expected that a new profession, now nascent in the work of management consultants, would emerge as the profession concerned with the design of such bonus systems and the measurement of economic performance. Indeed, such a new profession might be referred to as that of economic performance accounting, though the form of accounting would not be of the detailed character of profit accounting.

The canons of practice in measuring economic performance could also be expected to develop over a period. At first attention might be focused on such obvious factors as cost reduction and product improvement. Other factors relating to efficiency and economy and progress could be included. Also at the outset the measurement of performance and the bonus systems based on such measurements would be crude, but with experience and with greater discussion of the principles involved practice should improve. At the beginning it would be a great gain if the bonus system led to the adoption of a target rate of return that was not significantly above the competitive cost of capital and provided positive inducements to reduce costs and improve products. In time more refined and complex measures of performance could be developed and the bonus systems adjusted accordingly. Also, whether or not a crude or a refined system of performance bonuses were adopted, competition among the few would provide pressures toward technical advance as each big corporation strove to maintain or increase its share in the market.

The Economic Performance Act would not have to deal with these substantive problems. So long as it established the general concepts of economic performance and of bonus systems to induce this performance, the task of giving constructive meaning to these concepts would rest with business management and the emerging profession of performance accounting.

For much the same reason, the burden of judgment placed on the Treasury by such a tax provision would not be great. In essence it would be comparable to that involved in profit accounting for tax purposes. The measurement of performance is just as much a technical-professional matter as is the measurement of profit. Under present tax law, the Treasury is guided by the canons of good profit-accounting practice and usually accepts the corporate profit figures approved by a certified public accountant. With special tax treatment for performance bonuses, it could be expected that professional canons of good practice in measuring economic performance would play a similar role. While the measures of economic performance would not be as precise as those in profit accounting (and the latter are not as precise as many people believe), they could be sufficiently precise to relieve the Treasury from the necessity of policing collective enterprise.

With professionally approved performance bonus systems in operation, the Treasury could accept them as bona fide much as it does present day systems of profit accounting. Presumably it would have to set some limiting standards as it does now with profit accounting and be prepared to refuse the preferred treatment to bonuses where there was clear evidence that the bonus system was not bona fide. But the main task of "policing" would be done by the principles of "performance accounting" developed by the work of the performance-accounting profession. Once the professional criteria were well developed, the problem of actual policing would be of the same order of magnitude as that for profit accounting.

In the transition period, too, the Treasury could be relatively lenient, only refusing the preferential tax treatment to bonus systems which claimed to be based on economic performance but were quite obviously not.

The initial legislation would have to guard against certain possible abuses of the bonus tax privilege. The low tax rates on performance bonuses would provide an inducement to make all or practically all of the income from management take the bonus form. This could be prevented by limiting the bonus tax privilege to bonuses that do not exceed some specified ratio to salary payments with the limiting ratio set either in the legislation or by the Treasury. Also there could be a tendency to set maximum bonus payments too high and this also could be prevented by limiting the tax privilege to bonus plans whose maximum bonus payments do not exceed some specified ratio to total assets or total value added in manufacture.

A more difficult abuse to cope with is the possibility that the performance requirements under a particular bonus system would be made so easy that the *maximum* bonuses could easily be achieved year after year and so provide no significant drive for improved performance. It could, of course, be that a particular management team was so good that it rated the maximum bonus each year. But the burden of proof should be on the corporation to establish that this was so, not on the Treasury to show that the bonuses were not received for superior performance. This could be dealt with in the legislation by specifying that a given frequency in achieving the maximum bonuses under a given plan would place the burden of proof on the corporation to establish that its bonus system was a two words system to stimulate improved economic performance.

Even if the tax privilege were somewhat abused in the early years of its operation, it should produce results from big collective enterprise which would be no further from the public interest and usually a lot closer than those which come from a drive for corporate profits. And over a period of years both the measures of performance and the means for limiting abuse should improve until a high and improving level of economic performance was achieved.

ESTABLISHING LEGITIMATE TARGET RATES

A third section of the Economic Performance Act would deal with the requirement of reasonable target rates of return as the basis of pricing. It would provide that the special tax treatment would only be available where target pricing was employed and the target rate of return used in such pricing was the estimated cost of capital.

Under this section, a collective enterprise seeking special tax treatment for its management would be required to file with the Treasury four estimates with supporting data:

1. An estimate of the cost of capital to the enterprise which would be used as the target rate of return.
2. An estimate of the *average* rate of operation to be expected over a period of years which would be used as the standard rate of operations in target pricing.
3. An estimated schedule of the effect on earnings to be expected from operations at rates above or below the expected average.
4. An estimate of the total capital to be employed by the enterprise.

Initially, the first of these estimates—the cost of capital—would be the most difficult to arrive at, particularly where the enterprise had not been raising equity capital from the public.

Presumably the enterprise could arrive at a fair estimate of the cost of borrowing capital on the basis of its own borrowings and the rates paid by other borrowers. Also in the unlikely case that its past earnings had shown no trend of growth and no such growth could be expected, then its past earnings and the market price of its stock could be used as a direct indication of the cost of equity capital. And the *average* cost of capital to the enterprise could be estimated by weighting the cost of debt and equity capital according to its own capital structure.

However, where growth in earnings could be expected, the market price of the corporation's stock would reflect not only the current rate of earnings but also this growth. In order to use the price/earnings ratio as the basis for measuring the cost of equity capital, an adjustment for this growth factor would have to be made. As a result, the estimates of the cost of equity capital made by different experts could be expected to vary somewhat. With experience, and particularly with an increase in the equity capital obtained from public sale of securities, the range of expert estimates would undoubtedly narrow. But some range could always be expected. For this reason, the burden of proof should at first be placed entirely on the Treasury if it set out to reject a corporation estimate of its cost of capital on the ground that the estimate was too high. With experience, it might be possible to develop standards for the cost of capital such that an estimate falling above some limit, would place the burden of proof on the corporation to justify such a high estimate.

If, at the outset, the estimates of the cost of capital tended to be too high, this would not be serious. It is difficult to imagine that one of the big established enterprises would have to have an average prospect of 16 to 20 per cent return on its capital in order to obtain capital from the public when public utilities can obtain ample capital with an earning prospect on the sum of their equity and debt capital of less than 7 per cent. Any reduction in the target rate from the 16 and 20 per cent now used by some leading corporations would be a public gain. And with experience, the target rates could be expected to move reasonably close to the long-run cost of capital.

The estimate of the average rate of operation to be expected should involve less difficulty. For internal reasons, a corporation will usually have its own measures of capacity and of production and these would provide the basis for determining the average rate of operation in the past. Provided there had been no change in the methods of measurement, the average rate of operations in the past or a rounded figure close to the average could be accepted as prima facie evidence of the average rate to be expected in the future and the burden of proof should lie with the corporation if a different figure were used.

Similarly, the average effect of the rate of operation on the rate of earnings with a given target rate could be derived from a corporation's previous experience and the projection of this relation would be prima facie evidence of the relation to be expected. An estimated schedule which departed from this previous experience should place on the corporation the burden of justifying it.

The fourth estimate, that of the total amount of capital used by the enterprise, would involve no difficult problems in a long period of stable prices but a major change in price level would introduce the problem of valuation which was explored in the case of steel. With substantially stable prices, book values could be used and a corporation's capital would consist of its net working capital and the historical cost of its fixed capital, less the capital which had been recovered through charges to depreciation. In a period of rising prices, the Treasury would be required to accept these book values as the estimate of capital but the enterprise would have the option of revaluing the unrecovered capital represented by its fixed assets. For example, the law might allow the enterprise to take the average of the book value and the value reached by adjusting the unrecovered capital for the changes in the value of the dollar, a relatively simple accounting procedure. Of course, if a corporation elected to adjust the unrecovered book value of fixed assets upward for a rise in price level, it would commit itself to the reverse procedure if prices fell.

These four estimates would not only determine the target rate of return and the standard rate of operation to be used by the enterprise in pricing but, with the income data already required, would provide the Treasury with a substantial check on whether the indicated target rate and standard were being employed. If at the end of a year earnings on total capital were at a rate substantially above that called for by the target rate adjusted for the actual rate of operations, this would raise the question whether the appropriate target rate had been employed. In this case, if the difference were small the burden of proof that the proper pricing procedure was not used should rest with the Treasury, but if the difference were more than some specified ratio, the act could place the burden of proof on the enterprise to show that the difference in rate of return was not due to a departure from the appropriate pricing procedure but arose from some other source.

A MINIMUM OF GOVERNMENT INTERFERENCE

The introduction of a performance bonus system and legitimate target rates could be expected to re-orient the drives under which top management would operate and yet interfere to a minimum with management judgment in the actual operation of the enterprise. The Congress in passing the act would express its judgment that, for the companies whose pricing power was substantial, an average rate of return on capital equal to the cost of capital was in the public interest and would implement this judgment. But the decisions on the character of the performance bonus system and its details would be left primarily to management judgment. So also would be the decision on the estimated cost of capital and the average rate of operation to be used in pricing. There is no reason to expect that a management which sought to carry out the principles of the act would bring into play the judgment of Treasury officials. Only where a management *intentionally sought* to run counter to the principles of the act would Treasury judgment be set against that of management.

What is most important is that tax measures could be used to shift the focus of management from a drive for profits to a drive for economic performance, and this could be expected to bring about the operation of these great collective enterprises more nearly in the public interest, give management a more neutral approach to the conflicts of interest with which it necessarily has to deal, and provide management with a clearer guide to policy in operating the great engines of production for which they are responsible.

INDUCING ACCEPTANCE BY SECURITY HOLDERS AND THE COURTS

A fourth section of the Act would have to set up mechanisms which would induce security holders and the courts to accept the shift in focus. Undoubtedly management could make a certain amount of shift in focus away from the drive for profits and toward economic performance without getting into difficulties with investors or the courts. Statements by corporate management often suggest that such a shift is underway. However, management's action in this direction is usually justified as in the *long-run interest* of stockholders. And if there were no question of the break-up of collective enterprise or its regulation, it is clear that the complete shift in focus from profits to economic performance would not be in the long-run interest of stockholders, if, without the shift in focus, collective enterprise could make much more than a competitive rate of return on the capital used. To focus pricing policy around a target rate of return of 8 per cent instead of 16 or 20 per cent would result in fewer profits for the stockholders. The lower target rate should be easier to achieve on the average and, therefore, be more certain over a period of years, but the greater certainty would only make up in part for the lower rate of return in prospect. Clearly something would be taken away from investors by the shift to economic performance. Would stockholders stand for such a taking? Would the courts sustain management in such an overt shift?

First, consider the legal question. There has been considerable discussion among lawyers as to the legal status of management in the modern corporation. Should management be treated as trustee for the stockholders or trustee for a larger constituency? In 1931, Professor Berle took the first position, emphasizing the responsibility of management to stockholders and arguing that managers were trustees for stockholders.[2] In early 1932, Professor Dodd of the Harvard Law School took the second position, emphasizing the substantial public interest in the use of corporate property and arguing that management should be viewed as trustee for the enterprise as a whole—for the corporation viewed as an institution—not merely as "attorneys for the stockholders."[3] Berle and Means in 1932 summed up the problem in the following terms:

On the one hand, the owners of passive property, by surrendering control and responsibility over the active property, have surrendered the right that the corporation should be operated in their sole interest, —they have released the community from the obligation to protect them to the full extent implied in the doctrine of strict property rights. At the same time, the controlling groups, by means of the extension of corporate powers, have in their own interest broken the bars of tradition which require that the corporation be operated solely for the benefit of the owners of passive property. Eliminating the sole interest of the passive owner, however, does not necessarily lay a basis for the alternative claim that the new powers should be used in the interest of the controlling groups. The latter have not presented, in

[2] A. A. Berle, Jr. "Corporate Powers as Powers in Trust," *Harvard Law Review*, 44:1049 (1931).
[3] E. Merrick Dodd, Jr., "For Whom Are Corporate Managers Trustees?" *Harvard Law Review*, 45:1145 (1932).

acts or words any acceptable defense of the proposition that these powers should be so used. No tradition supports that proposition. The control groups have, rather, cleared the way for the claims of a group far wider than either the owners or the control. They have placed the community in a position to demand that the modern corporation serve not alone the owners or the control but all society.[4]

Then Berle and Means proposed a dual approach, acceptable to Professor Dodd, which went a long way in adopting Professor Dodd's position as the ultimate goal but insisted on the continuance of strict construction—the treatment of management as trustee for stockholders—*until* "a convincing system of community obligations is worked out and is generally accepted," saying: "Rigid enforcement of property rights as a temporary protection against plundering by control would not stand in the way of the modification of these rights in the interest of other groups."[5]

In the last twenty-five years the courts appear to have accepted some departure from strict construction in specific situations, notably in the case of gifts to community institutions, but whether the courts would apply the broad construction to a shift made at management's own initiative is by no means clear.

In any case it is not the objective of the program outlined here to focus on management as *trustee for the community,* but to provide management with a self-interest which will induce it to do those things in its own interest which also serve the public interest. Whether or not management's position is described as that of trustee, it is the inducements to self-interest, not the trust responsibility, which should be chiefly relied on to induce operation that serves the public interest.

The same approach can be applied to the interest of stockholders by setting up conditions such that a management shift to economic performance would be in the positive interest of stock-

---

[4] *The Modern Corporation and Private Property,* pp. 355-356.

[5] E. M. Dodd, Jr., "Is Effective Enforcement of the Fiduciary Duties of Corporate Management Practicable?" *University of Chicago Law Review,* 2:194 (1935).

holders as well as that of management. This could be done by making acceptance of the new orientation an alternative to corporate breakup or regulation. But a simpler way would be to introduce an excess profits tax which applied only to legally determined collective enterprises and only to those which failed to shift focus from profits to performance through a bona fide economic performance bonus system.

Under ordinary circumstances an excess-profit tax can lead to inefficient corporate operation and is, therefore, undesirable as an instrument of public policy. But in this case it is proposed as a means for inducing stockholders to accept the performance basis by taking away the profit advantage of adhering to the profit drive as the guide to corporate policy. This would not be an effort to coerce through arbitrary taxation but rather an effort to remove the illegitimate gains which arise from the use of pricing power. The two are closely akin but their moral and legal implications can be quite different.

An excess-profits tax which was acceptable to the courts could be so severe that a shift to economic performance would be in the positive interest of stockholders. The profits remaining after the excess-profits tax might be made less than those to be expected under the drive for economic performance particularly if a fairly liberal target rate of return was accepted.

Also, if an excess profits tax were placed on the collective enterprises which continued to operate under the drive for profits, the courts would find no difficulty in supporting management against minority stockholders on the ground that the shift to economic performance is in the interests of stockholders and not an invasion of stockholder rights. Stockholders might seek a finding that the excess profits tax law which reduced corporate profits was an invasion of property rights but it would be difficult to establish that, in the presence of such taxation, the shift to performance invaded property rights. Also, if use of pricing power leads to more than legitimate profits, the courts should have no difficulty in finding constitutional a profits tax which removed the excess.

The legislation creating the new legal status of collective enterprise would have to give ample time to make the shift. Enterprises might be given five years in which to develop a performance bonus system acceptable to the Treasury before the excess-profits tax became operative. In the meantime, the tax benefit for a performance bonus system would apply as soon as such a system was in operation.

The legislation should also provide that a corporation could avoid the legal status of a collective enterprise by a voluntary break-up into smaller units. Such an opportunity for voluntary break-up would mean that where the efficiency of big business was not significantly greater than that of smaller enterprises, management and stockholders might choose to break the big enterprise into many smaller units, thereby reducing the power to make excess profits rather than reorienting its use.

The net result of this legislation should be to give each big collective enterprise the choice between an excess profits tax, voluntary breakup or a focus on economic performance. Where big collective enterprise is significantly more efficient than smaller enterprise, the public interest lies in a focus on economic performance and the aim of the legislation should be to provide mechanisms which will induce management, stockholders, and the courts to accept economic performance as the basis of operation.

APPLICATION OF THE PROGRAM TO THE STEEL INDUSTRY

Let us consider how such a program would apply to the steel industry. Assume that, after a few years of discussion, legislation substantially along the lines already outlined is passed and becomes law and that a commission has been established concerned with determining which big corporations are to have the legal status of collective enterprise. How could the law be expected to operate in the steel industry?

First the commission could be expected to issue a preliminary finding that certain steel companies could and should carry the legal status of collective enterprise. In the steel hearings it was brought out that in 1956 the following eleven steel companies each had over $200 million of assets. The commission would examine published corporate records or get information directly from the bigger steel companies and might compile a list of the largest steel corporations similar to the list below which gives data for all the steel companies with assets over 200 million in 1956:[6]

	Assets (in million dollars)	Per cent of Blast Furnace Capacity	Per cent of Steel Ingot Capacity
United States Steel	$4,109	33.9	29.7
Bethlehem Steel	2,090	14.8	15.4
Republic Steel	924	8.9	8.3
Jones Laughlin Steel	732	5.3	4.9
National Steel	700	5.8	4.6
Armco Steel	623	2.9	4.5
Youngstown Steel	621	4.8	4.7
Inland Steel	618	3.5	4.1
Kaiser Steel	293		
Wheeling Steel	289	2.1	1.6
Colorado Fuel & Iron Co.	258	1.9	2.1

The commission would then have to decide which of these corporations should be listed for collective enterprise status. Presumably the commission would exclude the three smaller corporations since their influence on this industry must be relatively small. Whether the commission would include all of the eight corporations with assets over half a billion dollars is problematic. Because of their size, the burden of proof would rest with these corporations to show that they did not fit the legal requirements for collective enterprise. However, the commission might conclude

[6] *Hearings,* pp. 900-916 for assets and pp. 936-942 for capacities.

that, at least at first and perhaps permanently, sufficient improvement in the economic performance of the industry could be achieved if only the largest three which together operate more than half the steel capacity were to operate as legal collective enterprises. Let us assume that this is the case and the commission's preliminary list included only United States Steel, Bethlehem Steel, and Republic Steel.

The next step would be for the listed companies to decide whether they wished to accept the privileges and responsibilities of the collective status or to fight to retain the legal status of private enterprise.

First, the management would have to reach a decision. It might choose to fight the new status before the commission and in the courts or it might decide to accept it. At this stage it might put the issue up to the stockholders by asking for authorization to develop a proposal for economic performance bonuses for subsequent submission to the stockholders. If the management or stockholders decided in favor of the new status, the management would develop an economic performance bonus system and present it for a "yes" or "no" vote by the stockholders. The latter might vote down the proposal, in which case the corporation would become subject to the excess-profits tax, or to a court fight to preserve its private enterprise status. Or the majority might favor the new bonus system. Finally, even if a majority of stockholders approved the proposal, a single stockholder or minority group could go to the courts to resist the proposal on constitutional or other grounds or institute a proxy fight to replace the management.

It is not the purpose of this book to consider the legal complexities that could delay the shift to the new legal status. If the logic of the big collective enterprise is as compelling as it appears to be, the Congress and the courts will undoubtedly find ways to make the shift possible. Here it will be sufficient to consider what could be expected to happen if each of the designated corporations accept the new legal status of collective enterprise.

THE BIG THREE AS LEGAL COLLECTIVE ENTERPRISES

Let us assume that the top three steel companies have been designated by the commission as legal collective enterprises and that this status is acceptable to management and stockholders. The first substantive task then, would be the development of the new performance bonus system. The legislation would presumably allow a number of years (perhaps five) for the development and adoption of performance bonus systems, but the tax privilege to management could be obtained as soon as the system was in operation and, if the new status is acceptable, this would provide pressure for more rapid adoption. Even so, the development of the system would require considerable time and effort.

In the actual development of a bonus system, a big steel company might be expected to employ one of several management engineering firms which now act as consultants to big business. For this purpose, the management firm would have to expand its performance measuring techniques to cover the wider scope of economic performance. Perhaps it would have to add economists to its staff to help in giving the general concept of economic performance concrete meaning in terms of the everyday operation of a big business. The management firm, working closely with the management of the corporation would finally produce a bonus plan which in its opinion would meet the Treasury requirements for bona fide economic performance and fit the business requirements of the particular corporation.

Once the new bonus plans were adopted, the whole pricing procedure in the industry would begin to be modified. Each of the big three could be expected to make its initial pricing calculations in terms of the new target rates based on its estimated cost of capital. At first U. S. Steel, as the natural price leader, could be expected to recalculate the base rates which, in the light of its costs would yield the new target rate when operations were at an average ratio to capacity. The steel prices arrived at on this basis would undoubtedly be somewhat lower than the current prices and if set by U.S. Steel would also be initially adopted by the other two of the big three and by most of the rest of the industry. U.S. Steel would also begin to recalculate its book of differentials for different quantities and qualities on the basis of differential costs and the new target rates and published changes in its differentials would presumably be adopted by most of the industry.

Bethlehem and Republic would also calculate the prices which under an average operating rate would yield the new target rates of return. For some items, one of these corporations would presumably have lower costs than U.S. Steel, while for other items it might have higher costs and these would somewhat offset each other in terms of total earnings in this initial period. Then, as the economists and management engineers clarified the rules of economic performance and the rules were applied, the lowest total cost among the big three could be expected to play a larger role in the determination of price, and price could be expected to approximate the economic cost of production when the most efficient techniques of production are used.

For the enterprises that continued to operate as private enterprise with the drive for corporate profits, the competition of the big three would be more severe since steel prices would presumably be somewhat lower. Many of the smaller companies are specialists in qualities of steel or specialized services which are not provided by the big three and their power of survival would be little affected. But for those more directly competing with the big three, some would presumably be able to survive at the somewhat lower prices but would not be able to make higher than competitive rates of return on capital except as they were more economically efficient than the big three. Others, less efficient than the big three, that survive today only because of the umbrella provided by premium prices would have difficulty in surviving. This misfortune to stockholders—a risk of private enterprise—would be offset by the gain to the public in the transfer of output to the more efficient producers.

What would be the effect of the shift on the stockholders of the big three? The fact of the public concern with steel pricing has already been reflected in the steel hearings and in the government intervention in the steel strike. Undoubtedly this concern has been reflected to some extent in the price of steel—at least Chairman Blough of United States Steel gave as one consideration in setting steel prices ". . . the publicly stated desire of not only the President of the United States but of many other people in this country, to act as conservatively as all of us possibly could. . . ."[7] For the same reason, the shares of the big steel companies could be expected to reflect in some degree the possibilities of government intervention and therefore be lower, even today, than if this pricing power could be exercised without possible government restriction.

Also, the shift from the private to the collective status would not come suddenly and without warning. The discussions which finally lead to the adoption of an Economic Performance Act would extend over a number of years with an increasing likelihood of passage. In addition, the process of making the shift to economic performance would take time—particularly if it were resisted through court action. Altogether the shift might take a ten-year period during which it only gradually became more imminent. As a result, the reduction in the market value of the big company stocks implicit in the shift would be spread over a period of years and would not be in proportion to the actual reduction in corporate earnings. The change in value would not come suddenly and would be overlaid to some extent by the ups and downs of steel stocks for other reasons. But such a change is essential if the profits of big

[7] *Hearings*, p. 298.

steel are to be brought into line with the economic contribution of capital.

For the steel industry as a whole, the shift of the big three from a drive for profits to a drive for economic performance combined with competition both among the three big collectives and from the smaller private enterprises could be expected to result in prices closer to economic costs, better use of resources, more equitable distribution of income, and steadily improving technology. For the steel industry, therefore, where technology dictates huge units and limits competition to that between a few units with much of production concentrated in still fewer big collective enterprises, special tax treatment for bonuses based on economic performance could be expected to achieve substantially the goals of classical competition.

THE MORE GENERAL APPLICATION OF THE NEW APPROACH

The new approach outlined here would seem to have general application to big industrial enterprise wherever pricing power is so important that it creates a significant public interest and this public interest would not be served by regulating prices or by breaking up enterprises so as to reduce this pricing power. If it proved successful in the case of big industrial enterprises, it might well be considered as a substitute for price regulation in the public utility field. Also it might be adapted to the fields of distribution and service, though in these fields the relative ease of entry makes the big business problem quite different from that in the field of industry.

Even in the more limited field of industry, the new approach does not attempt to deal with many of the problems of bigness. If the new approach were adopted, it would modify and sometimes simplify the handling of other problems. Thus the conflict between labor and management would be importantly modified if the big corporations were operated under a drive for economic performance and not a drive for greater profit. It would strengthen the shift already evident in the statements of progressive union leaders, to emphasize, not the highest wages it is possible to squeeze from management, but wages commensurate with labor productivity and so shift the conflict from the realm of power to the realm of technical analysis. At the same time it would intensify the labor union's role in the consideration of economic performance and working conditions.

Similarly it would alter the framework within which discussion of corporate power and corporate democracy are carried on. Whether or not the principles of political democracy should be applied to the big corporation, their application *in order to obtain better economic performance* would not be needed under the new approach. It may be that under the drive for economic performance and well developed rules of economic performance a self-perpetuating management can provide both stability and high competence in corporate management while the stockholder's power to replace management through a proxy fight would help to protect the interest that would be most damaged by a failure to make legitimate profits. There would be the problem of preventing corporate raiding, and there would be problems of appeal from the arbitrary action of corporate management. The central problem of economic performance, however, would not be a problem of economic representation but of technical rules of performance in some degree comparable to the rules of accounting which now control one major aspect of management behavior.

The adoption of this new approach would also alter the role of the antitrust laws. In the industries dominated by collective enterprise, the function of the antitrust laws would be to maintain at least a few competitors and to make sure that the methods of competition are fair, but the function of maintaining sufficient competition to control prices in the public interest—a function for which these laws have been largely ineffective—would not be required.

Under the new approach these problems become peripheral to the central objective of high economic performance. And this objective is sought not through appeals to the trusteeship of management, or through a representation of competing interests, but by setting up conditions in which the self-interest of management is directly tied to economic performance and the guide to performance arises out of the technical rules of economic performance developed over the years by professionals outside the specific management. By such a procedure, the great potentials of modern technology can be made to serve the public interest without the centralization which comes from government regulation and without the fragmentation and waste that would come from the attempt to regulate prices through market competition. The freedom of enterprise would be retained but canalized to serve the public interest.

APPENDICES

&

INDEX

APPENDIX A

WERE STEEL PRICES REASONABLE IN 1942?

There are three ways to approach the question of the reasonableness of steel prices in 1942. One is to examine the recovery of steel prices from the depression. A second is to examine the reflation of costs. And the third is to examine the rate of profits. All these ways will be employed here.

THE REFLATION OF STEEL PRICES

That the recovery of steel prices from the depression was complete is suggested by the indexes of steel prices and wholesale prices from 1926 to 1942 which are shown in Table 28. As can be seen, the index of finished steel prices dropped much less than the wholesale price index in the depression and had more than recovered its pre-depression level by 1937, although the wholesale price index was still 11 per cent below its pre-depression level. Both indexes fell again in the 1938–1939 recession, but by 1940 the steel index was 3 per cent above the 1925–1929 level while the wholesale index was 18 per cent below. The finished steel price index then rose somewhat to 1941 and was at the same level in 1942. The 1942 level was 6.8 per cent above the average of 1926 to 1929 and 4.6 per cent above its 1929 average. Clearly, steel prices had recovered their depression drop by 1942 and had exceeded it by a small amount. If labor and other operating expenses in 1942 were the same as before the depression, one might conclude that steel prices in those two years were not unreasonably low. We must, therefore, examine costs.

THE REFLATION OF LABOR COSTS

Labor costs per unit of output appear to have just barely recovered their pre-depression level by 1942. Though exact data for all labor costs are lacking, we do have reliable estimates for production worker

Table 28—THE REFLATION OF STEEL PRICES

	Index of Finished Steel Prices	Index of Wholesale Prices
	1926-29=100	*1926-29=100*
1926	103.2	103.2
1927	98.2	98.6
1928	96.5	100.0
1929	97.9	98.3
1930	94.1	89.2
1931	87.4	75.3
1932	83.6	67.0
1933	82.7	68.1
1934	91.6	77.5
1935	92.3	82.6
1936	94.4	83.4
1937	113.1	89.2
1938	109.7	81.3
1939	103.1	79.7
1940	102.7	81.3
1941	106.8	90.3
1942	106.8	102.1 (Feb. 99.9)
1943	106.8	106.4

Source: BLS for Wholesale Price Index. Index of Finished Steel Prices prepared for the Joint Economic Committee, *Productivity, Prices and Incomes,* 1957, p. 222. (Based on *Iron Age,* Composite Price of Finished Steel.) If the BLS index for Steel Products had been used the picture would have been essentially the same.

payrolls per unit of steel output from 1926 to 1941, though not for 1942. But these figures are not a true index of labor cost per unit of output to the employer since they do not reflect fringe benefits per unit which increased importantly between 1933 and 1941. The U.S. Steel representative inserted into the record of the hearings data for 1941 indicating that for the steel industry as a whole employment costs per hour, including fringe benefits, were 5.3 per cent greater than average hourly earnings.[1] This figure includes not only the cost of paid holidays and vacations, which are included in payrolls, but also the cost of pensions, social security payments, and other costs of labor to the employer. If we accept this figure and assume that before the

[1] *Hearings,* p. 1451.

depression similar fringe benefits amounted to 1 per cent of average hourly earnings, a not unreasonable figure,[2] then three-quarters of the depression drop in wage rate had been recovered by 1941 as is shown in Table 29.

Table 29—PRODUCTION WORKER LABOR COSTS PER UNIT OF STEEL PRODUCED

	Index of Payroll Costs per Unit of Output (production workers only)	*Assumed Ratio of Fringe Benefits to Production Worker Payrolls*	*Index of Labor Costs per Unit of Output Adjusted for Fringe Benefits (production workers only)*
	1926–29 = 100	*Per cent*	*1926–29 = 100*
1926–1929	100.0	1.0	100.0
1933	79.9	1.0	79.9
1941	91.8	5.2	95.6

In 1942 steel's average cost of an hour of labor, including fringe benefits, was up 8 per cent over 1941.[3] How much labor costs per ton went up as a result, we do not have the data to determine. The change in product-mix toward special military steels makes it impossible to use the usual procedure in estimating labor cost. Did productivity in producing standard steels increase more than usual under the impetus of war patriotism or did the abnormalities of war cut into the usual increase? Between 1941 and 1947, the Bureau of Labor Statistics index of steel output per man-hour shows an increase of 15 per cent, or a cumulative rate of 2.3 per cent a year. If we adjust the 1941 index of employment costs per unit of output for an 8 per cent increase in employment costs and a 2.3 per cent increase in productivity, we get a 5.6 per cent increase in labor cost per ton. This would give an index value of 101 for labor costs in 1942, including fringe benefits to compare with the pre-depression index of 100. If we assume no increase in productivity we get an index value of 103.2 for 1942 or an

[2] No figures were presented for total fringe benefits before the depression, but U.S. Steel reported to the TNEC that the cost of pensions alone averaged .7 per cent of payrolls in 1927 to 1929.

[3] Source: *Productivity, Prices and Incomes*, p. 220, *op. cit.* Note that the figure for 1941 is based on the revised figure as given by the BLS and not the erroneous figure given in *Productivity, Prices and Incomes*. The latter gives the value of 75.9 (1947–1949 = 100) as the index of production worker payrolls per unit of output in 1941. The revised BLS figure is 70.2.

increase of 3.2 per cent in the production worker cost per ton. These figures suggest that production labor costs per standard ton in 1942 had only just a little more than recovered their pre-depression level and could at most account for only a part of the 6.8 per cent rise of steel prices above the pre-depression level.

Whether labor costs per ton for nonproduction workers (engineers, salesmen, clerks, and other white collar workers) rose more or less is difficult to determine. It seems likely that salaries and wages for this group kept pace with those of production wokers. Had the productivity of nonproduction workers also kept pace with that of production workers, the cost of their work per ton would parallel that of production labor. However, technical progress was more rapid than in nonproduction worker activity. This would mean that if employment costs per hour for nonproduction workers went up in the same proportion as that for production workers and productivity went up less, the cost *per ton* of steel for nonproduction workers would have gone up more. Thus total labor costs per ton could have gone up more than production labor costs. Though nonproduction workers at that time constituted only about an eighth of total steel workers, it seems likely that total labor costs per ton were about as much above the 1926–1929 level as the price of steel but it is doubtful if they had increased significantly more than the price of steel.[4]

REFLATION OF RAW MATERIAL PRICES

A similar conclusion seems justified with respect to the raw materials used in steel-making. The prices of basic raw materials for making steel (iron ore, scrap, and coking coal) were all above their 1926–1929 level while the general index for fuel, power and lighting was well below. These indexes are given in Table 30.

Table 30—THE PRICE REFLATION OF IMPORTANT STEELMAKING MATERIALS

	1926–1929	*1933*	*1942*
Iron Ore	100.0	104.7	103.5
Iron and Steel Scrap	100.0	60.1	139.2
Coking Coal	100.0	83.7	111.5
Fuel, Power & Lighting	100.0	74.6	88.3

Source: BLS.

[4] The American Iron and Steel Institute reports 108,500 salaried workers in a total of 891,000 steel industry workers in 1942.

If one makes a very crude price index for the materials going into steel production by giving a 40 per cent weight to iron ore, 20 per cent to scrap, 20 per cent to coal, and 20 per cent to fuel and power, the resulting index shows a rise of 9 per cent over the pre-depression level. A more reliable index might show a somewhat larger or a smaller rise in the prices of materials but the general magnitude is likely to be about the same.

In determining material costs per ton, account would also have to be taken of changes in the materials used per ton. With the lower relative cost of gas and fuel oil as compared with coal, some relative shift to the cheaper fuels could be expected, and with improving technology, some reduction in materials used could be expected.

When these economies in use are taken into account, it seems likely that the material costs per ton had increased by about the same magnitude as the increase in steel prices. Thus, the rise in labor costs and material costs could justify some rise in steel prices over pre-depression levels, but there is no evidence that steel prices in 1942 had not risen sufficiently to take account of the change in employment costs and material prices.

THE RETURN ON CAPITAL

This conclusion is confirmed by the evidence on steel profits. In comparing the rate of return on capital for this period, there are two important considerations which affect the comparison, the rate of operations and taxes.

The rate of return on capital is to an important extent determined by the rate of operations so that a comparison of profits between different years must either be made between years of about equal levels of operation or an adjustment must be made for the difference in rate. In 1942 steel operations were very close to capacity, while none of the 1926 to 1929 years were so close. However, as can be seen in Table 31, the rate was nearly 90 per cent in 1929 when the rate of return on capital before taxes was 13.8 per cent, the highest rate realized in the 1920's. In 1942 when the industry was operating at the abnormally high rate of close to 97 per cent, the return on capital before taxes to correspond with these rates would have to be close to 16 per cent. Since this is approximately the rate actually earned in 1942, as shown in Table 31, the return on capital *before* taxes in 1942 would appear to be in line with the rate earned in 1929.

But what of taxes? If we were dealing with two peacetime years,

Table 31—RATE OF RETURN ON STOCKHOLDER INVESTMENT, TOTAL STEEL INDUSTRY: 1929 AND 1942

	Per Cent of Capacity Operated	Rate of Return on Investment		
		Before Income Taxes	After Income Taxes	After Income Taxes at 1929 Rates
1929	88.7%	13.8%	12.1%	12.1%
1942	96.8%	16.2%	5.9%	14.2%

Source: AISI.

the appropriate comparison would be between profits after taxes. However, in 1942 heavy income tax rates were in effect both to finance the war and to remove some of the very high profits which could be expected from the high rate of wartime operation. In considering whether or not steel prices were reasonable in relation to costs, it would be appropriate to deduct peacetime taxes but not the extra war taxes. For this reason, Table 31 gives the rate of return not only after actual taxes but also after taxes at the prewar rates. The latter is the relevant figure for 1942. On this basis, the 14.2 per cent return on capital after peacetime taxes achieved in 1942 appears to be in line with the 12.1 per cent rate earned in 1929. Thus, the figures for profits tend to confirm the conclusion reached on the basis of the cost figures that steel prices in 1942 had fully adjusted to the change in costs growing out of the reflation.

This would seem to indicate that in the base year 1942 steel prices were in fairly reasonable relation to costs, provided war taxes are disregarded.

APPENDIX B

CAPITAL EMPLOYED BY THE UNITED STATES STEEL CORPORATION 1942 AND 1953

It is not difficult to arrive at reasonably comparable estimates of the capital per ton of capacity employed by the U.S. Steel Corporation in 1942 and 1953, both on the basis of historical costs and historical costs adjusted for the change in the general buying power of the dollar. But the book values in the two years are not wholly comparable and require some adjustments. Since 1936 the corporation has segregated its tangible fixed assets from its intangibles and carried its plant, equipment, and minerals at historical cost. However, the depreciation and depletion deductions which give the net book value introduce four matters that need to be taken into account.

The first has to do with the emergency plant constructed for war purposes. This emergency plant, amounting to $187 million, was written off over a five-year period. Thus, the whole of this capital investment was recovered and the plant was presumably written off the books by the end of the war. This rapid amortization involves a departure from the more routine depreciation procedures but for purposes of estimating the capital remaining in 1953, it will be treated here like other depreciation charges. Well before 1953 the emergency capital investment had been recovered, and it will be assumed that the physical assets created for war purposes were in fact "used up" before 1953 so that they should not be included as a part of the fixed assets at the later date.

The second matter is the shift in depreciation policy which took place in 1948. Prior to 1948 depreciation was in the main calculated on a modified straight-line basis. In principle the procedure was as follows. In the year of acquisition, the years of useful life were estimated, and the pro rata share of the cost was attributed to the use in that year and a corresponding charge to depreciation was made representing the recovery of this pro rata part of the capital. Then, in each subsequent year, the still remaining life was re-estimated and again the pro rata share of the cost not already recovered was attributed to the use in that year and charged to depreciation except that a less amount was charged to depreciation in any year when actual operating use of facilities in that year was less than a predetermined rate.[1] But in 1948 this procedure was modified to take account of the fact that, like automobiles and other durable goods, a new plant or new equipment loses value more rapidly in its first few years than in later years. To take account of this fact, "accelerated depreciation" was added to regular depreciation by adding 10 per cent of the cost of the facilities as extra depreciation in the first and the second year of their use except where operations fell below 70 per cent of capacity. This new policy results in the same total recovery of capital over the useful life of a facility but operates to charge a somewhat larger proportion in the first two years.

Between 1942 and 1953 such accelerated depreciation amounted to $201 million. This accelerated depreciation was not deductible from income for tax purposes but does reflect the corporation's estimate of the using up of the usefulness of facilities on which depreciation charges and the recovery of capital are based. It will, therefore, be treated here as a part of regular depreciation for present purposes. This seems particularly appropriate since this item of accelerated depreciation disappears from the corporation reports after 1952, while the principle of accelerated depreciation continues to be applied but in a form which new legislation made deductible for tax purposes and the depreciation thus arrived at is treated as regular depreciation.[2]

The third special matter involves a specific departure from accounting on the basis of historical cost. In 1948, at the same time that depreciation policy was revised, $270 million in the accumulated depreciation and depletion account was transferred to "earned surplus." This had the effect of arbitrarily increasing the remaining capital value of the corporation's fixed assets and making the fixed asset account in 1953 not strictly comparable with that for 1942. To make them comparable, either the $270 million should be added to the accumulated depreciation and depletion in 1953 or deducted from that account in 1942. The latter appears to be the appropriate procedure, since in

[1] The description of U.S. Steel's depreciation policy before and after 1948 is based on the more technical description in *Moody's Industrial Manual*, 1948, p. 1728.

[2] See chart, *Hearings*, p. 259, and U.S. Steel Corp. *Annual Report*, 1958, p. 35.

1935 an exactly equal amount, $270 million, was added to the depreciation and depletion account and charged to surplus, thus in effect writing down the net value of fixed assets without any actual recovery of capital being charged to operations. The 1948 write-up in the net value of fixed assets thus appears to be a reversal of the earlier write-down and, therefore, in seeking a strict historical cost basis of values, both will be disregarded and the accumulated depreciation in 1942 will be treated as if neither write-down nor write-up had occurred.

The fourth special item is the introduction of rapid amortization through certificates of necessity, beginning in December 1951. Where a plant was built under a special certificate of necessity issued by the Federal government, the cost of the plant could be amortized and recovered over a five year period and the amortization charges could be deducted for income tax purposes. However, this amortization represents a much more rapid recovery of capital than the using up of the facilities. To treat the whole of the amortization as "depreciation" would reduce the capital value too rapidly and yet some of it does represent true depreciation. However, up to the end of 1952 these charges had amounted to only $59 million and by the end of 1953 to $164 million or an average of $112 million for the year and the arbitrary allocation of one quarter of these charges to regular depreciation will not involve serious error. In the later period this matter becomes more important and will be given greater attention.

In addition to the adjustments in fixed capital, one adjustment in working capital is required. In 1953 working capital was abnormally low. By the end of 1954 it was abnormally high. To allow for this temporary abnormality, a separate estimate has been made on the assumption that working capital per ton was as great in 1953 as in 1942.

There is also a relatively small group of items designated here as miscellaneous capital, including "sundry parts and supplies," which are clearly part of the capital required for production, but also including some investments and deferred charges which should perhaps be segregated. In recent years the amount of this miscellaneous capital has been small and has changed little relative to total capital so that no effort has been made here to disentangle the two elements.

The capital investment of U.S. Steel according to the principle of historical cost is given in Table 32 for the years 1942 and 1953 along with figures for the capital employed per ton of steelmaking capacity.

Table 32—ESTIMATED CAPITAL EMPLOYED BY THE UNITED
STATES STEEL CORPORATION, HISTORICAL COST BASIS:
1942 AND 1953
(*in millions*)

	1942	1953	
Current Assets	$845	$1,093	
Current Liabilities	336	756	
Net Working Capital	509	337	
Plant, Equipment, and Minerals	2,412	4,057	
Depreciation and Depletion	1,057[a]	2,063[b]	
Net Fixed Capital	1,355	1,994	
Total Capital	1,864	2,331	
Capacity in Million Tons	30.9	37.5	
			Change 1942 to 1953
Working Capital per Ton of Capacity	16.47	8.99	—45.4%
Fixed Capital per Ton of Capacity	43.85	53.17	+21.3%
Total Capital per Ton of Capacity	60.32	62.16	+ 3.1%
Assuming same Working Capital per Ton in 1953 as in 1942, Total Capital per Ton would have been		69.64	+15.5%

Source: Moody's Industrial Manuals. Figures are for the average of the balance sheet assets as of December 31 of the current year and December 31 of the preceding year, except as noted.

[a] Excludes $270 million transferred from earned surplus in 1935 and returned in 1948.

[b] Excludes $84 million, three-quarters of the accelerated depreciation before mid-1953 (average of Dec. 31, 1952, and Dec. 31, 1953).

When the buying power principle is employed as the basis of valuation instead of historical cost, a substantially greater increase in fixed capital and in total capital per ton of capacity is shown between 1942 and 1953. Under this principle the useful values of fixed assets, calculated on the historical cost basis, have to be adjusted for the decline in the general buying power of the dollar.

To make such a revaluation, it is useful to distinguish between the plants, equipment and minerals which were on the books at the beginning of 1942 and the fixed assets acquired after the beginning of 1942. Most of the fixed assets held at the beginning of 1942 were acquired before the great depression and by 1953 the useful life remaining on the books was relatively small. At the end of 1941 this group of fixed assets had an historical cost of $2,411 million, and $1,034 million of this invested capital had already been recovered through depreciation and depletion charges to operations, leaving a historical value of $1,377 million for the remaining useful life. By the end of 1945, the historical value of these assets was around $700 million.[3] In the seven years to the beginning of 1953, a large part of the remaining historical value must have been recovered. If we place a historical value after depreciation and depletion on this remainder at $300 million for the beginning of 1953, this would seem to be reasonable. By the end of 1953 additional depreciation and depletion charges must have further reduced the remaining historical value, so that the average net historical value for the year 1953 for these pre-1942 properties would have been below $300 million. Here they will be valued at $272 million. This would be the unrecovered capital which they represented if one adhered strictly to the historical cost principle of valuation.

A revaluation of this $272 million on a buying-power principle to take account of the inflation from 1942 to 1953 would raise this amount to a value close to $450 million. The exact amount would depend on the index of inflation which is adopted. Between 1942 and 1953 the wholesale price index rose 71.5 per cent and the consumer price index rose 64.1 per cent. Revaluing the pre-1942 properties on the buying-power principle would give them 1953 values of $466 million or $446 million depending on whether the value was stated in 1953 wholesale or consumer dollars. These figures indicate the magnitude of the capital value in 1953 represented by the pre-1942 plant, equipment and minerals when valued according to the buying-power principle.

Most of the unused value of the fixed property held by U.S. Steel in 1953 consisted of plant, equipment and minerals acquired after the beginning of 1942. In the following eleven years U.S. Steel spent

[3] On Dec. 31, 1945, the historical cost of fixed assets was given as $2,410 million, of which $290 million had been acquired since Dec. 31, 1941. Depreciation and depletion for these assets amounted to $1,437 million (after deducting the $270 million not charged to operations), of which approximately $40 million would be depreciation on the assets acquired after 1941 if the latter were depreciated on a fifteen-year straight-line basis. This would leave $723 million as the remaining historical value of the assets acquired before 1942 and still on the books in 1945.

$2,334 million for new fixed assets. Of this, $187 million was written off on a five-year basis during and immediately after World War II. Also, some of the remainder must have been written off the books by 1953. Here it will be assumed that a total of $290 million had been removed from the books by 1953, an amount equal to the total fixed capital expenditures from 1942 to 1945, inclusive. If the remaining $2,044 million, i.e., the capital expenditure after 1945 is written off on a twenty-year straight-line basis, this gives a depreciated value of $1,722 million. When this is added to the $272 million suggested as the net value in 1953 of the fixed assets on the books in 1953, but acquired before 1942, the sum is just equal to the $1,994 million estimated as the net value of fixed assets in 1953.

Table 33—ESTIMATED FIXED CAPITAL OF THE UNITED STATES STEEL CORPORATION ON BOOKS IN 1953 WITH REMAINING VALUE MEASURED IN 1953 DOLLARS

Date of Acquisition	Fixed Assets Added at Cost (in millions)[a]	Estimated Depreciation and Depletion (in millions)[b]	Estimated Net Fixed Assets in Current Dollars (in millions)	Index of Buying power in Dollar Measured by Wholesale Prices	Consumer Prices	Estimated Net Fixed Assets in 1953 Dollars Wholesale	Consumer
Before 1942	$2,013	$1,741	$ 272	171.5	164.1	466	446
1946	201	70	131	139.9	137.2	182	180
1947	207	62	145	114.1	119.8	165	174
1948	275	69	206	105.5	111.3	217	229
1949	179	36	143	111.0	112.4	159	161
1950	179	27	152	106.8	111.3	162	169
1951	352	35	317	95.9	103.1	304	327
1952	470	23	447	98.7	100.8	441	450
1953 (one-half)	181		181	100.0	100.0	181	181
	$4,057	$2,063	$1,994			$2,277	$2,317
Increase in set fixed assets due to revaluation						+14.2%	+16.2%

Source: U.S. Steel *Annual Reports* as reported in *Moody's* for asset figures and BLS for price data.

[a] Assumes all fixed assets acquired from 1942 to 1945 had been written off by 1953 and all fixed assets acquired after 1945 were still on books in 1953.

[b] Assumes straight line 20-year write-off of fixed assets acquired after 1945. This rate of depreciation was adopted so as to give the pre-1942 acquisition a remaining value of $272 million.

The fixed assets acquired before 1942 and those added year by year after 1945 are given in Table 33, along with estimates of depreciation and indexes showing the decline in the buying power of the dollar and the net value of these assets in 1953 dollars. If the wholesale price index is used to revalue the total of fixed assets, the adjustment for change in general price level gives them a value of $2,277 million instead of $1,994 million, an increase of 14 per cent over the value based on historical cost. If the consumer price index is used, the value is raised to 2,370 million, an increase of 16 per cent over the value based on historical cost.

When U.S. Steel's 1953 assets per ton of capacity are valued in 1953 dollars, the increase in capital employed per ton of capacity from 1942 to 1953 is considerably greater than that found on the historical cost basis. The figures are given in Table 34 and show a 41 per cent increase in fixed capital and nearly 17 per cent increase in total capital employed per ton of capacity. The increase in total capital per ton would have amounted to 31 per cent if there had been no reduction in working capital per ton between 1942 and 1953. However, the increase in capital per ton for U.S. Steel would still be less than the increase shown in the cruder estimates for the industry as a whole and less than the 53 per cent increase found in the amount available for recovery and return on capital.

It could be argued that, if the capital invested is to be recovered in dollars of equal buying power, a construction price index should be used to measure the value of the dollar. This procedure would be based not on dollars in general but on dollars used in constructing capital plant and if attention is to be focused on the actual capital facilities, then the value of the dollar should be measured, not by how much steel, cement, lumber, and labor it can buy, but by how much productive capacity of what quality it can buy. But this is essentially the reproduction cost principle discussed in the text.

However, it may be useful to calculate the values which would be obtained by using construction price indexes instead of general price indexes and disregarding improvements in the design or increases in the efficiency in the use of materials and labor in the construction of steel plant. This has been done in Table 35 using the *Engineering News-Record* Construction Cost Index, which is very heavily weighted with the price of common labor, and the ENR Building Cost Index, which substitutes the price of skilled labor for common labor and is therefore more relevant to steel construction. The use of these two indexes yields figures for the increase in net fixed assets per ton of capacity from 1942 to 1953 of 37.7 per cent and 30.4 per cent, respectively. How much these figures should be adjusted downward for increases in efficiency in the use of materials and labor in the actual construction of steel plant and for the improvement in the design of such plant is difficult to estimate but it should considerably reduce the values attached on the basis of the building material and labor indexes.

Table 34—INCREASE IN CAPITAL EMPLOYED BY THE
UNITED STATES STEEL CORPORATION: 1942 TO 1953
(in millions)

	1942 Historical Cost Basis	1953 Historical Cost Basis	1953 In 1953 Dollars		
Net Working Capital	$ 509	$ 337	$ 337		
Net Fixed Capital	1,355	1,994	2,317		
Total Capital	$1,864	$2,331	$2,654		
Capacity in Million Tons	30.9	37.5	37.5		
				Change from 1942 to 1953	
				Historical Cost Basis	*Buying-Power Basis*
Capital per Ton of Capacity					
Working Capital	$ 16.47	$ 8.99	$ 8.99	—45.4%	—45.4%
Fixed Capital	43.85	53.17	61.79	+21.3%	+40.9%
Total Capital	$ 60,32	$ 62.16	$ 70.78	+ 3.1%	+17.3%
Assuming Same Working Capital in 1953 as in 1942: Total Capital Per Ton Would Have Been		69.64	79.26	+15.5%	+31.4%

Source: Tables 32 and 33.

Table 35—ESTIMATED NET BOOK VALUES OF CAPITAL EM-
PLOYED BY THE UNITED STATES STEEL CORPORATION
IN 1953 ADJUSTED FOR CHANGES IN CONSTRUCTION
PRICE INDEXES

Date of Acquisition	Estimated Net Fixed Assets (in millions)	Inverse of the ENR Construction Cost Index (1953 = 100)	Net Fixed Assets Adjusted by the 1953 ENR Construction Index (in millions)	Inverse of the ENR Building Cost Index (1953 = 100)	Net Fixed Assets Adjusted by the 1953 ENR Building Index (in millions)
Before 1942	$ 272	217.2	$ 591	193.7	$ 526
1946	131	173.4	227	164.3	215
1947	145	145.2	210	137.6	199
1948	206	130.2	269	125.0	258
1949	143	125.8	180	122.4	175
1950	152	117.7	179	114.7	174
1951	317	110.6	351	107.5	341
1952	447	105.4	471	103.7	464
1953 (one-half)	181	100.0	181	100.0	181
	$1,994		$2,659		$2,533
	Increase from revaluation		+33.4%		+27.0%

Source: Table 33 for asset figures and *Engineering News-Record*, March 24, 1960, for
construction price indexes.

APPENDIX C

CAPITAL EMPLOYED BY THE UNITED STATES STEEL CORPORATION, 1953 AND FISCAL 1959

To obtain estimates of the capital per ton of capacity employed by U.S. Steel in 1953 and fiscal 1959, the biggest single adjustment in the published figures is that for the excessive amortization arising from the five-year write-off of facilities under certificates of necessity already discussed. In 1959 the adjustment adds $535 million to the value of net fixed assets compared to $84 million for 1953. Account must also be taken of the abnormally low level of U.S. Steel's working capital in 1953. The adjustments for the buying power of the dollar follow the pattern already established for the 1942–1953 period.

The following three tables give the essential data for making the estimates. The increase in net fixed capital from 1953 to fiscal 1959 amounted to 29 per cent on the historical cost basis and to only 9 per cent on the buying-power basis. However, the very low level of working capital in 1953 makes for a much larger rise in total capital per ton; 37 per cent on the historical basis and 32 per cent on the buying power basis. If working capital per ton had been the same in 1953 as in 1942 (and about the same as in 1959), the increase in total capital per ton would have been 23 per cent and 18 per cent by the two methods of valuation. Main emphasis in the body of this book is given to the latter figures as more representative of factors which should affect pricing.

Table 36—ESTIMATED CAPITAL EMPLOYED BY THE UNITED
STATES STEEL CORPORATION, HISTORICAL COST BASIS:
1953 AND FISCAL 1959
(in millions)

	1953	Fiscal 1959
Current Assets	$1,093	$1,423
Current Liabilities	756	727
Net Working Capital	$ 337	$ 696
Plant Equipment and Minerals	4,057	5,600
Depreciation and Depletion	2,063	2,720[a]
Net Fixed Capital	$1,994	$2,880
Total Capital	$2,331	$3,576
Capacity in Million Tons	37.5	41.9[b]

			Change
			1953 to Fiscal 1959
Working Capital per Ton of Capacity	$ 8.99	$ 16.61	+84.8%
Fixed Capital per Ton of Capacity	53.17	68.74	+29.3%
Total Capital per Ton of Capacity	$ 62.16	$ 85.35	+37.3%
Assuming same Working Capital per Ton in 1953 as in 1942: Total Capital per Ton Would Have Been	$ 69.64	$ 85.35	+24.0%

Source: For 1953 figures, Appendix B; for 1959 figures, U. S. Steel annual reports,
using Dec. 31, 1958, to represent average for fiscal year except as noted.

[a] The published figure of $3,255 million for depreciation and depletion was adjusted
for the five-year write-off of part of the assets acquired after 1950 by converting the
write-off from five years to twenty years, thereby reducing depreciation and depletion
by $535 million and adding the equivalent to net fixed capital. Actual book values for
net fixed capital before any adjustment were Dec. 31, 1952 $1852 million, Dec. 31, 1953
$1970 million and Dec. 31, 1958 $2345 million. This gave $50.93 as the net fixed capital
per ton of capacity for 1953 and $55.97 per ton for Fiscal 1959, an increase of 9.9
per cent.

[b] Figure for January 1, 1959.

Table 37—ESTIMATED FIXED CAPITAL OF THE UNITED STATES
STEEL CORPORATION ON BOOKS AT BEGINNING OF 1959,
WITH REMAINING VALUE MEASURED IN 1959 DOLLARS

(in millions)

Date of Acquisition	Fixed Assets Added at Cost^a	Estimated Depreciation and Depletion^b	Estimated Net Fixed Assets in Current Dollars	Index of Buying Power of the Dollar Measured by			Estimated Net Fixed Assets in 1959 Dollars		
				Wholesale Prices	Consumer Prices	ENR Building Index	Wholesale Dollars	Consumer Dollars	Building Dollars
Before 1942	$1,635	$1,505	$ 130	185.7	177.0	236.5	$ 241	$ 230	$ 307
1946	201	131	70	151.5	148.0	200.4	106	104	140
1947	207	124	83	123.6	129.2	167.7	103	107	139
1948	275	151	124	114.2	120.0	152.2	142	149	189
1949	179	89	90	120.2	121.1	149.1	108	109	134
1950	179	81	98	115.6	120.0	140.0	113	118	137
1951	352	141	211	103.8	111.2	130.9	219	235	276
1952	469	164	305	106.8	108.7	126.2	326	332	385
1953	361	108	253	108.3	107.9	121.8	274	273	308
1954	227	57	170	108.1	107.5	118.0	184	183	201
1955	240	48	192	107.7	107.8	112.0	207	207	215
1956	312	47	265	104.3	106.2	106.9	276	281	283
1957	515	52	463	101.4	102.7	103.1	469	476	477
1958	448	22	426	100.0	100.0	100.0	426	426	426
	$5,600	$2,720	$2,880				$3,194	$3,230	$3,617
Increase from Revaluation							+10.7%	+12.2%	+25.6%

Source: U.S. Steel annual reports as reported in Moody's for asset figures and BLS and ENR for price data.

^a Assumes all fixed assets acquired from 1942 to 1945 had been written off by 1959 and all fixed assets acquired after 1945 were still on the books in 1959.

^b Assumes straight line 20-year write-off of fixed assets acquired after 1945. This rate of depreciation was adopted so as to give the pre-1942 assets a remaining book value of $380 million, a figure consistent with the $380 million given to these assets for 1953.

Table 38—INCREASE IN CAPITAL EMPLOYED BY THE UNITED
STATES STEEL CORPORATION: 1953–FISCAL 1959
(in millions)

	Historical Cost Basis		Buying Power Basis	
	1953	Fiscal 1959	1953	Fiscal 1959
Net Working Capital	$ 337	$ 696	$ 337	$ 696
Net Fixed Capital	1,994	2,880	2,317	3,230
Total Capital	$2,331	$3,576	$2,654	$3,926
Capacity (in million tons)	37.5	41.9		
Per Ton of Capacity				
Net Working Capital	$ 8.99	$16.61	$ 8.99	$16.61
Net Fixed Capital	53.17	68.74	61.79	77.09
Total Capital	$62.16	$85.35	$70.78	$93.70
Increase: 1953–Fiscal 1959		+37.3%		+32.4%
Assuming Same Working Capital per Ton in 1953 as in 1942: Total Capital per Ton Would Be	$69.64	$85.35	$79.26	$93.70
Increase: 1953–Fiscal 1959		+22.6%		+18.2%

Source: Tables 34, 36, and 37.

APPENDIX D

CAPITAL EMPLOYED BY THE STEEL INDUSTRY, 1953 AND FISCAL 1959

In making estimates of capital per ton of capacity employed by the steel industry in 1953 and fiscal 1959, the most difficult problem is to adjust the published figures for the five-year write-off under certificates of necessity. In the absence of data on the magnitude of the overamortization, it has been arbitrarily assumed that in both 1953 and fiscal 1959 this bore the same ratio to total fixed capital as in the case of U.S. Steel. On this basis, $179 million was added to the net value of fixed assets in 1953 and $1,422 million in fiscal 1959. There is considerable room for error in those adjustments and the resulting estimates of the increase in capital per ton during the period must be regarded as crude.

The estimates on the buying power basis carry the same crudeness but involve no additional difficulties. The adjustment for over-amortization has not been revalued in 1959 dollars, since practically all of it reflected facilities acquired at close to present price levels and because such an adjustment would be difficult to make.

The crude estimates developed in the three following tables suggest an increase of 28 per cent in the capital employed per ton of capacity on the historical cost basis and 19 per cent on the buying power basis.

Table 39—ESTIMATED CAPITAL EMPLOYED BY THE REPORTING
COMPANIES IN THE STEEL INDUSTRY, HISTORICAL COST BASIS
1953 AND FISCAL 1959

(in millions)

	1953	*Fiscal 1959*
Current Assets	$ 4,492	$ 5,706
Current Liabilities	2,243	2,188
Net Working Capital	$ 2,249	$ 3,518
Plant, Equipment, and Minerals	10,781	16,190
Depreciation and Depletion	5,262	8,468
Net Fixed Capital	5,519	7,722
Adjusted for Excess Amortization[a]	5,698	9,144
Total Capital	$ 7,947	$12,662
Capacity in Million Tons	112.6	139.8
Working Capital per Ton of Capacity	$ 19.97	$ 25.16
Fixed Capital per Ton of Capacity	50.60	65.41
Total Capital per Ton of Capacity	$ 70.57	$ 90.57
Increase from 1953 to Fiscal 1959		+28.3%

Source: AISI except as noted. For 1953, average of Dec. 31, 1952 and 1953; for fiscal
1959, data for Dec. 31, 1958.

[a] The depreciation and depletion figures as reported have been adjusted to take
account of the five-year write-off on the assumption that the industry's figures overstate
depreciation and depletion in the same proportion as the figures for U.S. Steel (see
Appendix C). The adjustment reduces the figures for 1953 by $179 million and those
for fiscal 1959 by $1,422 million, increasing the value of fixed capital by equal amounts.
Without adjustment, the net fixed capital per ton amounts to $49.01 for 1953 and $55.24
for fiscal 1959, an increase of 12.7 per cent.

Table 40—ESTIMATED FIXED CAPITAL OF THE REPORTING COMPANIES OF THE STEEL INDUSTRY ON BOOKS AT BEGINNING OF 1959, WITH REMAINING VALUE MEASURED IN 1959 DOLLARS

Date of Acquisition	Fixed Assets Added At Cost[a]	Estimated Depreciation and Depletion[b]	Estimated Net Fixed Assets in Current Dollars	Dollar Measured by Index of Buying Power of the			Estimated Net Fixed Assets in 1959 Dollars		
				Wholesale Prices	Consumer Prices	ENR Building Index	Wholesale Dollars	Consumer Dollars	Building Dollars
Before 1942	$ 4,810	$4,091	$719	185.7	177.0	236.5	$1,335	$1,273	$1,700
1946	365	316	49	151.5	148.0	200.4	74	73	98
1947	554	443	111	123.6	129.2	167.7	137	143	186
1948	642	470	172	114.2	120.0	152.2	196	206	262
1949	483	322	116	120.2	121.1	149.1	194	195	240
1950	505	303	202	115.6	120.0	140.0	234	242	283
1951	1,051	561	490	103.8	111.2	130.9	509	545	641
1952	1,298	606	692	106.8	108.7	126.2	739	752	873
1953	988	395	593	108.3	107.9	121.8	642	639	722
1954	609	203	406	108.1	107.5	118.0	439	436	479
1955	714	190	524	107.7	107.8	112.0	564	565	587
1956	1,311	262	1,049	104.3	106.2	106.9	1,084	1,114	1,121
1957	1,723	230	1,493	101.4	102.7	103.1	1,514	1,533	1,539
1958	1,137	76	1,061	100.0	100.0	100.0	1,061	1,061	1,061
	$16,190	$8,468	$7,722				$8,722	$8,777	$9,792
Adjustment for Excess Amortization[c]		−1,422	+1,422				1,422	1,422	1,422
Adjusted Value		7,046	9,144				10,144	10,199	11,214
Increase from Revaluation							+10.9%	+11.5%	+22.6%

Source: AISI for asset figures, and BLS and ENR for price data.

[a] Assumes all fixed assets acquired from 1942 to 1945 had been written off by 1959, and all fixed assets acquired after 1945 were on books in 1959.

[b] Assumes straight line fifteen-year write-off of fixed assets acquired after 1945. This rate of depreciation was adopted so as to give the pre-1942 assets a remaining value of $719 million, a figure consistent with the figure of $1,244 million given to these assets for 1953.

[c] For adjustment in excess depreciation, see Table 39.

Table 41—INCREASE IN CAPITAL EMPLOYED BY REPORTING
COMPANIES IN THE STEEL INDUSTRY: 1953–FISCAL 1959
(in millions)

	Historical Cost Basis		Buying-Power Basis	
	1953	*Fiscal 1959*	*1953*	*Fiscal 1959*
Net Working Capital	$2,249	$ 3,518	$2,249	$ 3,518
Net Fixed Capital	5,698	9,144	7,068[a]	10,199
Total Capital	$7,947	$12,662	$9,317	$13,717
Capacity (in million tons)	112.6	139.8		
Net Working Capital				
per Ton of Capacity	$19.97	$25.16	$19.97	$25.16
Net Fixed Capital	50.60	65.41	62.77	72.95
Total Capital	$70.57	$90.57	$82.74	$98.11
Increase 1953—Fiscal 1959		+28.3%		+18.6%

Source: Tables 39 and 40, except as noted.
[a] From Table 24 in text with a $179 million adjustment for excessive amortization.

APPENDIX E

REPRODUCTION COST AND
OBSOLESCENCE IN THE STEEL INDUSTRY

The importance of obsolescence in estimating reproduction cost in the steel industry is underlined by an analysis of steel ingot production made by two Kaiser engineers and presented before a meeting of the American Iron and Steel Institute in the fall of 1954.[1] This analysis compared the cost of producing ingots by the open hearth furnace, which at that time accounted for 90 per cent of steel ingot production in the United States, and the newly developed oxygen converter. The oxygen converter is in basic principle similar to the Bessemer converter but uses oxygen as part of the process and thereby overcomes the serious disadvantages of the Bessemer process. The quality of oxygen converter steel is reported to be "comparable to the finest product of the open hearth furnace" and this makes it a direct competitor of the open hearth.

The heart of the Kaiser engineers' analysis is their comparative estimates of the cost of constructing and operating open hearth and oxygen converter facilities for a medium sized plant and also for a large-sized plant. The results of this analysis are presented in Table 42. These figures are estimates, not reports of actual cost and they are presented by engineers whose parent company holds certain license rights for the use of the oxygen converter process in the United States. However, the increase in steel ingots produced by this process from zero in 1953 to nearly three per cent of national steel capacity in 1959 and the rapid expansion of this process abroad would seem to support the claims for lower costs.

These cost estimates assume the same prices paid for the labor and materials used in the construction of open hearth and oxygen converter and that both embody the most up-to-date design. Also the wage rates

[1] *Hearings,* p. 1386-1390. Paper presented at the AISI Meeting in Cleveland, Ohio, September 28–October 1, 1954, by W. W. Kueckel, Vice-President, Kaiser Engineers and J. W. Irvin, Associate Engineer, Kaiser Engineers.

Table 42—COMPARISON OF COSTS WITH OPEN HEARTH FURNACE AND OXYGEN CONVERTER

A. Estimated Capital Cost of Facilities Per Ton of Steel Ingot Capacity

	Open Hearth Furnace	Oxygen Converter	Saving per Ton of Capacity
For Medium-sized Plant	$39.61	$20.22	$19.39
For Large Plant	33.71	12.67	21.04

B. Estimated Production Costs Per Ton of Steel Production

For Medium-sized Plant (500,000 tons)			
Material Costs	$36.67	$37.41	—$.74
Other Operating Expenses	9.88	6.95	2.93
Fixed Charges	4.75	2.42	2.33
Total	$51.30	$46.78	$4.52
For Large Plant (1 million tons)			
Material Costs	36.67	37.41	—$.74
Other Operating Expenses	9.73	6.86	2.87
Fixed Charges	4.52	1.52	3.00
Total	$50.92	$45.79	$5.13

Source: Hearings, pp. 1388 and 1389.

and raw material prices involved in operating the furnaces are assumed to be the same.

If we take the estimates at face value, they suggest that much of the steel ingot capacity in 1959 must have been not only obsolescent but virtually obsolete.

First, consider the reproduction cost value of an existing open hearth furnace simply in terms of the cost of new ingot making capacity. If a ton of new capacity could be built on the oxygen converter basis for half what it could be on the open hearth basis, and both had the same operating expenses per ton, this alone would cut in half the value of existing open hearth furnaces when measured on the reproduction cost basis.

But in the present case, the lower operating costs would combine with the lower capital costs to eliminate the reproduction value almost entirely. For the large oxygen converter plant the sum of the operating *and* capital costs per ton would be less than the operating expenses alone with a brand new open hearth furnace. This suggests that a large open hearth furnace would have no reproduction value at all. It would be obsolete in the technical sense that just its cost of operating would be more than the reproduction costs including capital costs, for a new oxygen converter furnace. For the medium-sized plant, the combined capital and operating costs per ton for the oxygen converter would be just about the same as the operating expenses alone for an up-to-date open hearth furnace. This suggests that an existing open hearth furnace would have a very low reproduction value, particularly when its age as well as its obsolescence is taken into account.

There can be a considerable question whether the reduction in costs is as great as these figures suggest and it may be that, for some special situations, the open hearth has advantages over the oxygen converter or improvements in open hearth operations may in turn reduce its cost of operation, but the sizable reduction in costs and the increasing use of the oxygen converter could be expected to reduce the value of existing open hearth furnaces when valued on the principle of reproduction cost.

A similar situation may be developing in the case of steel rolling mills. Testimony was presented at the hearings by Mr. T. Sendzimir, a steel engineer well known in the industry, who developed the method of galvanizing steel sheet that is commonly used in the United States and throughout the world, and a cold-strip mill which is commonly used in rolling the more difficult steels such as stainless steel. His testimony dealt with a new type of rolling mill called a planetary mill which could take the place of the existing continuous strip rolling mills, at least for steel sheet of medium or smaller widths. According to this testimony, two planetary rolling mills were in commercial operation in England, one in Italy and one in Canada and while experience with this new type of rolling mill was still inadequate for firm estimates of cost, the capital cost per ton of rolling capacity was thought to be one-third that for a continuous strip mill, its operating expenses per ton were expected to be considerably less, and its product was equal to or in some cases superior to that of a comparable continuous strip mill.

What is important here is not the specific facts of particular improvements in technology. The evidence of increasing productivity—in the magnitude of 32 per cent between 1942 and 1953—is sufficient to indicate a progressive obsolescence of existing plants as they grow older. In the historical cost method of valuation, this obsolescence is taken into account in developing the estimates of the average useful life of a plant or piece of equipment which are used in allocating the capital cost over the prospective useful life. But in applying the reproduction cost principle of valuation to the steel industry, the superiority of new modern plant over plant built years earlier must not only be taken into account in valuing the existing plant, but can greatly reduce the current value as compared with historical cost when there is no change in price level or can offset a substantial part of the increase in costs due to a rise in price level.

INDEX

GETTING AND SPENDING:
The Consumer's Dilemma

An Arno Press Collection

Babson, Roger W[ard]. **The Folly of Instalment Buying.** 1938

Bauer, John. **Effective Regulation of Public Utilities.** 1925

Beckman, Theodore N. and Herman C. Nolen. **The Chain Store Problem.** 1938

Berridge, William A., Emma A. Winslow and Richard A. Flinn. **Purchasing Power of the Consumer.** 1925

Borden, Neil H. **The Economic Effects of Advertising.** 1942

Borsodi, Ralph. **The Distribution Age.** 1927

Brainerd, J. G[rist], editor. **The Ultimate Consumer.** 1934

Carson, Gerald. **Cornflake Crusade.** [1957]

Cassels, John M[acIntyre]. **A Study of Fluid Milk Prices.** 1937

Caveat Emptor. 1976

Cherington, Paul Terry. **Advertising as a Business Force.** 1913

Clark, Evans. **Financing the Consumer.** 1933

Cook, James. **Remedies and Rackets:** The Truth About Patent Medicines Today. [1958]

Cover, John H[igson]. **Neighborhood Distribution and Consumption of Meat in Pittsburgh.** [1932]

Federal Trade Commission. **Chain Stores.** 1933

Ferber, Robert and Hugh G. Wales, editors. **Motivation and Market Behavior.** 1958

For Richer or Poorer. 1976

Grether, Ewald T. **Price Control Under Fair Trade Legislation.** 1939

Harding, T. Swann. **The Popular Practice of Fraud.** 1935

Haring, Albert. **Retail Price Cutting and Its Control by Manufacturers.** [1935]

Harris, Emerson P[itt]. **Co-operation:** The Hope of the Consumer. 1918

Hoyt, Elizabeth Ellis. **The Consumption of Wealth.** 1928

Kallen, Horace M[eyer]. **The Decline and Rise of the Consumer.** 1936

Kallet, Arthur and F. J. Schlink. **100,000,000 Guinea Pigs:** Dangers in Everyday Foods, Drugs, and Cosmetics. 1933

Kyrk, Hazel. **A Theory of Consumption.** [1923]

Laird, Donald A[nderson]. **What Makes People Buy.** 1935

Lamb, Ruth deForest. **American Chamber of Horrors:** The Truth About Food and Drugs. [1936]

Lambert, I[saac] E. **The Public Accepts:** Stories Behind Famous Trade-Marks, Names, and Slogans. [1941]

Larrabee, Carroll B. **How to Package for Profit.** 1935

Lough, William H. **High-Level Consumption.** 1935

Lyon, Leverett S[amuel]. **Hand-to-Mouth Buying.** 1929

Means, Gardiner C. **Pricing Power and the Public Interest.** [1962]

Norris, Ruby Turner. **The Theory of Consumer's Demand.** 1952

Nourse, Edwin G. **Price Making in a Democracy.** 1944

Nystrom, Paul H[enry]. **Economic Principles of Consumption.** [1929]

Pancoast, Chalmers Lowell. **Trail Blazers of Advertising.** 1926

Pasdermadjian, H[rant]. **The Department Store.** 1954

Pease, Otis. **The Responsibilities of American Advertising.** 1958

Peixotto, Jessica B[lanche]. **Getting and Spending at the Professional Standard of Living.** 1927

Radin, Max. **The Lawful Pursuit of Gain.** 1931

Reid, Margaret G. **Consumers and the Market.** 1947

Rheinstrom, Carroll. **Psyching the Ads.** [1929]

Rorty, James. **Our Master's Voice:** Advertising. [1934]

Schlink, F. J. **Eat, Drink and Be Wary.** [1935]

Seldin, Joseph J. **The Golden Fleece:** Selling the Good Life to Americans. [1963]

Sheldon, Roy and Egmont Arens. **Consumer Engineering.** 1932

Stewart, Paul W. and J. Frederic Dewhurst. **Does Distribution Cost Too Much?** 1939

Thompson, Carl D. **Confessions of the Power Trust.** 1932

U. S. National Commission on Food Marketing. **Food From Farmer to Consumer.** 1966

U. S. Senate Subcommittee on Anti-Trust and Monopoly of the Committee on the Judiciary. **Administered Prices.** 1963

Waite, Warren C[leland] and Ralph Cassady, Jr. **The Consumer and the Economic Order.** 1939

Washburn, Robert Collyer. **The Life and Times of Lydia E. Pinkham.** 1931

Wiley, Harvey W[ashington]. **The History of a Crime Against the Food Law.** [1929]

Wright, Richardson [Little]. **Hawkers and Walkers in Early America.** 1927

Zimmerman, Carle C[lark]. **Consumption and Standards of Living.** 1936

HF   Means, Gardiner 231225
5417   Coit, 1896-
.M38
1976   Pricing power & the
          public interest